CW00552141

RAY BARRETT

AN AUTOBIOGRAPHY

RAY BARRETT

AN AUTOBIOGRAPHY

WITH PETER CORRIS

Random House Australia Pty Ltd
20 Alfred Street, Milsons Point, NSW 2061

Sydney New York Toronto
London Auckland Johannesburg
and agencies throughout the world

First published in 1995

National Library of Australia
Cataloguing-in-Publication Data

Barrett, Ray.
Ray Barrett: autobiography.

Includes index.
ISBN 0 09 183074 5.

1. Barrett, Ray, 2. Actors—Australia—Biography.
I. Corris, Peter, 1942- . II. Title.

792.028092

Cover designed by Graham Rendoth/Reno Design Group, Sydney
Typeset by Midland Typesetters, Maryborough
Printed by Griffin Paperbacks, Adelaide
Production by Vantage Graphics, Sydney

Dedication

To Gaye

For her undying confidence in me, her hours of typing and deciphering my handwriting, correcting my spelling, not months, but years spent keeping my scrapbooks comprehensive, and her constant encouragement when I wanted to give up.

Acknowledgments

For help in the preparation of this book thanks to Gaye Barrett, Wilfred Barrett, Barbara Battaglini, Anthony Buckley Productions Pty Ltd, Diane Cilento, Leonie Collins, Rosemary Creswell, Faye Denning, Patricia Donovan, Bob Ellis, Richard Lane, Leo McKern, Spike Milligan, Mike Noonan, Mollie Stewart, Walter Sullivan, Kate Turner, Jill Wearne, John West, David and Kristin Williamson, Peter Yeldham.

Peter Corris additionally thanks John Baxter, Graeme Blundell, Roger Milliss and Christine Morris.

Author's Note

This book came about after my old friend Al Thomas came around to my hotel in Sydney in about 1978 and asked if I would put some memories of my association with (Peter) Finch down on tape for the author of a biography on Finch shortly after his death. This I did. Most of them were funny experiences.

I then went off on location and promptly forgot about it. After a few weeks of filming I returned to my hotel to find a letter from the publisher thanking me for my contribution and saying how much everyone had enjoyed the stories. They suggested that I must have many tales about other people I had worked with over the years in various parts of the world and some amusing personal experiences also. They then insisted on a book from me.

My first reaction was one of horror. How could I possibly even attempt to write a book. I put it out of my mind. Subsequently, some of my actor friends supported the publisher's suggestion and convinced me that I should at least 'give it a go'.

I eventually started to put down some fond memories of characters I had worked with over the years, but became bogged down and abandoned the whole idea, until early one morning about two years ago I sneaked out of bed so as not to wake my wife and started jotting down recollections of my earliest childhood. I was amazed to find just how much was stored away in my mind and so I just carried on from there with many fits and starts.

I don't know whether the end result will be entertaining or of interest to anyone, but here it is anyway!

Foreword

To whomsoever is buying this book. This is to say that Ray Barrett is a good man. He gets pissed occasionally but doesn't beat his wife. Recently she has taken to beating him.

I have no idea what this book is about because I have had no time to read the manuscript nor do I bloody well intend to. So anyway give it a fair go, he needs something for his retirement and this book could be it.

Spike Milligan

Table of Contents

Prologue

Glen Kedron Lane, memory, fantasy and reality

The scene is Kedron, a suburb of Brisbane. The time is 1929 or 1930. The characters are Reginald Barrett, my father, and my uncle Cecil, his brother-in-law. I am two or three years old, in rompers, watching in amazement as a major transformation takes place. My father and uncle are working with picks and crowbars to uproot the stump of a huge Moreton Bay fig or camphor laurel on our allotment, adjacent to our house.

I have no comprehension of what is going on, no understanding that this massive labour has an end in view—the construction of a tennis court—but I am anxious to help. The memory is clear: I revelled in it, wanting to help and no doubt getting in the way. My enthusiasm is appreciated. I am a member of a happy family.

The next clear memory is of an ancient truck, labouring up the very steep hilly approach to Glen Kedron Lane. It must have been a very ancient machine and it is vivid in my mind that I was sitting on top of the precious cargo of ant-bed, possibly in rompers. After several attempts at the hill and lots of deliberations between my Dad and whoever the rest of the helpers were, my father, being the only driver, knew that reverse gear had the lowest ratio, so he reversed the wondrous machine up the dreaded hill with ultimate success.

They must have unloaded the ant-bed, spread and levelled and rolled it and built the court, putting in many man-hours, My memory of this work is hazy. But the truck, that was a different matter.

I recall its solid construction and steel tray, but wish I could remember its make. Was it a RIO? Perhaps. My father must have purchased it very cheaply for the purpose of fetching and carrying the ant-bed, and having served its purpose, it finally gave up the ghost and remained as a rusting wreck in the back-yard. In my fantasies though, it was my ship at sea and I spent hours on its stately 'decks', dreaming myself a seafarer. Boats seemed to have stirred my imagination from a very young age.

One day I cast a fishing line from the decks of my ship and was called in for supper or diverted in some way before I could reel it in. The line, baited with some morsel, stayed out all night and I came in for a severe chastising in the morning. I had hooked our neighbour's prize speckled hen—his best layer. The unfortunate bird had swallowed the hook and was running around the backyard in circles.

I never learned the details, but I believe the matter was settled out of court with Mr Dortkamp, money changing hands for the poor unfortunate bird which graced our table the following Sunday.

I

· 1 ·

Young Ray

I must go down to the sea again, to the lonely sea and the sky,
And all I ask is a tall ship and a star to steer her by
John Masefield *Sea Fever*

A stately home named Moredon Hall in Somerset in the west of England became the Barrett family seat early in the nineteenth century. It was built in the seventeenth century and remained in the family for many generations. A scrapbook we had at home contained a picture of it which used to intrigue me as a child. Barretts in the eighteenth century were professional people—a schoolmaster, a veterinary surgeon, a solicitor. William Barrett, a well-known landscape painter and painter on glass of the nineteenth century, is an ancestor of mine and apparently there were others prominent in the arts and sciences.

My great-grandfather was the first to come out to Australia. He made several visits in the mid-nineteenth century 'on business' before finally settling in Queensland. Family stories reveal little more. He must have prospered because my grandfather owned a considerable amount of property—160 acres at 'Chummy Town', an area settled by British immigrants some distance out from Brisbane. He also had a big house on twenty acres at Aspley, somewhat closer to the city, and cottages in the Brisbane suburbs—mainly around the showground area—from which he collected rents.

Poppa, as I called him, seems to have retired from active commercial life pretty early and occupied himself at the Aspley property as a sort of gentleman farmer. His large brood and their offspring were always welcome at Aspley. We spent almost every weekend there and my brother and I drew straws to see who would open the first gate to the property. It was a half mile run up to the house, and the lucky gate-opener got to ride the whole way to the next gate on the running board of the car. A big thrill.

As a child I remember going with my father, who was the eldest son, around the Brisbane houses to collect the rents. The rents were something like seven shillings and sixpence and twelve shillings and sixpence per week and Poppa refused all advice to put them up.

'No,' he said. 'They're good, honest working people in those houses and that's all they can afford.'

My father, Reginald Walter, was born and grew up in Brisbane. He enlisted in the 1st AIF and, because he could drive at a time when this wasn't a common skill, he was pressed into service as a driver. He spent some time in England between tours of duty. He didn't talk a lot about the war although he was in the thick of it, in the Somme and around some of the great battlefields like Ypres. He drove converted London buses with steel tyres loaded with ammunition and I remember him telling me that the soldiers thought nothing of brewing up tea on a primus in the back of one of these contraptions. A naked flame and tons of live ordnance—it doesn't bear thinking of. But he came through intact and not gassed although he suffered some sort of wound to one ear which I gather was pretty serious.

Dad returned to Brisbane after the war and took a job as a commercial traveller in hardware with a large firm named Wilson Tate. In those days the salesmen had to have the ability to estimate the materials required for building projects—some quite substantial, like bridges—and prepare quotes on the cost. It was skilled work. The Barrett house at Aspley had a tennis court (built by my father) and could accommodate weekend parties with people staying over—friends and friends of friends.

Dad met Mabel Armstrong Storey who was also working for

the hardware firm as a secretary. I don't know anything much about their courtship, but he was a likeable young traveller with a car and a few bob and she was English-born, attractive and a talented pianist. During the war she was part of a team that used to travel around with a piano on the back of a truck and stage impromptu concerts to raise funds for the war effort. Dad invited her to one of the Aspley gatherings. I have photographs of the scene—the men in blazers and boaters, the women in light frocks. All very jolly. Things must have gone smoothly. They were married in 1920 with my brother, Scott, being born in 1924 and me two and a half years later in 1927.

Mum had come out to Australia at age eleven because her mother was an asthmatic and had been advised to move to a better climate than that of North Shields, an industrial town in the north-east of England. I was touring that area many years later in a revue with Michael Bentine and Dick Emery and I thought I should go and take a look at the place where Mum was born and spent her early years. I actually found the cottage they'd lived in and I wandered around the rather grim area trying to imagine what life must have been like there in those days. In the window of a little general store I spotted a yellowed postcard with curled edges that looked pre-war. It showed some North Shields scene or other and I bought it. The shop-keeper must have thought I was crazy. I wrote on it something like, 'Grandfather showed great foresight in leaving this dread-ful place,' and posted it home.

Nostalgia didn't end there. On my walk I was hit in the eye by the sight, standing at the bottom of a hill, of a set of huge metal gates with an elaborate emblem. As a kid I'd sat on the lino floor of my grandparents' house in Herston, Brisbane, turning over the pages of a publication called *Smith's Docks Journal*. This was a sort of house journal with local news which the shipbuilding firm of that name posted out to Grandfather as an ex-employee. A photograph of the gates was on the front cover. Those gates were as familiar to me as the back fence and here I was looking at the real thing. I discovered later that my grandfather had been a metal worker and that one of his jobs had been as a blacksmith's striker. When I knew him he suf-fered severely from arthritis but he must have been a pretty solid fellow in his prime.

So there was considerable diversity in the family background and I can only describe my boyhood as rich, not in a material sense but in terms of the range of enjoyable and rewarding activities that were available to me. Aspley, Poppa Barrett's domain, was a delight. The house was built of chamfer board with a high-pitched, corrugated iron roof. It had sweeping, shady verandahs all around with a separate ten-bed dormitory and a semi-detached kitchen. The kitchen had an oil-burning stove and scrubbed white pine table. Under the large meat safe was a wicker basket where the cat had her kittens.

Just off the front verandah was Poppa's office with a wonderful roll top desk, a steel letter press and a leather sofa. Just inside the lounge room was a Polyphone. This intrigued me. It played sixteen inch steel discs with holes in them activated by prongs in a roller underneath, rather like the mechanism of a pianola. My special treat, if I had been a 'good boy', was to be allowed to listen to selections from *Naughty Marietta, The Belle of New York, Maid of the Mountains* etc.

Though it was all fascinating, some aspects of the property were rather frightening for a small boy. At home, I shared a bedroom with Scott; at Aspley we slept in our own rooms which were rather dark. In the outhouse bathroom was a hand pump that lifted the water up into a container something like a cistern. To shower you pulled a chain, released enough water to soap up, and then pulled the chain again to rinse off. Poppa Barrett was a frequenter of auctions and something of a bower bird. Collected in odd corners were unidentifiable pieces of furniture and odd items like ships' toilets.

The aviary and the horse paddocks were great attractions, as was the old sulky in the barn. A true 'surrey with a fringe on top', it served as a chicken roost as did the tank-like Buick tourer Dad used to drive. It was bought after he returned from the war but after he married it remained in the garage. No-one else could drive it. Smells and tastes. There were about fifty mango trees around the house and down by the stables were the apricots, mandarins, oranges and persimmons. Me, my cousins and friends climbed the trees and gorged ourselves.

Poppa was an intriguing man. He didn't say much but what he did say seemed always to have a message. He set himself certain standards. For example, he would never eat in the morning until every animal on the property had been fed. His choice of pets was odd—he had a huge carpet snake which used to drape itself over the sideboard in the dormitory and bask in the sun. I was terrified of it and gave it a wide berth. One day my Uncle Bert came upon it swallowing the last of a litter of kittens. He killed the snake, ripped it open and managed to save several of the kittens. I'm not sure whether I witnessed this event or only heard about it—but I would have been cheering for the kittens.

When the fruit ripened, Poppa would walk to the local school and invite the children to come and eat as much as they cared to and to carry away as much as they could. Once he caught my cousin, Bob Edwards, and I having a shot at some pigeons with our shanghais. I can't remember how he phrased it, but he got the message across that to harm a living thing for fun was ignoble. Sagely, he underlined the point by setting up a tin can on a fence and putting a sixpence in it.

'There boys,' he said, 'the first one to knock the tin off wins, and you can take the sixpence down to the shop and share it.' That shows a pretty sound grasp of child psychology I'd say.

I believe I wanted to get inside my grandfather's head, to understand him, but I never managed it. I have a memory of a time of severe drought, when the cracks in the baked ground were an inch wide. Poppa was hauling water in two kerosene tins from the dam back up the cow track to his garden. I trotted along with him, barefoot, making many trips. He was pouring the water on rows of Rosellas he'd planted. Even at that tender age the exercise seemed futile to me.

'Why are you doing that, Poppa?' I asked.

'You've got to try to keep them alive, son. It might rain soon.'

Poppa used to climb a high ladder which had several rungs missing, to clip and shape a towering brute of a bougainvillea hedge. Many a tumble he had from that ladder. He was no drinker, but often, after he'd completed every last chore around the property, he would walk to the pub and have two tots of rum. No more and no less. After Nanna Barrett died, the passion for life and living things went out of him. He lived alone; my Uncle Bert and Auntie Jessie, who occupied another house on the property about a quarter of a mile away, moved in to keep an eye on him. One day he went missing and Uncle

Bert found him slumped over the chaff cutter, dead. He'd been cutting chaff to feed the cows that morning as was his ritual. It was the way he would have wanted to go.

My memories of home are mainly of busyness. My mother was always busy with her hands, knitting, crocheting, cooking. My father likewise. He had a well-equipped workshop set up under the house with wood and metal vices, hand grinder and a grandiose tool chest. He had built a handsome wooden bench. A treasure trove to me. He was forever sawing, planing and nailing and I did the same. I have a vivid memory of my first carpentry set—saw, hammer, screwdriver, wondrous tools. I had access to wood, paint, nails, planes, rasps and the fascination with building things has never left me.

We spent our summer holidays in a grand tent on the shores of Moreton Bay, a place called Scott's Point. It was square with a tall centre pole and poles holding up the outer rim all supported by guy ropes. It had a carpet with a hole cut in it for the pole. My mother, an expert needlewoman, had manufactured a square dressing room in a corner of the tent, with hand-embroidered pocket compartments labelled 'underclothes', 'linen', 'handkerchiefs' and so on. To a kid, the tent was like a sheik's headquarters, a place for the imagination to run riot.

It was on those holidays that my conscious fascination with boats began. Several of my brother's friends had sailing boats and I longed to go out in them, but I was the 'nipper' and 'in the way'. I realise now that they were out to impress girls of their own age and a snotty-nosed kid could only have been a nuisance.

I desperately wanted a boat. I resurrected an old abandoned dinghy which was full of sand, got it to float and set out into deep water using a tomahawk as a rudder. I was plucked from it by older boys before it sank. The experience only intensified the need which became almost an obsession. I heard of a twelve foot skiff which was for sale for twelve pounds. I pleaded with my father to buy it for me. It would fulfil all my dreams. Obligingly, he came and inspected it with me where it sat under a house on the shore of the Brisbane River.

'No, Ray,' he said firmly.

I was thirteen at the time, a fragile age, and I hated him. I thought it was the most handsome vessel I had ever seen but he knew immediately that it was rotten. Resentful but undaunted, I began to buy and read magazines about boat-building. I found one, a ten-footer, which I thought might be within my capacity to build. Tentatively, I showed the plans to my father. To my great surprise, the timber arrived within a week.

'There it is,' Dad said. 'Timber and tools. Build it!'

It took time and I made false starts but I built the ten-footer and it was eventually launched on Nudgee Creek with me and my mate Ernie Burns aboard. It leaked a lot but it was a boat and Ernie and I spent many happy hours in her. I can't remember what became of my first boat, and if my father made an assessment of my effort as a master shipwright I can't recall the words. What I do remember is his encouragement. On reflection, the whole exercise must have cost at least treble the outlay for the rotten skiff. He was a wise and generous man.

Boats, boats, boats. I built four more after the leaky one and I venture to think that the construction methods improved along the way. One was a twelve foot open dinghy of a class peculiar to Brisbane known as a 'trainee'. It was designed by a well-known eighteen foot skiff sailor, Nip Thorpe, and as the name implies, was suited to training youngsters in the art of sailing. Sailing is a lot harder than it looks and it took Ernie and me a long time to catch on. We gauged our gradual improvement by measuring how far down the river we could get on each trip before capsizing. Capsizing was a foregone conclusion. I think getting sick of being dunked, being wet to the skin in cold winds and having to haul the boat out onto the foul mud with its buried dangers of broken glass and rusty tin hastened our progress as sailors.

A true obsession persists and mine did. I used to admire the lovely cruising boats heading down the river to Moreton Bay. I was confined to the Brisbane River but not in my imagination. I spent hours daydreaming of boats and drawing hundreds of detailed and no doubt impractical plans and designs. I took to spending hours after school haunting the boat-building yards. The names are fresh in my mind still—Norman Wright, Watts & Wright, Harold Spring, Crowley, McClear and Wherat etc.—all master craftsmen. To watch the building of a wooden vessel, from the laying of the keel, the fitting of the frames, the stern post and the tuck was a magical thing to me. Likewise the smell of red lead and linseed oil.

But although boats dominated my imagination and dreams there were other things going on in real life. To all outward appearances, I was an ordinary little boy. But this wasn't quite the whole story.

· 2 ·

Pianos and eisteddfods

The wireless in our house was a 'Crammond'. It was a pedestal model with a tiny dial that lit up, an ornate filigree grille and a sort of tapestry covering the speaker. It was all knobs and magic and the listeners actually sat around and stared at it, much as viewers now do at a television set.

Scott and I were allowed to listen to selected programs, one being a radio eisteddfod conducted on 4BH. It seemed to go on for years, with heats and semi-finals and finals. The winners were judged by the listeners who sent their votes in to the radio station.

My mother followed the common practice at the time, a hang-over from the Victorian era, of 'putting' the children to the piano. My brother and I were indeed put to the piano. I deeply regret to this day not having suffered the pain of tuition and carried it through.

If only Mum had been more careful in her choice of teachers. I desperately wanted to play. I remember listening in the hallway catching an occasional peek into the lounge whilst my elder brother, Scott, succumbed to his ordeal. Miss Bloxham, I'm sure, was a lovely lady and it was no fault of her own that her bad sight necessitated her wearing pebble thick glasses and possessing a shrill voice. I can still hear her and see her peering at the music sheet and saying: 'Is that a "D" or am I seeing things?' She had a habit, when one had hit a wrong note, of slapping one's small fingers with a wooden ruler. I have no doubt that Miss Bloxham's arrival at our house, to this day, denies me the confidence to even attempt putting my fingers on a keyboard.

After enduring a certain number of these lessons, I think it was a musical piece called 'Play of the Butterflies' that found me out. A tripping composition which involved playing cross-hands. Miss Bloxham twigged that I wasn't reading the dots but playing by ear. She was severe. The ruler came down. My fear of her must have been terrible because the next time I was due for a lesson I hid behind the hedge, confronted her at the gate, and announced, 'My mother doesn't want you to come here any more.' Scott certainly showed no signs of regret that his promising career as a piano virtuoso had come to an end at the hands of his young brother.

On reflection, my mother must have been pretty astute and she showed herself to be a capable bargainer. At that time it was common for a peculiar breed of person, known as an elocution teacher, to visit state schools and give lessons to students who volunteered. I was given the option—Miss Bloxham, the piano, the glasses, the voice and the ruler or elocution lessons from Alsace Rennison. I opted for the elocution, which would keep Mum off my back and get me out of a school lesson—with any luck, mathematics.

One of the exercises was the musical monologue. This was a discovery of Mum's. You told a story with the piano counter-pointing the words and vice versa. Some of the monologues were funny, some dramatic. It was a popular entertainment of the time, often heard on the wireless and available in published form and on 78 rpm records. Our Brunswick phonograph had pride of place in the family sun lounge along with the 'Crammond'. We listened to the exponents of the musical monologue on HMV and Regal Zonophone 78s and tuned in to the radio eisteddfods and talent quests. It was a wonderful world of sound that stimulated the imagination—a world I was to enter at the tender age of 12!

Mum was a very accomplished pianist and I practised my

renditions with her. I must have had my own ideas about how pieces should be put across, because we had many disagreements over interpretation during these sessions. Her insistence on set times for practice was anathema to me. I was only eleven years old, very much an out-of-doors sort of kid, and the jibes and insinuations of my mates were hard to take. But it was the lesser of two evils—Miss Bloxham or this—grin and bear it.

'Just play, Mum, and let me do the talking.'

I was eventually entered in the very radio eisteddfod Scott and I had listened to for so many months. It was sponsored by Fraser Edmiston, a leading Brisbane optometrist. I had entered and performed creditably in other eisteddfods before this, hauled around by my mother to suburban town halls in my suit and with my hair slicked down. I hated competing against the other children and I'm sure most of them felt the same. The adjudicators were remote figures with hyphenated names, like Robert Dally-Scarlet. The only apparent winners were the mothers, who glowed with pride when their offspring came out on top. But this was different. This was on the wireless!

After twelve gruelling heats, I emerged the winner, performing a musical monologue entitled 'Paddy'. It was about a dog. Fraser Edmiston, a tall lean individual, immaculately suited and bespectacled as befitted his trade, presented me with a magnificent cup. I have very little memory about the final except that I was sick with nerves. I had never seen a microphone before this contest, let alone a broadcasting studio (the heats and final were held in the 4BH auditorium with some of the broadcasters I had heard present). I must have stammered out a response. The photograph of the ceremony shows me beaming up at Fraser Edmiston. I have no recollection of my emotion. It might have been relief that the ordeal was over.

If I had a personal ambition at that time it was to be a boatbuilder. I wasn't to know it, but winning the eisteddfod had set me on a different course.

· 3 ·

School and after

Moriarty: How are you at Mathematics?
Seagoon: I speak it like a native.

Spike Milligan *The Goon Show*

My first schoolteacher made a big impression on me but unfortunately it was negative. Mrs Craze was the teacher of 'first babies' at Kedron State School where I was enlisted at the age of four and a half. She was a woman of immense proportions and terrifying authority. Mrs Craze's daughter Jeanette was in the class and the scratching on our slates was periodically suspended while Jeanette went up to her mother's desk, mounted on a platform at the front of the room, to get her glass of milk. I suspect that Jeanette must have at least reached her mother's ample proportions. I know that this early reaction of dislike and fear directed at a teacher disinclined me towards scholarship, especially mathematics.

I always found the subject baffling and its laws questionable. When told that two and two equalled four, my natural reaction was to say, 'Why? Who says so?'

My second grade teacher, a Miss Hamer, was much more sympathetic and was inclined to overlook my shortcomings in maths and encourage me in other directions.

The humanities were more the go for me, especially English and Geography. The attraction of the latter is obvious, most of the world is covered by water. As for English, my elocution training stood me in good stead. Particularly in the class run my Mr Coots. This teacher figures in my memory as the obverse of Mrs Craze—he *encouraged* me and gave me confidence. While accepting that I was a dunce at mathematics he must have recognised some flicker of talent in me in other directions. Invariably I would be chosen to read aloud to the class from the story or recite the poem under study.

If I was strapped or caned at primary school it could not have been very often or very hard because it left no scars. Discipline at home was pretty loose. Dad had a razor strop hanging in the bathroom and Scott and I would get it around the legs only if we pushed the poor man beyond endurance. Like all boys we were mischievous and careless. On one occasion, Scott and I, inspired by what we had seen at the 'Ekka'—Brisbane's annual Royal Agricultural Show—sheared a neighbour's prize red setter named Skipper. Dad, of course, had hand shears in his workshop. Events like that brought the razor strop into play, but it was seldom wielded.

My parents were a devoted couple. My father was a sweet-natured, tolerant man. Mum always seemed to be busy. She was somewhat disorganised and when we opened the cupboard in the hallway that contained our tennis rackets, forgotten balls and untidy skeins of wool were likely to fall out. For many years she collected newspaper clippings on my doings, but her method was simply to tear them from the paper and toss them into a shoe box. She liked her bed and I can recall my father bringing her in her Gilbey's gin and ginger ale nightcap. Never a cross word between them.

At school rugby league football had no appeal for me. Instead I played tennis at which I was good enough to represent the school. I tried out for cricket but didn't quite have the talent. I was probably thought of as a sissy by my mates for my classroom reading, tennis and avoidance of football, but I didn't care.

My boyhood relations with Scott were generally good with some low points. He was a great ideas man, full of schemes to make money or achieve some desired end, but most of them came to nothing. A great starter but a fader at the finish. Where I was always building things Scott was inclined towards demolition. He lopped the head off his teddy bear to see what was inside and carelessly dismantled a billy-cart I had painstakingly constructed. His intention had been to improve it, but he lost interest and there it lay in bits.

I had won a Cyclops scooter as an eisteddfod prize. It was red with a footbrake, everything a boy would want. Unfortunately, I was confined to bed with mumps and couldn't ride the scooter when it was delivered, all glistening new and wrapped in cellophane. Imagine my anguish when, looking down from the bedroom window, I saw Scott and a couple of his mates strip off the wrapping and begin to ride the scooter. We had a cement pathway that ran down to the garage and then forked off in the direction of the old outdoor dunny. Scott and co. found it great fun to roar down the path and jump off at the fork, letting the scooter run where it would. It got scratched and dented. I howled and beat on the window, smashing a pane. I got the razor strop for that one.

I suppose these are the standard events of a suburban childhood, but I have one memory from about this time which I have never understood. I vividly recall standing in the little bathroom in Kedron, gazing intently into my own eyes reflected in Dad's shaving mirror. Inside my head was a message I was sending to myself. *You are going to do something. You are going to do something.* It was no clearer or more focused than that. It was as if I was aware of something ticking inside me that I wanted to give expression to. But to say any more about it would be to embellish it. The memory is crystal clear, the meaning of it is not.

A few days into my time at Brisbane State High, after Scott had left school, about a dozen of his pals who had stayed on decided it was time for my initiation[1]. They grabbed me and pinned my arms back around a pillar under the school. Passing seniors were invited to thump me in the ribs which they did. Next was to 'see the goldfish'. This involved putting my head into each toilet bowl in the lavatory block and flushing them. *That must be it*, I thought. But no, they positioned me above the

[1] I had known this was coming and used to hide from them every day until I decided at last to face the music.

tennis court, hanging by my fingers over a drop of about twenty feet, and took turns in treading on my fingers until I fell. I was stuck in a garbage bin, bum first and rolled down a hill, smeared with strawberry jam, banana skins and other rubbish and eventually stripped and rubbed with the leaves from what we called the 'itchy tree'. The scratches itched like hell. My clothes were then filled with the fine grass clippings from a nearby bowling green and my shoes were tossed up into the branches of a tree. I had to throw stones at them to bring them down.

When I eventually got back to the classroom I was lamentably late and in a deplorably dishevelled condition. This brought on six of the best with the long cane from the headmaster. His name was Isaac Waddle so naturally his nickname was 'the Duck'. He was so small that he had to stand on a stool to cane me and I was no great height. But he could whack. Altogether a traumatic day, and I got into more trouble when I arrived home, after two long tram rides, for the state of my clothes. To this day, I don't know why the ritual was so brutal and sadistic.

Perhaps the greatest trial of my adolescence was the raging acne that plagued me throughout my teenage years. I have since learned that it is a condition brought on by body chemistry and to do with the composition of the fatty cells beneath the skin. Not primarily a matter of diet and nothing much to be done about it. Certainly the patent preparations available at the time were ineffective and sometimes made the complaint worse. It was a severe embarrassment at the time. My somewhat pitted skin became a sort of distinguishing feature and an asset more than a liability.

I even had some innocent fun out of it years later in Britain when I was making a horror film at the lovely old Bray Studios by the Thames. John Gilling was the director, a man found difficult by some actors for his abrupt style, but I liked him and we were in the habit of taking our lunch in a nearby pub. John and I looked forward to escaping from the studio canteen, the constant shop-talk and preening. One day the publicity department informed me that a lunch had been arranged for me in the studio dining room with a journalist from one of the glossies. I resented missing my salad roll and half of bitter with John at the local but realised that it was an actor's duty to perform these little chores.

Cold lasagne and a lady of the blue rinse brigade. An hour of boredom or what would have been an hour if I hadn't had the foresight to brief the second assistant to call me fifteen minutes early. When I got the call she stammered, 'I just have one more question to ask you. I don't know how to put it really.'

The false eyelashes lowered to her note pad. I knew what was coming and decided not only to put her out of her misery but to give her a scoop.

'You mean the boat race,' I said. 'The face?'

'Well, yes. I know it must be terribly embarrassing to you.'

'Oh, not really,' I said. 'But you must understand that I don't like talking about it.'

She apologised again.

I paused, lowered my eyes and spoke quietly. 'There always has to be someone to throw himself on the barbed wire to let the other chaps over.'

I had the pleasure of reading it in glossy print some time later.

My complete puzzlement at all branches of mathematics and my preference for drawing boats to conjugating French verbs brought my school years to an inglorious close. Competence in English, History and Geography could not paper over the cracks and I failed the Junior Certificate. For most youngsters that would have closed off a lot of avenues but I had another string to my bow. Between 1939 and 1942 I won eighteen eisteddfods. I appeared in radio plays and school programs. At that time, the actors wore full evening dress to perform in plays that went out over the airwaves. There I would be, along with the gentlemen in their dinner suits and the ladies in their long frocks, wearing a cut-down stiff dicky, bow tie and long black socks, standing on a box to deliver my lines into the microphone. A clipping preserved by my mother indicates that I contributed to school broadcasts such as 'Health and Hygiene', 'History and Geography' and 'Drama and Poetry Speaking'. I also played the flexitone, an instrument something like a cross between a musical saw and a jew's harp. A metal strip mounted on a frame is vibrated and struck in a way to produce a variety of high-pitched notes. The flexitone used to figure in drummers' kits but it has long gone out of use and I hope it is never rediscovered.

It was while working on 'Health and Hygiene' with a Dr Gutteridge, that I first heard my own recorded voice. I had spoken my lines and was called in to listen to the result which had been recorded on acetate. I heard the voice and recognised the words but was puzzled.

'Why did you get another boy to say my lines?' I asked. I could not believe that the thin, piping tones I'd heard were my own.

As a result of this radio work, people in the business had kept an eye on me. I applied for and got the job of office boy at 4BH, the scene of my radio eisteddfod win. I was fifteen, not long out of short pants, terrified in this new world. I must have given satisfaction though, because I quickly advanced to a job in the record library.

That was the equivalent of a musical Pandora's box for me. There was no question of 9 to 5—I could quite happily have lived in the place. I quickly acquainted myself with the best in all the various compartments from classical through semi-classical to jazz and pop. I learned about Caruso and Galli-Curci, Crosby, Whiteman and Sinatra. Around Mum's piano the favourites were Gilbert and Sullivan, excerpts from *Chu Chin Chow* and the like. We all had a go at 'crooning' the latest hits, but Mum's virtuosity didn't run to the modern stuff. She couldn't handle improvisation and could only play strictly the 'dots'. Working in the record library greatly broadened my musical horizons.

Charles Carson, the station manager, kept a fatherly eye on me and not long after I'd turned sixteen I was summoned to his office. My knees went to water at the prospect of being reprimanded for some misdemeanour or act of negligence. Not that Mr Carson was a frightening figure. Quite the reverse. He was a middling-sized, comfortable sort of man with a benign manner and a wonderfully resonant voice. He'd been one of the early announcers in radio's infancy. Still, he was the boss.

To my astonishment he looked me directly in the eye and said, 'Ray, my boy, I'm going to take a chance on you and put you on air. I want you to take over the midday program from 12 to 2. Do you think you could do it?'

My initial fear had turned almost to paralysis but I managed to stammer out, 'Yes, sir. Thank you, sir.'

I don't recall any training sessions or rehearsals. The day arrived when the seconds ticked away to noon. I could barely summon the strength to pull down the switch to open the microphone. That my voice was going out over the ether was scary enough, but the terror was compounded by the knowledge that my kindly mentor would be monitoring my performance. The phone on the console rang at intervals—Mr Carson giving me encouragement and advice. I made a number of nervous mistakes such as announcing a number from Debroy Summers dance band as a selection from the Ninety Naughties. I rendered the name of a firm of ladies' wear called Overelles in the Valley as overalls in the valley and gave their special as 'ladies mayonnaise pantettes'. Milanese, of course. Two o'clock seemed like an eternity away.

When it finally came I gratefully handed over to Dulcie Scott for her women's afternoon program. The studio was a mess with 78 rpm records, running schedules and advertising copy scattered all over every surface and the floor. I was exhausted and limp. There was silence, no phone call of approval, no comment. The end of my hopes had arrived. I didn't want to leave the studio in case I encountered other staffers. I waited until I could see a clear course to the record library. I dashed through, returned my records and headed for the toilet block where I sat with my head in my hands, stunned. I contemplated fleeing down the fire escape into the backyard where the morticians, Cannen and Cripps, had their premises. That seemed fitting.

At last I summoned the courage to return to the record library and at least go through the motions of preparing my program for the next day. I avoided eye contact on the way. Mr Carson was waiting for me. He put his hand on my shoulder.

'Not bad, son. You'll be better tomorrow.'

I was in a transported daze all the way home to Kedron on the tram. I remember an odd feeling of having no strength in my limbs such was the joy in my heart. Charles Carson's faith and endorsement had given me an enormous injection of confidence without which I couldn't have hoped to succeed as a an announcer, let alone as a performer in other fields.

I progressed to the breakfast program—6.00 am to 9.00 am, five days a week. I had to get up at 4.45 am and I would get a wake-up telephone call at that time. Because I didn't want to arouse the whole house that early, I schooled myself to wake up just before the phone rang so that I could snatch it up at the first ring. It was a pretty rigorous regime for a young man. Winter mornings can be chill in Brisbane and I had a longish walk to catch the 5.25 tram from Lutwyche which passed the door of 4BH in Adelaide Street at approximately two minutes to six. The designated stop was roughly a hundred yards further on so I perfected the art of jumping from the tram's platform while it was still moving. A dangerous exercise, but necessary if I was to open the station on time. The ride itself was an experience. At that hour the people on the tram were absolute regulars, shift-workers mostly, and each had his favourite seat which the others would protect.

'Hang on, you can't sit there, young fella. That's Bert's seat. He'll be getting on at the next stop.'

The trams had closed sections at each end and were open in the middle. Everybody smoked in those days (I didn't yet), and as I've always been a bit claustrophobic I found the smoky compartment oppressive. I'd often end up out in the open, shivering.

The drill was to run upstairs to the studio and officially open the station with the call sign. This had to be done right. 4BH was owned by one John Beals Chandler who was then Mayor of Brisbane. You had to deliver the line, 'This is radio 4BH, Brisbane—a *Chandler* station,' with the right amount of gravity. Then I'd slap on a standby record, race up the stairs to the record library, collect my bundle of 78s and advertising copy, scoot down the stairs and settle into the three hours of broadcasting. The 78s were very brittle, slipped easily out of their paper sleeves and I lost count of how many were broken in those mad rushes. I might add that, at election time, one of the duties of those in the lower echelons was to carry the quite weighty electoral material for Mayor Chandler to the GPO for posting.

Looking back it seems extraordinary that I could be given such an opportunity (and responsibility) at such an early age. The war had depleted the work force and provided opportunities for young men and women that didn't exist in peace time. The voice was obviously critical. I don't remember my voice breaking so perhaps it settled into a mature mould without difficulty. The elocution, acting and performing in public must have helped as did the singing lessons I embarked on at about this time. In any case, I was doing what I was fitted for and enjoying it. Some mornings of course went better than others. Sometimes it seemed that the ten minute breather that came when we switched to the hourly news bulletin from the Macquarie Broadcasting Service would never come. Other days I skated through it.

The war did not touch the family closely. Scott was in the air force, posted to Canada for training. More or less as a joke, Mum had made him a stuffed kangaroo. It was felt, beautifully stitched and packed, complete with a joey in the pouch. Scott wrote saying how much the other blokes in his squadron admired the 'roo, how it had become the squadron's mascot, and what a boost to morale it would be if he had some more he could distribute. I can remember Mum working hard to produce quite a number of kangaroos, all of excellent quality. They were shipped over to Scott who, we later learned, was raffling them off and earning himself some useful pocket money.

More serious was the news from New Guinea, not far to the north, and the consciousness that Brisbane was a garrison town, presided over by one General Douglas MacArthur. American troops were everywhere, well-dressed, well-fed and well-paid. PX stores and clubs catered to the Yanks' needs and some great dance bands were playing. Top musicians, drawn from bands like Tommy Dorsey's and others' were performing. Artie Shaw visited and it was a thrill to have the opportunity of singing with some of these great outfits.

One night I arrived at a jazz club on the south side to do some singing. The black Americans were stationed on the south side, segregated from the whites. They attended the club in the company of some very pretty girls. It was my first sight of the 'zoot suit'—long draped coat, trousers tight at the ankle and long gold watch chain tucked into the pocket. Jackie Thompson, one of the musicians; greeted me as I approached the bandstand.

'Hi, Ray. Staying for the fight?'

'What fight?'

'Hang around. There'll be one in a minute.'

I believe I saw the first punches thrown in what became known as 'the battle of Brisbane'. The Australian 7th Division had just returned from Africa to find the city overrun with free-spending Americans. They had had it pretty hard in North Africa and were now preparing for the worst of it in New Guinea and the islands. The Australian authorities were to blame for permitting such a glaring disparity to exist between the conditions enjoyed by the Americans and what the Diggers had to put up with. As far as I could see the only amenity that existed for them was a hole in the wall where they queued for miles for their smokes.

Buildings in the vicinity of the fight were reduced to matchwood; an American MP shot and killed one Aussie soldier and several were seriously wounded. Some of the smarter Diggers profited from the affluence of the Americans. They would position themselves in the queues outside the brothels in Alice and Albert Streets and as they approached the head of the queue would sell their position to a Yank for whatever they could get. Then the trick was to go to the end of the line and repeat the procedure until satisfied with the day's takings.

I turned eighteen four months before the end of the war. I had put my name down for the navy, thinking more of the deck beneath my feet and the smart uniform than the dangers and discomforts of service life. But the Japanese were on the retreat and I was not called upon to serve.

· 4 ·

On air and on water

Will I ever find
The girl in my mind
The one who is my ideal . . .

'My Ideal' (words by Leo Robin,
music by Richard Whiting and Newell Chase)

At the age of eighteen or thereabouts, I was frantically busy with radio programs, singing with dance bands at places like the 'Four Aces Club' and acting in radio plays and with the Brisbane Repertory Theatre. But I was still living at home and home and family still exerted a big influence over me. Politics had never loomed large in the Barrett household. My parents voted conservative automatically. Labor was equated with uncouthness and, I suspect, communism. Religion was more important but still low-key. My father was an Anglican and attended church regularly. He also tended to show his devotion by service—volunteering to paint the Sunday school and mend the church fence. I don't recall any theological discussion at home. Scott and I went to Sunday school and church as Dad wished us to. Out of respect for him I was confirmed at the appropriate age, but I have to say that I was never a true believer.

Mum baked cakes for church socials but seldom attended church. She always appeared to be too busy for such a sedentary activity. Nevertheless, their Protestantism was steadfast. Aunt Eva, my mother's younger sister, committed the great crime of marrying a Roman Catholic and 'turning'. She was regarded as a traitor. We kids coming home from the state school would chant at the Catholics:

Catholic dogs
Jump like frogs
In the holy water

While across the street the Catholic kids responded with:

Protestant mugs
Crawl like slugs . . .

Poppa Barrett had married a Catholic and they were devoted. Once, when he was having one of his regular sessions with the mean old Jersey bull named Barney, the bull got the better of him and had Poppa bailed up in the barn. Barney was butting and prodding at him and pawing the ground. Poppa's only weapon was the empty kerosene tin from which he had been feeding the animals. He bashed the beast across the head with the tin shouting, 'Piss off, you bloody old Roman Catholic!'

Never a joiner by nature—Boy Scouts, school cadets, church boys brigade—not for me, I nevertheless became a Mason following in the footsteps of Dad and Grandpa Storey. I went through the various initiation rituals and attended meetings regularly. But it never appealed to me; from the first I regarded the rituals as pointless. I abandoned Freemasonry altogether after I left Australia for England.

To say that is to jump forward to 1954, but the years after the war until that move were formative and productive. I was forging a career at an age when people are still studying or casting about for their vocation. This is not to say that I wasn't still learning, I was—about announcing, singing, acting and life itself.

As the war drew to a close my time on the air increased. I was doing the breakfast program as well as the midday show and I had the option of fronting the Children's hour between 5pm and 6pm if I chose. I was then drawn into a Sunday afternoon session called 'Smokes for Sick Soldiers'. This was a singalong program featuring invited celebrities who would perform and induce the listeners to phone in with promises of cash to purchase cigarettes for hospitalised soldiers. Incredible to think of today. The Japanese were killing our soldiers to the north and we were putting sick and wounded ones at home on the way to lung cancer and heart disease. To give up one's Sunday afternoon as I did was looked on as an honour—'doing one's bit'. Good intentions, dire results.

I helped compere these events along with chief announcer George Hardman, introducing the participants, conducting the group singing and doing duets and solos. One of my tasks was to show the slides that put the words of the songs up on a screen. It always got a laugh when I put the slides in upside down. Sometimes this was deliberate.

I had begun to take singing lessons from Bessie Dougal, one of the old school, very strict. There was talk of some connection between her and Melba. I wasn't allowed to sing a note for the initial three months which was spent entirely on breathing exercises. You had to breathe in slowly, filling your lungs to capacity without lifting 'those' shoulders, so as to expand the lungs and the rib cage. Then exhale slowly, holding a mirror to the mouth. If the mirror fogged even slightly you were exhaling too quickly and were reprimanded. This exercise was painful, but I remain eternally grateful to Bessie Dougal for teaching me breath control—a great asset for an actor!

Bessie Dougall was a stickler for doing things the right way. She would refuse to give a lesson if the pupil was tired. Sometimes I would knock on the door of her studio on the second floor of Penney's Building at the appointed hour after a week of morning and afternoon radio and doing the 'Night Owl spot' on Saturday night. She would take one look at me and say,'You're tired. Go away!'

I must have often been tired, but I was young, earning good money, wearing hand-tailored suits and living at home paying a nominal board.

At the end of the war the Australian Labor Party opened a broadcasting station, 4KQ. I suspect the motive behind the venture was party propaganda rather than entertainment but the manager of the station, Les Andrews, made me a tantalising offer—ten pounds a week!

I was sorely tempted. I didn't want to leave my beloved 4BH

and felt an allegiance to my mentor, Charles Carson, but I felt I was worth the extra money and steeled myself to ask 4BH to match the offer. The man to see was the Managing Director, Mr Mitchell, a plump forbidding person. I was sick with nerves when I knocked on his door. I told him of the offer from 4KQ and my wish to stay where I was.

'Could you see your way clear to give me a two pound a week raise, sir?'

He looked at me cold-eyed for what seemed like a very long time. Eventually he grunted, 'Who put you up to this?'

'No one, sir,' I stammered.

The Buddha-like figure bent forward in his leather chair, elbows on the desk, hands propping up his three chins. Once again the unblinking stare. 'We don't take kindly to blackmail, young man. The answer is No!'

He did me a favour. An actor has to be prepared to change direction and move on. I've been doing so ever since.

I had a few good years at 4KQ. Being a new station they were anxious to acquire an audience and ready to try new things. I devised the Night Owls Club, which ran until midnight on Saturday, very late in those days, where I had people telephone me in the studio to talk on air—an early version of the chat show. People called the station from parties or just at home to ask for special requests and to send messages. It proved to be popular. I compered the 'Swing Show' which featured dance music and also did some singing. I was mentioned in the press as 'the crooning announcer'. For a time there was a Ray Barrett fan club composed of what one newspaper called 'Bobby sox radio fanettes'. My signature tune was, 'My Ideal'.

My love of boats persisted through this time. In 1947 while at 4KQ I persuaded the station manager to give me the job of broadcasting the Queensland Cruising Yacht Club race, from Brisbane to Gladstone, from the deck of the Commodore's yacht. It was the inaugural race, 360 nautical miles and I was desperate to be in it but my working commitments prevented me. 4KQ was a new station, anxious to build up a listening audience. I convinced the manager that such a unique broadcast could attract advertisers—ships' chandlers, boating equipment manufacturers, food and drink sellers—who would welcome the kudos of being associated with the first broadcast of an ocean race from a participating yacht.

We approached the army and they gave us full support, installing their transmitter and signals gear on the Commodore's yacht, the ketch *Sari Marais.* I neglected to tell the manager that once at sea the yachts would scatter and I would have no further contact with them. This was long before it was compulsory for yachts to have radios and keep regular 'skeds' with maritime monitoring stations.

There were only six boats in that first race which made it a bit easier for me to more or less imagine where each one might be. Knowing the boats as I did and their individual performances under varying conditions, I was able to give a pseudo-accurate description of their positions.

'It seems that *Hoana* has got the best of the outgoing tide and is off Point Cartwright. *Norseman* has her spinnaker set and is inshore avoiding the southerly set . . .' All slightly vague and imagined, but it sounded authentic and who was to challenge me? The main point for me was, I was part of the race.

As the fleet spread out I thought it best not to push my luck, so I threw in some descriptions of the weather conditions, our encounter with an imaginary whale, sharks travelling north, the sunrise, conditions on board our boat etc. I did live to air interviews with the skippers and crew on arrival in Gladstone. All in all, it came off. It was a sneaky thing to do, but it got me out on the water and the broadcast *did* attract advertisers to the station.

Twenty years or so later on my return from the UK, I was invited to broadcast the race from Gladstone to Cairns. This time I was aboard the mother ship, *Royce.* All mod cons were on hand, such as ship-to-shore equipment installed and controlled by AWA. It was a much more efficient exercise, but to me not nearly as much fun.

I had built a boat of which I was immensely proud. I commissioned an apprentice boat-builder at Watts & Wright to draw up plans for a twenty foot hard chine drop bow sharpie. Being familiar with the river and docks area, I had noticed a pile of packing case timber—ideal for setting the frames for the building of the boat. I plucked up the courage to ask the boss of the yard if I could have the timber.

'If you can take 'em away you can have 'em.'

Great, but how to transport the load. The only solution was Dad. I asked him for help in getting the timber. He gave me a strange old-fashioned look as if to say, 'Oh, my god, here he goes again. We'll have the yard piled high with junk.'

He was non-committal and I despaired. I was sure someone was going to get in first and pinch 'my' precious timber or that the yard man would set a match to it. But not long after Dad said, 'You'd better be in this afternoon. Herman Kratzman's truck will be delivering that stuff you want. Stack it behind the garage.'

I've been a father myself now long enough to guess what was going through his mind. *I wonder if the little bugger can actually do it? Be interesting to see.*

Herman Kratzman (of the family that has produced the famous tennis player) duly delivered the load. The next problem was a construction site. Not in our backyard near the tennis court. Think of the horrible little kids arriving with their Mums. Think of the destruction they would wreak on my beautiful creation! Our neighbour directly across Glen Kedron Lane was Horrie Doolan, a more than adequate bush carpenter. He was the owner of Skipper, the red setter Scott and I had shorn, but I was on reasonably good terms with him again by this time. I must have played on Horrie's wish to be my mentor and instructor for I outlined my intentions, gave him my plans to look over and humbly asked for his advice. I also knew that Horrie had dabbled in the sailing lark in the past. Horrie and his wife Rene eventually allowed me to build my boat in their backyard, with, I suspect, a little gentle persuasion from my Dad.

I set up the rough frames on which the boat would be built and had a look. *Too stubby-looking,* I thought. After some deliberation I decided to add another four feet to her length and widened her out by twelve inches. I agonised for some time over this. If the finished product turned out to look like a narrow cigar I would be laughed off the river. I took the chance.

This job was going to take some time and it had to be done under cover. Thus began the 'temporary dwelling'. This was quickly and roughly knocked up by me from scrap 4 × 4 hardwood and the remains of the case timber. It boasted a malthoid (a tar-impregnated material) covering that could be battened down over the ungainly-looking 30 feet by 15 feet structure.

So far so good. Next problem. It was wartime and the local Council acted under instructions from on high relating to the erecting of temporary structures. A neighbour (probably more concerned at the effect the ugly structure was having on property values than wartime security) dobbed me in and a portly gentleman arrived, presented his Council credentials, and announced that the 'illegal building' had to go. I explained the purpose and pleaded my cause. Perhaps the official had progeny of his own or liked boats, in any event he relented. The neighbours (I had my suspicions of Mrs Doyle and Mrs Haslett) were assured that the structure would be completely demolished by a certain date, and I was able to proceed.

After further trying my father's patience by turning away three or four pieces of timber delivered to the house on account of imperfections, I finally settled on a thirty foot piece of six by four stringybark, very wet and unseasoned with a beautifully straight grain—perfect for the keel.

With the help of Horrie and Nev Willis, a mate from trainee dinghy days, we laid her out and set her rises fore and aft, supported at both ends by Dad's cast-off cement rollers from the tennis court. I bought a beautiful piece of tallow wood for the stem (how I love wood!) and gently cut the rebate into her and set her up, supported by the knees cut from Nudgee Swamp ti-tree. Cutting the knees involved one person climbing up the tree and working a cross-cut saw from above while another pulled on the rope tail below. Bloody hard work and the resultant timber is immensely heavy because of the sap it carries. How we transported these heavy loads on our bikes I'll never know but we did. When it dries the ti-tree is iron hard and virtually unbreakable, much the best stuff for the job. The tuck was dowled and glued on Dad's work bench; the chines and sheers were set in place and the boat began to take shape.

Launching time eventually arrived. I hadn't given any thought to transporting the boat from Kedron to Breakfast Creek, a couple of miles away. Eventually a crane and a low-loader did the job. I refused to leave my beautiful craft and sat in the stern sheets during the entire operation.

I was scared stiff that she might sink or settle to starboard or port or set by the bow or stern. She took in immense amounts of water which is natural for a newly-launched wooden boat before she takes up at the seams, but, to my utmost delight, she rode perfectly. My heart filled with ecstasy.

Now to rigging. I had intended all along she should be gaff rigged and I was lucky enough to find advertised in the local rag an oregon flagpole. On inspection this was just right, perfectly grained and square at the bottom. I set the base above the keel in a cradle across a span of approximately three feet square, thereby spreading the stress and avoiding the thrust directly on the keel. I don't profess to know about stresses and formulas, but I worked out that a greater radius of stress across a larger area made sense. As the boat was cross-planked from keel to chine, I was afraid of springing the planks directly at the base of the mast. I was rather proud of that arrangement, the product of many hours of thought and calculation. I was given a wonderful ten foot bowsprit taken from *Tangalooma,* a famous old eighteen foot skiff, by Alex Wright of Watts and Wright.

I gave the boat's plans to Chick Ware, head sailmaker at Paul & Greys, one of the oldest ships' chandlers in Brisbane. He cut me a fine mainsail and jib and I scrounged old balloon jibs and a spinnaker from various boaties so that I had a full set. The centreboard was five feet of half inch plate steel fitted with a stainless steel pin made by an old German toolmaker. I can see him now, turning the pin on his lathe. Why, I wondered, wasn't he interned with the other Germans in the indiscriminate round-ups of those wartime years? The board had an arm with a series of holes about four inches apart with a steel pin placed in the appropriate hole to indicate the depth of the board between fully down and fully up. This was achieved by a double purchase block and tackle from the mast to a cleat beside the centreboard case.

The boat was twenty-four feet long, but when fully rigged, her boom extended about six feet over the stern and with her jib, which was set on an outhaul on the bowsprit about six feet from the bow, she had a fore and aft spread of approximately thirty feet. The main had two sets of reefing points with the old-fashioned sewn-in tails, which laced under the bolt rope on the boom. I named her *Countess.* Aristocratic names like *Princess* and *Duchess* were fashionable then and I thought my boat the equal of others so-named.

Her maiden voyage was from her mooring on the Brisbane River to the Broadwater at Southport, quite an intrepid expedition considering that I knew very little about navigation in those days. The Shell oil company put out a map of Moreton Bay with its islands and beacons marked. It cost a shilling. That was my first chart. Setting forth into the unknown vastness of Moreton Bay from the security of the Brisbane River was, or should have been, a daunting exercise, but we got away with it.

Countess was a pure sailing vessel. An engine was out of the question. I disguised the reason for not having one by declaring myself a purist. In fact, I could not have afforded an engine and wouldn't have known how to start it anyway.

Moreton Bay is shallow, only navigable along channels marked by beacons—a stiff challenge to the novice. Local knowledge is a great advantage and every sailor has to learn how to sail his own vessel in the tricky waters. I arrived at a set of procedures that worked for me. On approaching a narrow entrance, I would keep the swing centreboard down and when it hit the bank I would go about on the opposite tack and repeat the process until I was in deep water and a safe anchorage.

My horizons were expanding on land as well as at sea. While working at 4KQ I had been appearing in ABC radio plays and receiving good notices. Sydney was the Mecca for that kind of work and I was having serious thoughts about moving there when I was invited to an interview with one of the big-wigs in ABC management. To my astonishment I was offered a one-year contract to work as an actor exclusively for the ABC. This may not sound so remarkable now with the many opportunities that have opened up in the media, but it was unprecedented then. I was the first actor to be hired in this way. It was a great honour, the money would be good and I would be able to concentrate on acting, extend my range and widen my experience.

So Brisbane was to hold me for a while yet. In some ways it irked me to be living at home but in those days it was unusual for young people to leave the parental home unless they married or moved away to work. Gradually the notion of being home by a particular time dropped away and I was more or less free to come and go. Most importantly, my relations with Mum and Dad had always been good. How could they not be with the encouragement they gave and the tolerance they displayed?

I remember coming home late one night after a drinking session. I was unused to drinking and had probably been trying to impress some female. I struggled desperately to put the key in the back door without making a noise. Those old timber houses were like a sound box. The lino creaked. No need for a light, I had a mental chart of the rooms and their furniture. *Successfully past the kitchen door and no response from the parental bedroom. Now past the kitchen table and turn right into the lounge room. Feel to the right and gently glide past the sideboard. Now take stock. It's about three feet from the edge of the sideboard to the door jamb. One foot at a time. Yes, the hallway! Almost there. Feel with the fingers. Yes, that's it, three more feet past Dad's desk and you're there.*

What a relief to find the bed, one of two iron-framed beds my brother and I had occupied since childhood. The bed then seemed to take off and rise slowly towards the ceiling, move clockwise and then anti-clockwise around the room with ever increasing velocity until it landed with a gigantic thud on the lino floor. The casement windows danced and changed shape mysteriously. They lost the shape they had when I helped my father put them in. I just made it in time and unloaded the alcohol out into the Golden Glow (Mum's favourite climbing vine) below.

The first sound I heard in the morning was the scraper on the tennis court roller. Dad was at work preparing the court as usual and it was accepted that I would help him. Somehow I struggled out and got through the rolling and scraping between fainting spells in the hope that I could decently and with a clear conscience return to my sickbed. No. He pointed to a tin.

'There's the lime. Would you mind marking the court?'

Oh, god, I thought. *This'll be the death of me.* Fighting the hang-over I mixed the lime whitener and applied it along the lines with a whitewash brush. He had a system of pegs and cords to mark out the playing area. Through the sweat and nausea I became aware of just how very many yards there are in the lines on a tennis court. Finally I finished and was about to stagger back to bed. Dad called me aside and pointed to a strip of white running down the beige weatherboard beneath my window sill to the garden.

'See,' he said, 'what gin does to paint?'

My income went up when I worked for the ABC and more of my time was my own. I recall inviting two ABC hands, Ian Neil and Mervyn Eadie, to join me in a cruise. Mervyn was the duty newsreader that night and we planned to collect him after his bulletin at 11pm. Ian and I passed our time at a pub known as 'The National', a fine old building with verandahs graced by ornate wrought iron brought as ballast in the old sailing ships. 'The National' is just one of the many fine Brisbane buildings whose passing I mourn. Approaching 11pm we decided it was time, not only to collect Mervyn but to help him out. Well-oiled, we admitted ourselves to the news studio and read the broadcast as a triumvirate, announcing at the end, 'That was the news read by Mervyn Eadie, Ian Neil and Ray Barrett.'

There were no reprisals.

On returning to Bulimba Point I found that I had completely forgotten the rapid fall of the tide and it was no longer possible to step into my tiny pram dinghy which was now twenty feet down at the end of the rickety old jetty. Somebody had to scale down the slippery barnacled ladder. Being the skipper, I decided it was my responsibility. I managed to board the dinghy. The overnight bags were handed down to me and I stowed them, placing the precious square bottle of Bundaberg rum, so necessary for the warding off of mosquito bites, on the top.

At that precise moment the tug *Forceful* chose to pass at ten knots, creating a wake which capsized the dinghy and me and the contents. Retrieving the overnight bags was no problem, but what was more important was the square bottle. Urged on by my companions still up on the jetty, I performed an underwater gardening exercise, feeling around with my hands in the sticky mud until the precious cargo was saved.

With my friends eventually safely on board, we let slip the lines and went out on the tide around Bulimba Point. Fortified with Moreton Bay porridge (rum and milk), our spirits high, we set the spinnaker and made good speed. After a few miles sailing free under the reliable early morning westerly, spinnaker drawing beautifully and with the warmth of the Moreton Bay porridge in our bellies, life was worth living. Then I became aware that the dinghy was bumping into the stern. I remarked that the tide seemed to have changed early. Gradually, through the Bundaberg haze, I realised that the centreboard was firmly in the mud. We had made our first landfall!

Thirty years or so later I was back in Brisbane attending a function in my brother's boat showroom at Breakfast Creek, when he pointed to one of the guests. 'That's the bloke you sold the *Countess* to,' he said.

We chatted for a while and I asked him casually if he knew where the boat had ended up.

'Ended up,' he replied. 'She just came past here half an hour ago. She's up on Tripconny's slip.'

I was dumbfounded. I knew she had been through two cyclones. The desire to see her was strong but I resisted. Perhaps it would be a sad experience. Then I thought of the painting of the boat that my son Reggie had on his bedroom wall in London since childhood. That was the catalyst. I walked around to the slip. There she was, unmistakable apart from a hideous built-up cabin. She was now a motor sailer and there was a guy underneath anti-fouling her.

'Who owns her?' I asked him.

'I do.'

'What's going to happen to her?'

'She's up for sale. She's got a good bottom in her.'

'I know,' I said. 'I built her!' As soon as I spoke I knew I was hooked.

'You're not Barrett?'

After I confessed to being Barrett he took me into the boatshed and showed me the spars, wooden blocks, the bolt turned by the old German and other relics of her earlier days. We negotiated a price on the spot and I bought her for roughly what it had cost me to build her originally.

Reggie was amazed when I told him I had actually bought

the original of the painting on his wall. Later I had many enjoyable fishing trips in her before I had to go overseas for a long spell and, rather than leave her unattended, I gave her to the girls' Sea Rangers where she acted as Mother ship to the sailing fleet. A fitting finale for the *Countess*.

· 5 ·

Some characters and incidents

John Henry Benjamin Borey had an important and long-lasting influence on me. Known as Jackie, he was of Portuguese and Aboriginal descent, and possessed great wisdom and the ability to impart it. He made his living from his oyster beds and fishing, and his sensitivity to everything connected with his occupation was remarkable. I recall fishing with some friends and Jackie off Peel Island. He had positioned the boat, baited our hooks and put us on to a run of schnapper. Highly excited, we all pulled in about three each.

'Up lines!' says Jackie.

A wail of protest from the townies.

Jackie looked at each of us in turn. 'Can you eat more than three of those?'

We had to admit that we couldn't.

'Well,' says Jackie, 'leave them where they are. They stay fresher down there.'

I remember sitting on a beach with Jackie and Charlie Campbell one morning, their dinghies with their nets aboard at anchor, when Jackie remarked, 'It's going to be an early winter, Charlie.'

I was intrigued. 'How can you tell?' I inquired.

'The hardgut mullet are coming in.'

To my unaccustomed eye it was just water.

'How many cases do you reckon, Charlie?'

'Oh, about fifty to sixty.'

'Christ,' I said, jumping to my feet. 'Let's go and and get 'em.'

'Sit down, Ray,' said Jackie. 'They'll be there tomorrow.'

Jackie used to take me walkabout in the scrub behind Myora on Stradbroke Island, looking for stakes for his oyster beds. The sun beat down on the sandy tracks and the first time we made one of these expeditions I remember that I picked up the pace, anxious to get into the shade of the scrub.

'Slow down,' Jackie said.

'Why?' from the townie.

'Because you've gotta come back.'

A medium-sized man, who moved slowly and gracefully, Jackie was a fine bushman. Carefully selecting a spot, he would clear all leaves and twigs in about a six foot radius and meticulously set his fire, boil the billy and cook some snags. After this simple fare, he would say, 'Put your head down for a while, Ray. I'll be back in an hour.'

I'd nod off and he moved so quietly there was no chance I'd hear him returning. He then carefully poured the cold tea in the billy over the fire and replaced every leaf and twig exactly as he'd found them. Whether this was an Aboriginal practice I don't know, but no man ever left a camp site in as undisturbed a condition as Jackie. On the return journey we'd cross small streams on the wallaby pads. The wallabies knocked down bunches of tall reeds across the wet and marshy spots, laminating them for firmness and hopped across them. By taking a good run we could manage to do much the same and cross without getting too wet.

We would break our journey home with a swim in Myora Springs, a beautiful place with its waterfall coming down from Brown Lake. There Jackie would show me how the seasons were marked out by the layers of oyster and mussel shell in the ancient Aboriginal midden. Such feel as I have for the natural and human history of this fascinating part of Queensland, I owe to Jackie Borey.

He had a dreadful stammer, especially when attempting a long statement, and, like most stammerers, he had devised ways to pass the barrier and get the words flowing. Jackie would sidle up to a sentence with something such as, 'Like, what I mean to say,' or 'Watchamacallit.' One night, in the tiny cabin of the *Countess*, with a bottle of Bundaberg rum on the centreboard case between us, I informed Jackie that I was going to cure him of his stuttering. He seemed quite pleased and patiently allowed himself to be taken through all the rigmarole of my endless elocution lessons.

'It's all in the mind, Jackie,' I told him. 'Think of what you want to say, keep calm, take a deep breath, relax and just let the words flow.'

Come 4 am and Jackie climbed into his old tarred oyster 'flattie' and I bade him farewell.

'Like, watchamacallit ... I mean to say ... I'll s-s--see you l-l--later J-J-Jackie.'

I stuttered for a month.

Jackie was on the way to see me for a visit the night he died. He'd stayed overnight with some friends, cooked a meal and died of a heart attack in his sleep. The news of his death hit me hard, leaving a terribly empty feeling and sense of disbelief. Someone so kind and gentle, without a malicious atom in him, shouldn't have died at sixty-three. We buried him overlooking the entrance to the One Mile, an Aboriginal settlement on Stradbroke. I'm proud to say that on the Admiralty Charts the flashing green beacon that welcomes all sailors into safe anchorages in these waters bears the name, 'The Jackie Borey Beacon'.

Another interesting waterman and Stradbroke Island character was Bonty Dixon, a resourceful and gregarious man who was also an historian and poet. Small and bustling, he had theories and views on every subject under the sun, and would expound them at length if encouraged. During the war, most of the boatbuilders on the Brisbane River were commissioned by the government to make wooden vessels such as Fairmiles, MTBs, work boats for the army and navy. I have already mentioned the suitability of mangrove and ti-tree for the manufacture of 'knees' for the support of stern posts, sterns and general strengthening of the craft. Bonty was too old to join up, so he determined that his contribution would be to supply as much of the invaluable material as possible.

He had an old wooden flattie on which he rigged a small sail. He would pack enough provisions for a few days and set off, using the tide up the Rainbow Channel to run past Myora and Amity Point, to where he knew the ti-tree grew in abundance. He would secure his dinghy and set forth into the scrub with axe, compass and paper and pencil. When he sighted a suitable bend, one that could be shaped into a knee, he would make an axe cut on the tree trunk and mark its position on the rough chart he was drawing of the area. After a couple of days in the bush, with a dozen or so likely knees marked, he would return to Dunwich using the tide again and his small sail. Then he'd sharpen his axes and cross-cut saws and collect up the rope and other things he'd need.

Back in the scrub, he'd begin the harvest. Often, to get the correct angle required, he would have to cut three or four times the amount of wood necessary. Trees were very seldom obliging enough to grow exactly to the required shape. Once the branch with the desired piece was felled and the extraneous limbs trimmed off, Bonty carefully marked its location on his chart and proceeded to the next tree until he calculated he had as many branches as his flattie could carry.

The first time he made one of these expeditions, Bonty realised that he had an unforseen problem. When first cut, ti-tree is full of sap and these large pieces of timber weigh an enormous amount, too much for a man to lift. Using a sapling as a fulcrum, Bonty rolled the knees inch by inch to the banks of the tidal stream where his dinghy was beached. Getting them into the boat was the next problem. He agonised for hours, watching the tide come in, floating the dinghy. Suddenly the answer came to him. *Heavy objects under water are more or less weightless. Sink the dinghy, float the knees in and secure. That's the answer. But how does the dinghy refloat?*

Before the tide was halfway out he had the solution. Back down the Rainbow Channel to home to collect a brace and bit and a dozen corks. Returning to the stream, he carefully bored a dozen holes in the bottom of the flattie and waited for the tide. The dinghy filled, the knees were floated in and secured. He had some tucker and rested until the tide went out. The dinghy drained and he inserted the corks and settled down to wait for the next incoming tide when the dinghy and its cargo would float. It worked like a charm. I was always very impressed by this exercise in patience, determination and making use of natural forces. Bonty continued to supply the knees all through the war until the invention of the laminated knee. One man's war effort!

When the Benevolent Asylum at Dunwich closed, Bonty bought all the old iron bedsteads and placed them on his oyster bank to catch the spawn oysters. It was a sight to see at low tide—50 or so beds on an oyster bank. Newcomers to the area could be forgiven for doubting their sanity. On the incoming tide the bream fed on the young spawn and the fishermen were waiting for them in numbers. Frequently, after hooking a fish, the line would become snagged on one of the iron bedsteads. On the low tide all Bonty had to do was simply go out to his bank and fill his dinghy with prime fish. A truly resourceful man.

Bonty had the first shop on Stradbroke Island, a corrugated iron structure with a dirt floor, which housed among other things a pianola. Many a good time was had by boaties, me among them, frequenting the One Mile anchorage.

I invited Johnny Herbert, an old school mate from Brisbane State High, to join the crew of the *Countess*, for a race on Moreton Bay. Johnny figures in the story later, but at this juncture he had no experience whatsoever as a sailor so I put him in charge of the runners. A gaff-rigged boat carries running shrouds, port and starboard, as extra support for the mast when the boat changes tack. This was the simplest task I could find for Johnny. All he had to do was let one shroud go from the cleat on the order and secure the other when we went about.

The race was run in dirty weather. The tension ran high. The skipper's language was salty, and the new chum did pretty well under the circumstances. We were all relieved when it was over and we could anchor for the night in the calm water in the lee of Bishop Island with a few convivial Bundys to soothe the nerves.

The next day the wind had abated; the sea was dead calm so we decided on a leisurely jog around the bay. There are hundreds of islands in Moreton Bay and it is a sailor's delight. Time to go about, and I gently asked Johnny to pull the runner on, which he had forgotten to do in the casual atmosphere of the cruise. I repeated the request.

'Would you mind swearing at me, Ray,' he said. 'I can't understand you otherwise.'

During the war, communications and broadcasting facilities were to be protected at all costs in case of enemy invasion.

An underground bunker, housing several studios, had been constructed at Alice Street, opposite the Botanical Gardens. The ABC shifted most of its operations here from Penney's Building. However, for reasons unknown to me, the news studio was kept at Penney's. The studio was entered through two huge soundproof doors with a space of about two feet between them, designed to absorb all sound. The newsreader was under strict instruction to carefully lock the first door from the inside, then the second door in the same way, thus rendering himself secure and safe from foreign invasion. The newsroom studio microphone could only be activated from the bunker studios at Alice Street, a quarter of a mile away.

Then, as now, news bulletins were broadcast on the hour, although in those days the evening duty reader was required to wear a dinner suit while he performed his task. This schedule gave the reader quite an amount of time to fill. Directly across Adelaide Street there happened to be a watering hole of dubious reputation, The Royal—a convivial place to while away the time between bulletins.

Frank Carswell was one such newsreader. I remember him with affection, an ebullient character with a huge Henry Lawson moustache. I found it fascinating to listen to his readings and note the transition from precision and authoritativeness in the early bulletins to a more relaxed delivery as the hours passed. Frank was a frequent visitor to The Royal. I recall one night when I was listening, waiting to see how he would shape up in his final bulletin at 11 pm.

Now in Edward Street, near Penney's, there was a transportable pie shop, something like Woolloomooloo's famous Cafe de Wheels. It opened at 6pm and was strategically located to attract the custom of people who spent some of their time in the many pubs in the area. On the night in question, Frank, feeling the effects of his visits to The Royal, evidently thought it prudent to partake of some sustenance before his 11 o'clock bulletin. He bought what was affectionately known as a 'floater'—a meat pie with peas and mashed potato, swimming in a generous amount of gravy. A great favourite at the time.

Frank, wisely giving himself plenty of time to consume the repast, locked himself as per regulations into the news studio and set out the dish in front of his console and prepared his news sheets. From the bunker came the words:

'This is the ABC. The time is eleven o'clock. We now cross to the newsroom. Here is the news read by Frank Carswell.'

I cocked an ear, knowing Frank was well-oiled.

Silence at first, then slowly followed a drowning, slurping sound with occasional snorts. This lasted for a minute or so before the duty announcer, safe from invasion in his bunker, said:

'We apologise for this slight technical fault. We'll be back just as soon as these technical difficulties can be sorted out.'

I heard later that security guards were alerted, the axe in the glass case was broken out and the impregnable bastion of the news studio was stormed in the nick of time to save Frank from drowning in a 'floater'.

· 6 ·

A big fish in a small pond

I was a late starter in the sex stakes. I remember asking Betty Dortkamp over the back fence for a fuck. She said: 'No, but J...... round at 8th Avenue would.' I didn't know J...... very well and felt too embarrassed to go around and ask her. So my entry into the love-making business was put on hold for some time.

The pictures, the 'flicks', were an opportunity to gain sexual experience. We went to the old Crystal Palace at Windsor, run by 'Baldy' Fenwick. There were cartoons and serials and the feature was often a Western. As a kid, it was a fun and games sort of thing—rolling your bottle of Kirks ginger ale down the wooden floor at the end of the film to the ire of 'Baldy'. Later, sex was the object. The seats in the back row were canvas, very comfortable, especially when you got back there with a girl. I was shy with girls and seldom managed to get very far with them. Any kind of a decent grope was regarded as a major triumph to be boasted about.

There were all sorts of inhibitions operating—parental, religious, medical (the horror of venereal disease), and above all, the great fear of 'getting her pregnant'. The pill was a generation away, condoms were an embarrassing purchase to make and reputedly unreliable. It's a wonder there was any pre-marital sex at all in those days, but there was. We fumbled our way to an uncertain competence in the backs of cars, on beaches and in borrowed bedrooms. I had a few brief affairs, nothing important, and then I met Joy Bettanay.

It was a typical Brisbane party in a typical Brisbane house—lots of beer in a big airy place with verandahs all around, the piano playing. The party was given by a school friend whose father was a big noise in business. I was smitten by Joy who was very attractive. I had to go into town to collect someone to bring to the party. A mate of mine drove and I took Joy along for the ride. She worked at the Commonwealth Bank, liked tennis and music. We got on well. I didn't know at the time that she had been brought to the party by a bloke named Johnny Herbert who I had known at high school and who was later to become a great friend—boat crew and a golfing partner—when I met up with him again in Sydney.

'Here's the bastard,' Johnny would say, almost as a party piece, 'who stole my girlfriend.'

'And you should go down on your bended knees and bloody well thank me,' I would reply.

Joy turned out to be a flirt and a tease and a semi-professional heart-breaker. She delighted in tricks like accompanying her beau of the moment to a tennis party and leaving with someone else. She dumped me in due course to my great distress. A little while later I met her sister Audrey who worked as a secretary in various ABC departments. I found something inherently fascinating about the difference between the two women. Audrey was attractive too, but had none of Joy's capriciousness. There was an element of 'on the rebound' about the relationship no doubt, but the attraction was there and I was looking for stability. Audrey and I were married in 1951.

I have pronounced home-making instincts. One of my games as a kid was to construct a private sanctum under the house at Kedron, to wall myself in and lay out possessions just as I liked them. When I married I got the first chance to express this impulse in a significant way. I found a house to buy at Norman Park, across the river from New Farm and a respectable distance from Kedron. Here was a house right on the river where I could keep my beloved *Countess*. Objectively, it was a terrible place, built of fibro, up on stilts of course, and with a mountain of work to do to make the house livable. But I was up to the job. I ripped out walls and put in new floors and windows to give a view of the river.

Like most of my projects, the work on the house was a family affair. One incident demonstrated the differences between my two grandfathers. Poppa Barrett, as I have said, was a capable man and quite astoundingly energetic. Much and all as I loved him, I could not say that energy and application were Grandpa Storey's strong attributes. I had a plan to convert the wooden shack at the bottom of the property into a boathouse and to put in a slipway below it. To do that I would have to reclaim some land that had been nibbled away by tides and backwash. I had the retaining wall rebuilt with some beautiful stone supplied free by the council. There remained a hole filled with rubbish which was a home for water rats and other vermin. The only way to clean it out before filling it in was with fire. I lit the fire and stationed Grandpa nearby in a comfortable chair with a hose.

'There you are, Grandpa,' I said. 'Just play it on the neighbour's fence and make sure the fire doesn't get away.'

Dad and I went on with the job of building a wash house around the other side of the main house. About an hour later the neighbour on that side arrived home and hung over the fence.

'How you goin?'

'Gidday. Fine,' I said.

'You're doin' a great job there.'

'Yeah, not bad.'

'By the way, Ray,' he said in exactly the same tone of voice, 'your shed's on fire.'

I raced around the house to find the shed blazing and the hose running away uselessly. The fire had got beyond the hose stage; fanned by a northerly, it was burning fiercely and threatening the next-door house. Fortunately, Audrey had called the fire brigade and they arrived in the nick of time.

'What happened, Grandpa?'

'Oh, Mabel said tea was ready.'

I put a lot of sweat and a fair bit of money into that house. Painted it inside and out, top to bottom. I measured up and built, in Dad's workshop, an entire kitchen which I then slotted into place. I restored the jetty and eventually there the *Countess* rode, in pride of place, at the bottom of the garden. When I left Brisbane I sold it to the King of the radio quiz shows, Bob Dyer and his wife Dolly. Bob was a passionate fisherman and wanted a place to keep his big boat.

I keep jumping ahead but I shouldn't minimise the importance of those years under contract to the ABC in Brisbane. I had the great good fortune to work under the direction of Dion Wheeler, who headed up the drama production unit in Brisbane. Dion was dedicated and imaginative and I admired him immensely. It was really a dream job and a bit of a doddle. I was kept very busy doing things for the Children's program, rehearsing and so on, but I enjoyed it so much it didn't seem like work and you've got the game beaten if you can get into a situation like that. I'd go in to the drama department where Dion and his assistant Phillip Dodds would be working at something and Dion would toss a bundle of scripts at me.

'Have a read of these, Ray, and give me your opinion.'

I'd sort through the scripts picking out the ones I found interesting. We'd have a bit of a discussion, settle on one, and Dion would say, 'Well, say we do this one. What part d'you fancy?'

'Well, I like the General but he's seventy . . .'

'Oh, you can have a go.'

We'd read through and make notes. Hard to imagine a more ideal situation for an actor.

My contract, which ran for a year, called for me to perform in one play each week. In some ways it was an education in drama—I was Mark Antony one week and the archdeacon in Trolloppe's *The Warden* the next. Among the many plays I appeared in, I remember Sidney Howard's comedy-drama *They knew what they wanted*, Marlowe's *Dr Faustus*, Jules Romain's dark satire on the doctor-patient relationship, *Dr Knock* and Douglas Stewart's terrific play about Scott of the Antarctic, *Fire on the Snow*.

The Stewart play illustrates a couple of points. The part of Scott was played by one Robert Speight, out from England. We locals had to defer to English actors which was galling, especially if they weren't very good. This happened from time to time. I played Wilson, the doctor, and of course we all ended up dying in our tent. Dion hit on the idea of having us all lie down on sofas and on the floor to get that constricted sound into our voices. It worked.

Another memorable Dion Wheeler production was *Morning Departure,* a great play about a submarine sunk in the North Sea. The situation is—the sub's stuck on the bottom, all the electrics go and it's impossible to get out through the hatches or torpedo chutes. It's about the last hours of the crew, but the divers come down and tap on the hull and try to make contact. The Stratford Shakespearian Company was touring Australia at the time and some members of the company were in the cast of *Morning Departure,* including Clement McCallum who played the captain. There was a need for different sets of sounds—in the stricken sub, above in the rescue vessels and the sound of the divers tapping. Dion was prepared to experiment with sound and settings which seems like a natural thing to do in radio but was very forward-thinking of him at the time. He decided to use the studio for the surface level work and he discovered that he could get a terrific atmosphere in the gents' toilet on the sixth floor of Penney's Building in Adelaide Street where the ABC studios were. Tapping on the pipes provided the ideal sound for the divers' attempts to communicate and the large and cavernous toilet, with its marble and tiles, was perfect for the interior of the sub.

After achieving the variety of sounds he wanted, Dion realised that he had a problem—the noise created by the regular flushing of the cisterns every few minutes. Resourceful as ever, he applied to the local council to have the water cut off in the building for the duration of the broadcast. Imagine trying to explain to some Council 'Executive Head of Lavatories' that we wanted the water turned off in urinal number 80 for four hours as we required it to be a submarine! The council must have thought they were dealing with a madman, but Dion got his way.

The play had enormous emotional clout. I remember that when the time came for the scene when all we trapped submariners realised that we were finished, Dion had us huddle together in a sort of tent constructed from heavy blankets to muffle the sounds and restrict our breathing. The captain read

ABOVE: Me helping Dad and Uncle Cecil build the garage at Kedron, 1930.

LEFT: Scott and me, 1928.

FROM LEFT: Nanna Storey, Dad, Uncle Cecil, me, Scott, Mum and Grandpa Storey in the Ford Tourer.

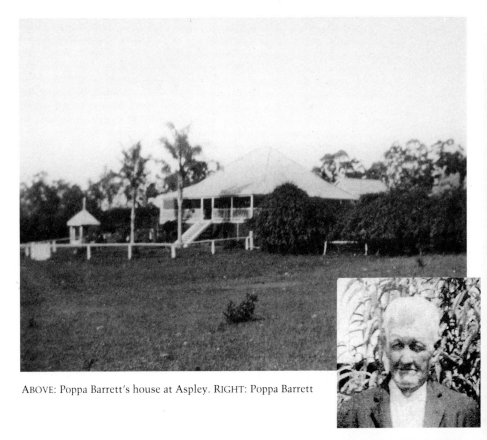

ABOVE: Poppa Barrett's house at Aspley. RIGHT: Poppa Barrett

Grade III, Kedron State School. I'm sitting to the right of the boy holding the slate.

LEFT: Me at 11 years of age receiving first prize in the 4BH Radio Eisteddfod from Fraser Edmiston, 1938.

RIGHT: As the prince in the tower, with a costume lovingly made by Mum, 1939. *(Regent Studios)*

Me on Aby, Scott on Trixie, Mt Beppo, 1939. Guess who's got the only saddle?!

Family photo, 1942. Scott is 17, I'm 15.

TOP: Me on 'Saturday Morning Sing Song' at age 18, with rampant acne, interviewing Chips Rafferty. Commenting on his height, he said, 'I lie long in bed'. *(W.A. Jones and Co.)*

BOTTOM: 7th Avenue, Kedron

LEFT: Building the temporary dwelling with Horrie Doolan, 1945.

BELOW: Building *Countess*, 1945. Just completed the drop bow.

The *Countess* finished, 1945. Ready to be taken to launch.

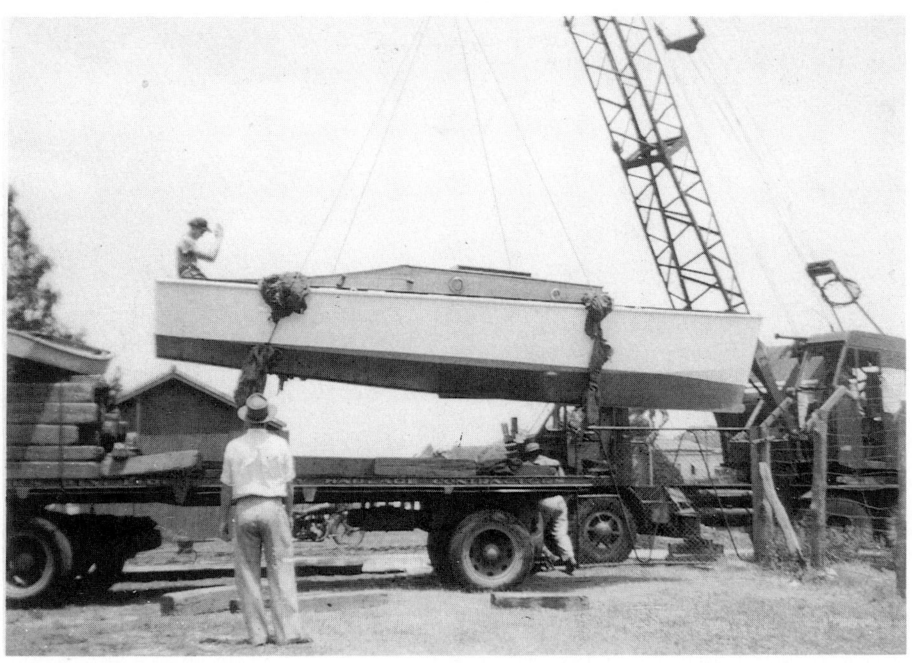

Me praying during a nervous moment. I'd come too far to leave the ship!

ABOVE: *Countess* launched. Me with mate Nev Willis, 1946.

LEFT: *Countess* under sail.

RIGHT: Camping it up at Tugun Beach, 1949.

BELOW: Nanna and Grandpa Storey at my 21st birthday.

Me at 4KQ, 1950.

At our wedding reception, 1951. Audrey is sitting at the piano with Don Bennett.

Me in the grey gaberdine and polka-dot bow tie at a play broadcast in the Fish Bowl at the Royal Agricultural show, Brisbane. *(Camera-Craft)*

LEFT: Audrey with Sue Ellen, aged 12 weeks.

BELOW: As Nosey Parker in *Tea with the Thomases*, with Al and Vonney Thomas, 1955. *(Norman L. Danvers)*

RIGHT: The bow tie, 1956.

BELOW: Three of the 'Idiots' in *The Idiot Weekly*. From left: me, Spike Milligan and John Bluthal, 1958. *(ABC)*

More 'Idiots'. From left: me, Michael Eisdell, John Bluthal, Bobby Limb, Reg Goldsworthy and Spike Milligan. *(ABC)*

Publicity shots. *(Norman Dewhurst)*

ABOVE: *Time Remembered* with Margaret Rutherford and Darlene Johnson. Elizabethan Theatre, 1958. *(Gordon F. De'Lisle)*

RIGHT: With Fulton McKay in *Naked Island*. Arts Theatre, London, 1960.

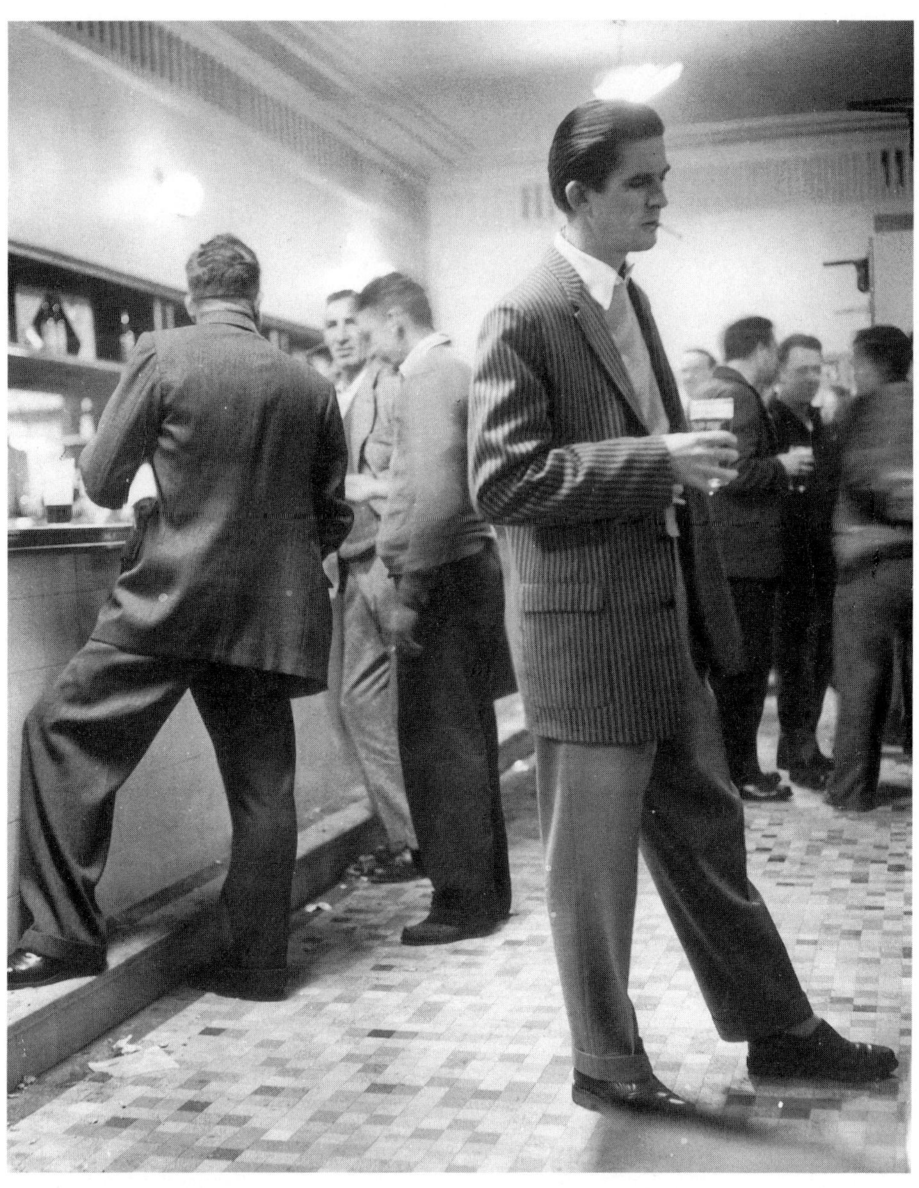

Absorbing lines and beer for *Look Back in Anger*. A pub near the Elizabethan Theatre, 1958. *(Elizabethan Theatre Trust)*

a prayer, gasping for breath. I had tears in my eyes.

We did it live of course, and it happened that my mother and father were listening up at Grandpa and Nanna Storey's place at Herston. Dad picked me up and we went back there to have supper. Dear old Nanna had really got carried away by the play, especially the scenes where we said our last prayers and expired dramatically.

'Mabel, get him a nice hot cup of tea,' she said in her Geordie accent. 'He must be very cold being under that water for so long.'

Radio in those days had a wonderful way of touching the emotions through the imagination. There has never been anything quite like it since in my opinion.

As well as plays I did readings from novels like Paton's *Cry the Beloved Country* (which must have involved some tricky stuff with accents, T.A.G. Hungerford's *The Ridge and the River*, a very popular book in its day and another best seller called *Road Going North*. Sometimes film scripts were adapted to radio. In 1953 we did *No Highway* which was an adaptation of the film of Nevil Shute's immensely popular novel about a plane flight. The engineer who built the plane is aboard and knows that its construction has flaws that could bring it down before the flight is complete. A classic nail-biter. The film starred James Stewart and Marlene Dietrich and was a great success as was our radio version.

There was also a very limited amount of community liaison work in keeping with the ABC's charter as a public body. In 1953 the very accomplished actress Margo Lee and I were sent off to Armidale under the ABC's auspices to work with the local amateur theatrical group giving what would now be called workshops on radio acting.

One day, out of the blue, the Talks department more or less issued me with a directive: take a technician with a wire recorder and go down to the port and record an interview with this skipper who was torpedoed three times during the war. He lost three boats and we want his story.

I was a boatie, but I couldn't see that I had any other qualification for the job. I said, 'I'm not an interviewer. I wouldn't know how to go about it.'

The bloke from Talks said, 'We contribute five pounds a week to your salary. We want you to do it.'

This was the first I knew of an arrangement whereby other departments—Talks, Music, Children's—kicked in to my salary and had a call on my services. Up to then, I thought that odd bits of work I'd been doing for them was out of the goodness of my heart.

Down to the port I went with the recordist and my notes.

'Captain so-and-so,' says I. 'You were torpedoed in the Mediterranean in 1942?'

'Yes.'

'And then you were sunk in the North Sea in '43?'

'Yes.'

'And you and the crew were rescued by HMAS whatsit?'

'That's so.'

A disaster! It wasn't until years later when I got to England and did stints on the BBC relieving people like Pete Murray on their holiday breaks that I learned the technique of drawing subjects out in interviews.

Nowadays, like most people, I dress casually most of the time. It is amazing to look back at photographs taken in the 1950s and see how dress codes have changed. We wore lounge suits on occasions when jeans and a sweater would suffice now. Of course I had a greater need for suits than the average man because I was still singing with dance bands around Brisbane, compering concerts and appearing in public and for those occasions nothing but the best would do. A radio colleague named John Tuttle was always very smartly dressed and I asked him who his tailor was.

He looked me up and down as if wondering whether this individual was worthy of the information. Eventually he told me in a manner resembling a spy divulging secret information.

'Fred Hoey.'

Off to Fred Hoey in Adelaide Street I went and he made me quite a few suits over the years. I can still remember him crouching there, a small, stout, balding man, with the tape measure around his neck, making chalk marks, fussing away. It took quite a few fittings before he was satisfied with his creation and he insisted on a thorough measuring-up each time. His hand-tailored suits were really beautiful—double-breasted, silk-lined, gaberdine and other top quality materials, worn with a polka dot bow tie as often as not, expensive shoes and shirts. Very suave. How I managed to achieve this elegance on eight pounds a week I can't imagine.

When my daughter Suellen was born in 1954 domestic expenses mounted, but it was certainly a prosperous time for Audrey and me. I had begun to smoke for reasons I can't now quite recall. It was almost like a social attribute one picked up along the way. Cigarettes were cheap and so was alcohol. Unlike a lot of people in show business, I've never been a gambler and for this I am very grateful. I've seen many big talents run into the ground through an addiction to gambling.

Not that I had any inclination towards it, but a story told by Spiro Aroni, a very successful fish shop owner in Brisbane, underlined the futility of gambling. Spiro was the sponsor of the 'Hillbilly Half Hour', a show I did on 4BH. One day he invited me down to one of his shops in Fortitude Valley for a drink. He had Australians working for him and I asked him how he'd managed to become such a success after arriving in Australia with nothing.

'Ray, you Australians knock off when the bell goes. We knock off when we finish.'

He went on to say that he was a great punter. I was sceptical.

'Ray,' he said, 'every Saturday we close the shop and I go home. I have a bath. I get into my pyjamas and dressing gown. I go through the form guide; a hundred quid on this one, two hundred on that. I've got my bookie's number all ready by the phone. Then I go into my bedroom, pull the curtain and go to sleep. That's the way to make money on the horses!'

As I've said, I had begun to think of moving to Sydney earlier but the ABC contract offer forestalled me. After four years the impulse arose again. Brisbane was very much the poor cousin of Sydney as far as radio was concerned. From time to time the leading names from Sydney, who were household names in Australia—John Cazabon, Lyndall Barbour, Neva Carr-Glynn—came to Brisbane and we local actors performed with them. ABC plays and episodes of the Lux Radio Theatre introduced by Harry Dearth or Caltex Playhouse would be performed live or recorded and would attract tremendous studio and home audiences. These luminaries were usually charming and professionally impressive, but I couldn't help feeling the difference in status between the metropolitan star and the provincial performer. I felt I could more than hold my own with them.

Towards the end of 1954 Wally Pym, one of the leading producers in Sydney commercial radio, came to Brisbane to organise one of his productions and he phoned me.

'I've got a Caltex Theatre production coming up,' he said. 'And I very much want you to play the lead in it. Do you think you could possibly come down to Sydney?'

His timing couldn't have been more perfect.

· 7 ·

The Big Smoke

The ABC released me from my contract which still had several months to run. Eric Scholl, the Brisbane manager, was very reasonable about it although of course he had to consult with all those departments who'd been chipping in for my salary. I travelled to Sydney by plane and the plan was to bring Audrey and Suellen down later. Ordinarily, going from the security of a contract to the uncertainties of free-lance work would be alarming, but I walked straight into leading parts in Lux Radio Theatre and Caltex Playhouse productions and my Sydney radio career was off to a flying start. I'd only been to Sydney once before, some years back when I farewelled Audrey who was off on a trip to the west. I retained only a memory of its size and of being lonely there. Sydney was many times the size of Brisbane and life moved at a much faster pace.

Lady in Edinburgh for the Caltex Playhouse was my first job and I was feeling pretty apprehensive when I turned up at the 2GB auditorium in Phillip Street for the first rehearsal. Pretty daunting. Radio in Sydney was booming and here was I stepping right into the middle of it in a leading part. The Sydney actors were a pretty cliquy lot, protective of their status, wary to the point of being resentful of newcomers. I recall that Buddy

Tingwell, one of the leading lights, turned up late to the rehearsal almost as if by right, and the others kept a close eye on me to see if the brash boy from Brisbane would step in it.

I can't remember one thing about *Lady in Edinburgh* but everything went off all right and I soon found myself getting along fine with the established players. Actors are much the same everywhere in my experience—watchful, jealous, intensely competitive (they have to be due to the high unemployment rate), but ready to be welcoming, especially over a few drinks. There were going to be quite a lot of drinks during my Sydney sojourn. One watering hole was the Australia on the corner of Castlereagh and Rowe Streets where Evie presided in the 'Long Bar'. This was a famous meeting place where people who had been out of town for years would go, confident that they would see some familiar faces. Actors, writers and bohemians, along with colourful characters like Errol Flynn and sundry remittance men, drank there over the years. Later, we frequented the Carlton, also in Castlereagh Street, with Betty behind the bar, and the old Journalists' Club in Phillip Street.

At these pubs and the club, women couldn't drink in the public bar, only in the lounge or saloon, but that was beginning to break down. At the Assembly Hotel, near radio station 2GB, the infiltration of women was well underway. We drank there quite regularly and I recall that E. Mason Wood ('Woody'), one of the leading producers, delighted in hiding women in the public bar—Lyndall Barbour, Pamela Page and others.

'Now we'll just stand around here,' he'd say. 'Yes, gather round the corner and we'll poke Pam Page in the passage.'

One of the first steps was to get an agent. There were quite a few of them in business. Mine was Nora Burnett. The agents played a fairly passive role for their ten per cent. All they had to do was answer the telephone, keep track of your diary and tell the producers when you were available and when not. There was none of the manoeuvring and pressurising of producers and casting agencies that goes on now. No need for it. The agents also collected the money and you'd go in on Thursdays and pick up your pay packets—cash in a brown envelope with the tax already deducted. All very straightforward. If you were constantly in work as I was, the rewards were substantial. Two hundred and fifty pounds a week wasn't uncommon—very good money for those days—and anything under two hundred quid felt pretty light on.

Before television changed everything completely, there were 85 serials and plays going out on the radio every week. They were made by various production houses (AWA, EMI, ARC, Grace Gibson and others) that were going flat out—*Biggles, Tarzan, Superman, Portia Faces Life, Night Beat, Larry Kent* ... the list goes on and on. The serials tend to blur a bit in the memory and I sometimes wonder if the writers didn't just change the names and use the same dialogue. I had the title parts in *Robin Hood* and *Tarzan* and was in *Portia, Address Unknown, Around the World in 80 Days, No Love for Linda, Mary Southern* and many others. As an introduction to Robin Hood I set the mood by singing 'Greensleeves'. In a total change of pace, I was a cowboy in *Brand of Justice*. That required an American accent of course. I took over the Tarzan role from Buddy Tingwell who had taken it over from Rod Taylor, so that I ended up imitating Tingwell imitating Taylor. We all had a laugh about that. For Tarzan I used an English accent (he was Lord Greystoke after all), but my Jane, Joan Landor, spoke American.

As Richard Lane points out in his book *The Golden Age of Radio Drama,* recorded Australian serials were exported to America and were popular there. Those dollars must have been useful to the production houses. There were about 40 actors in full-time work meeting this demand and about another 25 involved part-time. Occasionally there were protests in the radio press that the same voices were being heard over and over again. Fair comment, but in fact the same *names* were involved more than people realised—you had to have a number of voices in your repertoire. I was lucky to be good at accents, lighter and darker voices, older and younger tones.

In addition, and very beneficial to the pay packet, were the commercials. I did a lot of that kind of work, along with people like Brian Henderson and Roger Climpson. It was the hey-day of the cigarette ad of course and I did those and everything from hair oil to corn pads. I was the Ford Pills man, which involved recording the word 'Ford' dragged out and given an echo. Buckley's Canadiol Mixture was another. The message extolling the virtues of this cough medicine was played against the background of a howling Arctic gale.

The production houses were dotted around the city and we literally rushed from one to another, riding on the running boards of trams, hopping off and scooting through the traffic to get to the next appointment on time. Sometimes I forgot what character I was playing.

'Who the hell am I?' I'd ask the production assistant while riffling through the script with one hand and grabbing a glass of water in the other.

'The old man with one eye and the limp.'

'Oh, yes.' Essential information if I was to remember how to play a character who might have been out of the serial for six episodes and wasn't fresh in my memory.

For the serials, some of the sound effects—tyres shrieking, sirens etc.—were recorded, but many were done manually with various pieces of equipment, such as a particularly squeaky chair which was a sailing ship at sea. Woe betide you if you accidentally sat in that chair. It had been everything from the *Hispaniola* to Nelson's flagship. My favourite was the gravel box which was set next to the door in its frame, complete with metal knockers, buzzers, bells etc. When a minute had to be found somewhere one of us who wasn't involved in the dialogue at the time would get into the gravel box and simulate footsteps coming up the path while whistling or humming a tune. All the time with eyes on the production booth, getting the signals as to how much time to go. Knock on the door. *Not yet! Hum a tune!* Getting nearer. Another knock.

Door opens.

Actors' voice: Yes, can I help you?
Oh, is this the Smith residence?
No, I'm sorry—two doors down.
Oh, I am sorry to disturb you. Good day.

Back in the gravel box, musing, Funny, I thought it was number 25 . . . and more walking until thumbs up from the booth.

There were coconut shells for hoofbeats and so on. The sound effects man was a handy person to know. One of the great sound effects men of the time was Oscar Lansbury of the famous theatrical family. His sound effects cupboard, where he kept all his equipment, was a closely guarded sanctum. He had a sort of mini-bar in there and knew everyone's tipple. Some mornings some were more in need than others, but you had to be in the know. If you got the nod, you could get a heart starter from behind the horses' hooves.

Because we were so hard pressed rushing from one thing to another, recording batches of five episodes at a time, we were often late and the producers had to be ready to make adjustments. The scripts were marked with optional cuts and indications of where the pace might have to be picked up and we had to keep an eye on the production booth while the piece was going to air or being recorded. A 'scissors' sign meant make the optional cut; 'thumbs up' meant that everything was running to time. There were lots of tricks to this pacing, from coughs and whistles to more elaborate strategies. *Tarzan* was an easy show to make up time on. I'd just give Joan Landor the nod, put my finger in the script and say,

'Oombu! Imbibolo meh umatutuilo. Wahey? Imbe? Toboeooomba ha maka!'

Joan: 'What did he say, Tarzan?'

Me: 'They went east.'

Sometimes we'd 'fly' an episode which meant do it without rehearsal—either because one player was late and there wasn't time for the run-through or because the producer was going for spontaneity. Usually a mistake, that.

The same procedures and hectic pace applied to recording the adverts. We all became very adept at making cuts and speeding up to get the timing right. Because we saw each other all the time a real camaraderie developed, often expressed in the form of practical jokes.

'Jesus, Ray,' Tingwell might say as I cleared my throat ready to launch into my role in *No Love for Linda*, 'What are you doing here? They're looking for you over at AWA for *Address Unknown*.' Just for a second, if the rush had been frantic enough, I might be taken in.

I returned to Brisbane, packed up Audrey and Suellen and we drove back to Sydney. The road was a rough old track in those days and it was a long haul. I remember that I drove a good part of the way in my underpants on account of the heat. Our first Sydney home was a dreadful flat in Cross Street, Double

Bay. It was a dreadful place, dirty and uncomfortable and the landlady was a real Miss Haversham type—eccentric and quite mad.

We stuck Cross Street for about six months and then I found a big, old Victorian block of flats in Darling Point Road. I took a long lease and did a lot of work on our flat myself so that it ended up very comfortable. My home life was very agreeable. Audrey was a natural home-maker and she was very understanding about the erratic hours and habits of an actor. I adored my daughter and spent as much time in fatherly pursuits as I could—somewhat ironically, considering what I was doing for my living all day and half the night—I got a great deal of pleasure out of reading to her. One advantage of radio work was that it was possible to leave it behind at the end of the day. I don't recall agonising over scripts or roles or inflicting any of the actor's angst on Audrey. One journalist reported that I scared the life out of Audrey the first time I tried out my Tarzan call at home. That points up the danger of relying on newspapers for information. Such a thing never happened. There was no need for me to practise the Tarzan call—it was recorded!

At the time every radio was tuned in at 5 o'clock waiting to hear the unmistakable Tarzan call. One day the little kids next door greeted me with a quizzical look when I arrived home. I wondered what was on their minds. One said, 'Are you really Tarzan, Mr Barrett?'

'Yes, my darling.'

A long sceptical appraisal.

'You don't *look* much like Tarzan!'

I was extremely thin in those days.

We worked hard and played hard, especially at the end of the week. Pub sessions and long dinners were common, but not long lunches. If you were busy in radio you had to remain sharp throughout the working day, after that, there was a fair amount of pressure that needed a release. The Journalists' Club was one of my main safety valves and I was often there after work. The brilliant cartoonist Brodie Mack, who I called 'my Falstaff', was one of my drinking mates. It wasn't uncommon for me to arrive at the club, find Brodie the worse for wear and take him home in a cab to Rose Bay. I'd put him through the door and say something like, 'Goodnight, mate. Get some sleep.' I'd return to the club only to find that Brodie had somehow got his second wind and beaten me back there.

Some of the legendary characters had departed from the Sydney scene by the time I got there, but the stories lingered. In particular there were many stories about Arundel Nixon whom I had met in Brisbane not long before he died at forty-four. He had been a leading radio actor and producer in Sydney but his drinking and chaotic personal life had got him into difficulties and he had eventually fallen foul of E. Mason Wood, leading producer on the Macquarie network. Nixon took me aside and said, 'I hear you're going to Sydney. Could you put in a good word for me with Woodie. Tell him I'm on the dry.' He wasn't of course.

The story was told of him filling in as a producer at the Grace Gibson production house. At that time he was a charming English remittance man, very handsome with a Ronald Colman moustache but overly fond of a glass. He was producing a serial, rehearsal for which began at 10 am—precisely when the pubs opened. The studio was so situated that the morning sun shone through the windows straight into the faces of those in the production booth. They wisely had a holland blind installed for their protection. The actors were never consulted, just had to blink and swelter.

Arundel Nixon learned that the back lift, accessible from the booth, led almost directly down to the Metropole Hotel. Usually, he would arrive with a hangover. His address to the cast would be on these lines.

'I know it's Monday morning, but remember energy, energy. Don't think I'm being rude but I know you all so well I want to divorce myself from you as it were. Get yourselves together and get on with it. As this isn't a visual medium, I propose to receive your efforts like an ordinary listener.'

He would then pull down the blind.

He would instruct his assistant to 'take the timing' and immediately leave by the back lift for the Metropole. He would keep a careful eye on his watch, knowing how many brandies he could have per episode. Returning just as the rehearsal was finishing he would lift the blind and direct the performances. He was the only man in the business ever to rehearse five episodes in one morning, record them and not hear a single word.

Given Sydney's magnificent climate and wonderful waterways, it was inevitable that sailing would loom large in my life. I was working with Wally Sullivan, the actor who played Bertie in *Biggles* along with lots of other roles, on some soapie or other and I overheard him say, 'I must get my boat on the slip.' Of course my ears pricked up.

'What sort of boat?' I asked.

He told me it was an American star design with a Marconi rig and said it was moored in Mosman Bay and he'd be getting it on the slip on Saturday morning.

'Well, what time? I'll give you a hand.'

'Ten o'clock. Good of you to offer, Ray, but I don't suppose you'll show up. Nobody ever does.'

He was flabbergasted when I not only turned up but knew what was involved. We put the boat on the slip and got to work on it. I was his forward hand for the next few years and we raced in the Sydney Amateurs' club. I'm competitive by nature and old Wally was more relaxed about things. We'd be belting along off Double Bay and he'd point and say, 'Oh, look at that lovely house up there. That's the Fairfaxes' place you know.'

And I'd say, 'Are we in a race here or are you giving me a fucking harbour tour?'

I remember one race that we were actually winning. We were well ahead running down to the marker in Watson's Bay and I'd done everything right—cottoned up the spinnaker[1] and set it at just the right moment so that we rounded the mark in the lead. How wonderful! And as we rounded the mark to go back on the tack to the Sow 'n Pigs do you think I could get the bloody spinnaker down? No chance. The halyard had jammed between the mast and the sheave which had become worn and loose. Lack of maintenance. I could've killed him. For the rest of the windward leg I had to gather the spinnaker, still up the

---

[1] This was done previous to the race. One used knitting wool to loosely tie up the bunched sail. The ties were about three feet apart so that when the sail was hauled up the mast it resembled a string of sausages. After a point was rounded the procedure was to haul the sail up, push the pole out and haul on the tack which breaks the first tie; the wind then fills the lower portion of the sail and it breaks dramatically out of the ties.

mast, roll it round as tightly as I could and move it from one side of the mast to the other as we went about, all this while managing the jib sheet as well. We didn't win the race.

But the sailing was great fun. After the race we'd put the boat to bed and jump in our cars and shoot round to the beautiful Clifton Gardens pub at Cremorne, looking out towards the heads. That's where all the yachties went to celebrate or commiserate. Great days!

Wally Sullivan became a life-long friend. We corresponded regularly over my almost 20 years in England, and still sail and play golf together when opportunity presents. He is my daughter's godfather and was best man at my third and last wedding. Such is the camaraderie of the boating fraternity.

I'd played a few games of golf in Brisbane at the Victoria Park course and liked it, but I really got interested in the game in Sydney. Again, the climate is a factor. If you have a regular tee-off time booked in Sydney you're unlikely to be prevented from playing more than three or four times a year by the weather. A group of radio people—Max Osbiston, Nigel Lovell, Wally Sullivan, Reginald Goldsworthy, Leonard Bullen and others—had a regular booking for 8.30 on Saturday mornings at Long Reef. After a few games I decided I needed some instruction and I had a couple of lessons from a professional who worked in Bert Oldfield's sports store. Bert had been the Australian test wicket-keeper in the 1920s and 30s. As many people have found, the lessons completely stuffed me up and I reverted to my own unorthodox swing. I have very small hands and wrists and I found that I needed a very flat swing to get distance. Anathema to the purists who favour a very upright swing plane. It worked for me though.

The arrangement was very loose at Long Reef; four people might turn up or a dozen. We had our own handicapping system whereby the person who won had two strokes docked from his handicap for the next week. We each put in a brand new ball and that was the kitty. I became a pretty good golfer although I never had as much time to put into it as I would have liked. It sounds like skiting, but I don't think any surviving members of the Long Reef Radio Golfing Association will contradict me when I say that I bought very few golf balls in my Sydney days.

I had my name down for membership at The Lakes but one day I was taken as a guest to a new course at the Monash Country Club, a predominantly Jewish club. At that time Jews couldn't join clubs like The Lakes or Elanora and some enterprising spirits bought this tract of land out on the Powder Works Road at Warringah. It was elevated above the Elanora course and the Monash members made jokes about being able to piss down on the Gentiles. The course was still being built at that time and on some holes you had to tee up on the fairways to protect the grass. After the round I was approached in the bar by two members, Barry Cherlian and Hymie Isenberg, who asked me if I'd enjoyed the course. I had and said so. They slapped a membership application down on the bar.

'There you are. Sign that.'

I signed. 'How much do I owe you?'

'Nothing. You are now a fully paid-up member of the Monash Golf Club.' Hard not to like people of that stamp. I got involved in the building of the course and enjoyed many rounds there. I never regretted not joining the Lakes.

The money was so good that after a few years in Sydney I was able to buy a new car and to pay cash for it—two firsts for me. The Saturday I picked it up I spent the morning rehearsing with an orchestra about six different songs for a huge marionette show called *The Tintookies*. I was supplying many of the characters' voices. I had prearranged to meet a friend after the rehearsal and head off for a game of golf.

I arrived outside 2GB in my brand new blue Austin A40. It still had the cellophane on the inside of the doors and the unmistakable odour of new leather. I showed it off to all and sundry and when my mate arrived I took him through the car's amazing features finishing with the then revolutionary self-locking doors.

'Very nice,' he said. 'You must be very proud, but I hope you've got a spare set of keys because I think you've just locked yours inside in the ignition.'

Sure enough, I had. The spare set was miles away at home so I called the NRMA. It was a steaming hot day and when the NRMA man arrived in his van he didn't seem to be in the best of moods. I suppose dealing with flat batteries and flooded engines in the hot sun will do that to you.

'What's the matter?' he growled.

'I've locked my keys in the car. I wonder if you would be so kind as to open it for me.'

'Is this your car, sir?'

'Of course it's my car. I only picked it up today. Nice, isn't it?'

'What's the number?'

'Oh! Well . . .' We were standing by the driver's door. The number plate was out of sight and I hadn't yet memorised it. I tried to explain that to him and why my membership badge still held the number of my previous car.

'I see.' No softening in his attitude.

'Ah, there's a tin of paint on the floor. Bought it this morning.'

'Yes, I can see that. What's in the glove box.'

'A Refidex road map,' I said. *That should do it*, I thought.

'Yes, most cars have one of them. We get a fair few cars stolen this way, sir. It'd help if you knew the number.'

Golf time was ticking away and panic was setting in when inspiration struck. I remembered the manuscript on the back seat. 'D'you read music by any chance?'

'No, not one of my accomplishments.'

'Well, that folder on the back seat contains the score of a new puppet extravaganza called *The Tintookies*. Perhaps you've heard about it?'

'Can't say I have.' He backed off, looking as if he'd encountered a sunstruck madman.

'Tell you what I'll do,' I said. 'I'll sing you one of the songs from the show and you can take the manuscript away and have it played for you. Then you'll know I'm on the level.'

Whereupon, in the middle of busy Phillip Street, I gave him a rendition of 'The Emu's Lament':

> Boo Hoo, Boo Hoo
> You're never quite a bird if you're an emu

This was too much. 'You win.' He swiftly unlocked the car and roared off. My strong advice to motorists, especially absent-minded ones, is always to carry some sheet music of a song you've rehearsed well somewhere in the car.

Serials and advertisements provided a firm financial base for a career in radio, but the real artistic satisfaction and possibility for development of the craft of acting came in the extended radio plays and stage work. Lux Radio Theatre, the General Motors Hour, Caltex Playhouse at the Macquarie auditorium, I performed in them all as well as in radio dramas on the ABC. In many ways the work was similar to what I'd done in Brisbane, but the pay was better and the profile was higher. *Libelled Lady* was adapted from an MGM hit film of 1936 which had starred Spencer Tracy, Jean Harlow, Myrna Loy and William Powell. The American film star Ann Miller was visiting Australia at the time and she appeared in the play along with Lyndall Barbour, Bruce Stewart and me. That got a lot of press.

The range of roles was enormous from high drama to farce and everything in between. I remember playing Henry Higgins in *Pygmalion* and enjoying the part so much that I lusted to do *My Fair Lady* later but never got the chance. *The Caine Mutiny* was a great success on radio. I played Lt Maryck, twitching and fidgeting his way towards justice. I played all eight parts in *Kind Hearts and Coronets* and this was the occasion of the only photograph of me in drag.

Although we wore street clothes when recording plays and evening dress when going live to air with an audience, we had to get into costume for publicity photographs that appeared in the press. So I had to put on the wig and the uniform as Captain Cook, the cassock as the priest, the trenchcoat as the detective and so on. The front cover of one issue of the *Listener In*, a magazine of radio programs and news, was completely taken up by a photograph of me as Robin Hood along with Will Scarlet, Friar Tuck and Little John. Tights, feathered cap, long bow, the lot. For *Kind Hearts* the publicity shot was of me as Lady Agatha in a crinoline with an impossible bosom. I suppose it was all good practice for the tremendous amount of 'suiting-up' you have to do as a stage, film and television actor.

The formally presented plays were remarkable events. People dressed up and came long distances from the suburbs, often using public transport in those days when not everyone owned a car, to sit in perfect silence while a group of actors in evening dress read scripts into a microphone. They could have been listening to the same play in the comfort of their living rooms.

Of course, it was 'a night out' and a nice change, I suppose, from going to the pictures.

When Harry Dearth was producing the Lux Radio Theatre, the audience had a bit more to watch. Unlike other producers, Harry did not stay in the control booth. He was out on the stage, listening to the lines through a set of earphones attached by long leads to the microphone. He jumped about, waving his arms and the script, kicking cables out of the way, directing the actors and sound effects crew and playing shamelessly to the audience. Harry had been an actor himself and never lost the taste for it. Some members of the audience were hardcore radio fans and would queue up outside the auditorium with their programs and autograph books clamouring for signatures.

In 1957, the ABC approached me to narrate Prokofiev's *Peter and the Wolf* with the Sydney Symphony Orchestra. I was delighted at the prospect, especially as the guest conductor was the great Nicolai Malko. The performance was to be the highlight of a youth concert season at the Sydney Town Hall.

I arrived early for rehearsal watching the members of the orchestra unpacking their instruments and experienced a familiar griping sensation in my intestines. One's first reaction, I have found, is to locate the nearest toilet and the fire escape. I was put more or less at ease by the friendly understanding of the resident conductor, Mr Joseph Post who took me aside, gave me a manuscript and assured me that Maestro Malko was a kindly man. All the musicians, he told me, were feeling similarly apprehensive, but we would proceed, very slowly, section by section. He advised me not to give a performance, but to gently deliver the narration and watch the baton of the Maestro. 'Remember, Ray,' he said, 'you are as important an instrument in the orchestra as any other.'

Joseph Post turned out to be right. Malko was a nice man and very amusing. We had many laughs during rehearsal and along with the musicians I was beginning to enjoy myself. On the morning before the final rehearsal in the Sydney Town Hall, some thoughtful person had taken Malko to the famous Taronga Park zoo. He was more than impressed. When we came to the triumphal march where Peter leads the wolf home and his grandfather announces, 'Now we'll take him to the zoo,' Malko tapped his baton on the stand, stopped the orchestra and took me aside. He pointed to the text in my score and spoke in his thick, Russian accent.

'Now vee change deese vords! Instead of "Now vee take him to da zoo", vee say, "Now vee take him to Taronga Park."'

Joseph Post was horrified and argued strongly in favour of Prokofiev. It took a great deal of time to persuade the great Russian conductor that he should respect the work of his fellow countryman.

I was very nervous when performance time arrived. This was a new experience for me—a very long step from the musical monologues of my eisteddfod days. I stood at my lectern beside the great conductor in front of the renowned Sydney Symphony Orchestra with every seat in the house occupied, the reception applause slowly fading. The soft rap of the conductor's baton, the gentle entry of the strings beginning the story and we were off into the extraordinary piece of music where the instruments produce the sounds of the bird, the duck, the hunter's gun etc. It was a very moving experience to be part of that fine orchestra and to feel the audience's total involvement and utter enjoyment.

At the end of the performance the house stood and we took our bows. Malko ushered me through the orchestra, I shook his hand, thanked him and prepared to leave. I learned then how much the Maestro knew about how to milk an audience. I lost count of how many times we returned to receive our ovations, how many times the orchestra was asked to rise.

Many years later, my wife Gaye and I happened to see a midday presenter on television utterly crucify *Peter and the Wolf*. Gaye recalled attending, at the age of fifteen, a youth concert in the Sydney Town Hall with the SSO being conducted by Nicolai Malko. She remembered that she had been entranced by the performance.

'Who was the narrator?' I asked.

She couldn't recall.

'Well,' I said, 'great impression he must have made. That was your husband!'

I was still doing book readings, like Jon Cleary's great outback novel *Justin Bayard*, and I was the quiz master for a show entitled 'We're asking You'. I sang with Jim Gussey's ABC dance band. In the midst of all this microphone work I hadn't given up live performance. I did revues at the little Phillip Street Theatre opposite the Journalists' Club. Phillip Street became a cult thing and actors from all branches of the profession appeared there—Margo Lee, Johnny Ewart (sadly missed), Max Oldacre ('ancient arse' as we used to call him), Buddy Tingwell, June Salter, Gordon Chater, David Netheim. Bill Orr was the producer and John McKeller was one of the main writers. It was great experience and turned out to be the springboard of many performers' careers. I recall *Hit and Run* and *Happy Returns*, satirical revues, singing and dancing, greasepaint and applause, who could resist it?

· 8 ·

On the boards

'But, dear boy, you are a *local* actor.'
James Mills to RB, 1957

Did I sense in 1957 that the golden age of radio was coming to an end and that it was time to jump ship? I don't think so. As I remember it, I felt 'saturated' with radio. I had been at it on a full-time basis for fifteen years and had trodden all of its highways and by-ways—announcing, singing, compering, quiz mastering, acting. It wasn't that I was in a rut—there were always new parts coming up, new directors to adjust to, old roles to re-interpret, but sub-consciously I was always ready to move on. I'd been thinking about going to England for some time and might have done so earlier except that a new and exciting opportunity arose at home.

In 1957 the Australian Elizabethan Theatre Trust was formed with a brief to develop drama in Australia. Quite sensibly, the Trust decided that it should use overseas stars in its initial productions to attract the audiences and get the company off on a firm footing. Margaret Rutherford, then a big star of stage and screen in England and much loved by Anglophile Australians, came out for a six-month season to perform in two plays, *The Happiest Days of Your Life* and *Time Remembered*, a gently romantic piece by Jean Anouilh. Margaret had been a great success in the 1950 film version of *Days* along with Alistair Sim and Joyce

Grenfell. I was offered roles in both plays—as the stupid house master Billings in *Days* and the Prince in *Time Remembered*. I would be earning a fraction of what I was getting in radio but I didn't hesitate. I saw it as a great opportunity to get stage experience alongside an artist with an international reputation.

We opened at the Elizabethan Theatre in Newtown and the plays were a great success. We took them on tour to Melbourne and Adelaide and, because Margaret wanted to see Tasmania, we went there and played Hobart, Burnie and Devonport. In Devonport we had to put the set up ourselves because there was no-one there who knew how to do it. It was a great experience for me, that tour. I learned a lot about stagecraft and the travelling broke me out of a kind of insularity that was common in Australia at that time. There were many people who never travelled out of the state in which they had been born. It was as confined as that, but it was good to get a better sense of the vastness and variety of things.

Margaret was a wonderful person and I grew very fond of her. She had been a piano and elocution teacher, liked younger people, and knew how to get on with them. She adopted me in a way and we spent a great deal of our time together while on tour. The Trust had made her very comfortable as befitted her status. Her dressing room was fitted out with a nice carpet, chaise-longue, easy chairs and a refrigerator. Margaret always insisted on me joining her husband, Stringer Davis, and herself for drinks after the curtain. It wasn't always convenient but Margaret insisted.

'Stringer, tell Ray he *must* come and have a gin and tonic.'

She would keep on insisting as we were taking curtain calls and in the end it was easier to comply than protest. So almost every night I would sit in Margaret's dressing room while Stringer, an actor who appeared in all of Margaret's films and was affectionately nick-named 'Lightning' because it took him an age to do anything, served the drinks.

Margaret would relax in her lounge chair, still in her heavy makeup as the Duchess of Pontebronc. Night after night she would open with the same question.

'Ray, *darling*, do you know Morley?' Her face would screw up in that endearing manner everyone loved.

After a time I finally said, 'No, Margaret, I don't know Morley. I told you last night and the night before and the night before that. I would dearly love to know Morley, but unfortunately I do not know Morley.'

She sat back, closed her eyes and said, 'Pity, you'd like Morley.'

She asked the question and we went through the same routine many times subsequently.

Years later I was in a lift in the BBC when who should walk in but Robert Morley. I couldn't help myself, it was an automatic reflex. I went straight into my Margaret Rutherford impersonation saying 'Hello, Morley,' just as Margaret would have rendered it.

Morley didn't turn a hair. 'Hello, dear boy,' was all he said.

There was another actor in the lift. Morley surveyed him from his great height. 'What ails you, dear boy. You're looking somewhat down today?'

'If you must know, Robert, I'm in tax trouble.'

'Ooh, my dear fellow. How much might one ask?'

'Five thousand bloody pounds.'

'Dear, oh dear,' Morley said. 'That will never do. You really must get it up a bit. I'd say to thirty thousand at least, like me. D'you know they take me to lunch every month!'

Behind the scenes, actors are always playing games, sometimes bitchy sometimes not, but always trying each other out. I'm a bit of a mimic and I'd fallen into the habit of imitating Margaret's voice, mannerisms and expression for the amusement of myself and others. Entirely affectionately. Someone had told her and one evening, as 'Lightning' was attempting to organise the drinks, she took me completely unawares.

'Come on now, Ray. Do me!'

Like being wrong-footed at tennis, there's no comeback.

Margaret loved swimming and there are few better places for it than Sydney. I took her to the Redleaf pool, a sharkproof enclosure in the harbour with a tiny strip of sand and a wooden catwalk all around. Margaret insisted on wearing the latest swimwear fashions although she didn't quite have the figure for them. I suspect they were always one size too small. In vogue at that time was a rather unfortunate garment called the playsuit—Margaret's was frilly, pink and was worn with a rubber bathing cap complete with applique rubber flowers. Her only stroke was a stately breaststroke and I was swimming alongside her when the top half of her anatomy fell out. Without missing a stroke or changing expression, she said, 'Can you pop them back in, darling?'

I did and nothing further was said.

For some reason Margaret was interested in the penal settlement at Port Arthur and insisted on making a visit there. We made the rather uncomfortable bus journey and then went on a conducted tour of the remains of the prison. We were shown the tiny, dark cells, the minute exercise yard, the shackles and other instruments of restraint. I supposed that this was all the stuff Margaret had wanted to see and I turned to get her reaction. She was nowhere to be seen. I asked Stringer where she was.

'She finds herself to be not very proud of this aspect of our heritage,' he said.

Margaret was an utterly professional actor but otherwise she was an assembly of quirks and attitudes that made up a genuine English eccentric. She was devoted to her equally eccentric husband. I recall one night in Hobart's Wrest Point casino. We had a great meal and went into the coffee lounge where there was a beautiful grand piano. We had an excellent actor and musician in the company named Eric Rasdell and he played 'On the Air' which had been made famous by Carroll Gibbons and his Savoy Hotel Orpheans, a band that broadcast weekly on the BBC from the Savoy Hotel. Whereupon a very drunk man, claiming to be a property developer, a millionaire and Carroll Gibbons' dearest friend, shouted for the waiter and ordered Veuve Cliquot. He was a bit of a pain, and Margaret asked me to get rid of him, but I discovered that whenever Eric tinkled 'On the Air' the man would leap from his seat and exclaim, 'More Veuve Cliquot!'

I gave Eric the nod and he played 'On the Air' whenever the bubbly ran out. I believe we drank the casino dry of Veuve.

I danced with Margaret but the Veuve caused us to end up on the floor where we watched Stringer laboriously attempting to play the drums four beats behind Eric.

'Isn't he wonderful,' Margaret said. 'His troops adored him.'

Soon after I arrived in England in 1959 Margaret invited me

to lunch at her house in Highgate. I'd forgotten that she found Australian barbecues diverting but was instantly reminded when Margaret introduced me to her fifty or so lunch guests.

'Here is my leading man from Australia. He is going to barbecue lunch for us all.'

She had hired a barbecue which stood inside the wall immediately over which was the grave of Karl Marx. I was required to cook for fifty people in an English winter—naturally it was pissing down rain. Such details couldn't deter Margaret. I cooked the wet bangers and soggy steaks with one hand while holding up a British brolly in the other. It must have been a very funny sight. I imagine only a few of Margaret's formidable g & t's got me through it. We kept in contact throughout my time in England and her death in 1972 saddened me.

Days was a great success. One reviewer noted that 'laughter held up the action for minutes at a time' which was gratifying. I got good notices for both plays and before the return run in Sydney was over I was offered the part of Jimmy Porter in the play that had signalled the arrival of 'kitchen sink drama' and the 'angry young men'—John Osborne's *Look Back in Anger*.

I only had ten days for rehearsal and most of those sessions were squeezed in during the day while I was doing evenings and matinees in the two other plays. But I seemed to have adrenalin and energy to burn. I'd dash from the theatre and go into a nearby pub to eat some lunch and learn my lines. Funny choice you might think but it worked for me. It was a rowdy Sydney pub with the tiled walls and the terrazzo floors, the kind they could hose the vomit out of after closing time. Terrific din bouncing off the walls. I'd prop the book up on the bar and for some strange reason the noise blocked out all distraction. Some of Jimmy Porter's rantings go on for pages and I was able to absorb it all, just soak it up along with the food and a few beers. Of course it's a bravura part, what with the trumpet and everything. Great fun to play.

It so happened that the opening night was on the day Margaret and Stringer sailed for home. I saw them off and wandered back to the theatre to sniff the hurdles, try to settle myself down. I knew I was too wound up to have a nap but I thought it would be a good idea to go to the dressing room (I'd been assigned the same one Margaret had) and stretch out on the chaise-longue for a rest. I opened the door and for a second I thought I was in the wrong theatre. Then I thought I was in some kind of delirium and had lost my mind.

The scene I'd been accustomed to for the past weeks was brutally erased. Gone were the blue carpet, the chaise-longue, the Parker Knoll chairs, the refrigerator. In their place were the torn brown lino, the paint-spotted kitchen chair. I was irate. I summoned Hugh Hunt and James Mills, two Englishmen who were running our indigenous theatre, and demanded to know what the hell was going on. Their faces showed wonderment and disbelief at my belligerence.

'But, dear boy, you are a *local* actor!' James Mills said.

Their attitude was typical of theatrical management's practice at the time. No matter how second-rate the foreign actors who appeared in Australian productions of imported plays were, they were billed and treated as 'stars'. The management had the best of both worlds—they could tout their 'stars' and be confident that they could have the pick of the local actors for the supporting roles. Parts were few and actors were many. The management could pay the minimum and assign the 'locals' to shared dressing rooms below the stage or near the alley. One chair and a cold tap—complain and you're out. It was a scandalous situation which still hasn't changed as much as it should.

Perhaps anger over this treatment fuelled my performance or perhaps a little bit of Jimmy Porter was rubbing off. On the first night I had trouble controlling the volume of my voice. One reviewer said that I seemed to be about six decibels up on the other players. He added that I was 'an interesting performer'. It was sheer nerves, of course. I settled into the role and got good notices, along with Darlene Johnson as Alison and Alan Hopgood as Cliff. It was very gratifying to get a rave review from Elizabeth Riddell in the *Daily Mirror*. She was already a well-known poet and was to become one of Australia's leading poets. She referred to Osborne's 'whiplash words'—exactly right.

The production, however, was not a commercial success. Australia was still being force-fed on light West End social comedy and Broadway musicals and was not yet ready for the angry young men. And theatrical management wasn't ready to mount drama performed by Australian professionals. At some time in the morning of the last day the play was on, the management ordered all the front of house dressing—the various displays and photographs and what's called the '24 sheeters'—the large posters that are pasted up in sheets—to be taken down. I was furious when I was told about it after the matinee. There was no sign that there would be a performance of the play that night.

Outraged, I went to see James Mills. 'Couldn't you have had the courtesy to tell us we're not playing tonight. I could have gone home.'

He was very taken aback. 'What d'you mean? We've got a full house.'

I took him out and showed him the devastation. 'As far as I can see, we're not playing. I'm going home and so is everyone else.'

'Well what do you want me to do?' he blustered. I told him that unless the complete dressing was restored, along with the '24 sheeters', there would be no performance. They did it and we went on, but the brutal disregard that had been shown left a very sour taste in my mouth, especially as the theatre was going to be dark for the next month until the opera came in to lose more money.

My next major job after the Osborne play closed was again a new departure. I worked with Spike Milligan on the weekly ABC radio show, *The Idiot Weekly*. Spike had a great success with *The Goon Show* and this was an attempt to reproduce some of the same kind of humour in the colonies. I greatly enjoyed the change after the emotion-draining intensity of *Look Back in Anger* and there was no better person from whom to learn about that kind of comedy than Spike who combines a unique sense of humour with a deep concern for humanity and all things around him. The program was billed as 'madder than the Goon Show' and it was certainly mad. I had enormous fun working with Spike and John Bluthall and Bobby Limb. Who else could have written this lyric but Spike?

Australia, Australia
I think of you each day.

Australia, Australia
Though you're so far away.
I think of you each morning
I think of you each day.
I even wake at midnight
To think of you again.

My only venture into Australian television was at this time in a show devised by Spike. When pressed by the ABC publicity people to give it a title he resisted, suggested some unprintable names, but eventually came up with, off the top of his head, 'The Gladys Half Hour, sponsored by Footo, the wonder boot exploder.' It was mad-cap stuff. I remember one sketch in which we were RAF POWs in Stalag something or other. We wore immaculate uniforms above the waist and as the camera pulled back it revealed that we wore only our underpants below. We had shaving soap on our faces having waited three years for the Red Cross parcels with razors, and at one point Milligan identifies someone *not* as Squadron Leader so-and-so but as Commander such-and-such by the taste of his shaving soap.

'Give me that rope,' Milligan says.

'What rope?' says I.

'That rope you've been knitting for three years. We all want to get out of here you know.'

I hand over the rope and it's barely two feet long.

I said: 'But we're *six* storeys up!'

Spike: 'Don't worry, we'll just have to jump the rest.'

Then the head of a German guard crosses at the window.

'Take no notice of him. That's Lofty Heinrich, one of the tallest guards in the German army!'

The scene cuts to the BBC studio where we are being interviewed about our escape. We are all on our knees with our jackets reaching to the floor and our shoes just poking out underneath—reduced to half size by our six storey jump. And so it went on. Spike had trouble finding a bridge between scenes. As it was going out live we needed some time to change clothes and set up for the next sketch. He solved the problem by simply putting me on a swing hanging by my legs upside down. The swing was pushed and I came into shot saying, 'I'm not mad you know. I just do this until they're ready.'

At the end of the show there was a cross to Michael Charlton in the newsroom which was just a set adjacent to ours. Very plummily, as was the fashion in those days, Michael Charlton launched into, 'Good Evening. This is Michael Charlton with the news. Today . . .'

Spike wandered onto the set. I followed him and we went into an impromptu routine:

'What's the weather like, Michael?'

'Any good news, Michael.'

Outrageous.

There were only a handful of films being made in Australia during the time I was in Sydney. Charles Chauvel's *Jedda* was the only truly local product of any quality, and while Peter Finch came home to do *The Shiralee* for Ealing and *Robbery Under Arms* for Rank, the future didn't look rosy for 'local' actors. Finch, by then, wasn't local. I had a small part, playing a fop, in the *Long John Silver* series in which Robert Newton was starring. It wasn't a good series. I must have said something to Bobby Newton about intending to go to England. We were rehearsing a scene and Bobby was laughing.

I said something like, 'Get out of my eye line will you, Bobby. It's hard enough playing this bloody fop without you laughing at me.'

He looked me up and down in my absurd outfit—wig, powder and patch—and said, 'I wasn't laughing at you. I was just thinking about you going to England. They'll love you over there. They all behave like that.'

I felt there was nowhere else to go in Australia. I was bouncing off the ceiling in Sydney. Doing this, doing that, going up and down. I knew I could continue making a good living but it would all be just more of the same. I had tried everything. I'd missed the war and had never been out of Australia. I was 31 and I thought it was time to find out if I could hold my own in the international scene. I was completely open-minded about it. Have a go! If I wasn't up to it, fair enough. At least I'd tried. I could always come home and pick up where I had left off. I had no desire to go to Hollywood. I always had London in mind. I preferred England. I guess I had ties there, Mum was born there and Dad had spent time there during the war and it was also my ancestral home. And of course the lure of London's West End. It was time to go.

II

· 9 ·

Getting away

Sooner or later, most Australian actors thought of going overseas and many did so. There were two options—England or America. Pioneers like Dick Bentley, Joy Nicholls and Bill Kerr had taken the London route in the late 1940s; Ron Randell and Michael Pate had gone to America. They had been successful and provided encouraging models. Remarkable as it may sound now, a great many Australians, including some radio actors, left for England in late 1952 and early 1953 to be in London for the coronation of Queen Elizabeth II. Among them were Ruth Cracknell and Kitty Bluett. Madge Ryan and Buddy Tingwell had also gone to England.

'Getting away' was a constant background possibility and people seized the chance when it came. Rod Taylor, with whom I worked in plays and serials, made the break in 1955. At the time Rola refrigerators, whose prize model was a rounded, sort of art deco construction, were sponsoring plays on 2CH which were produced by Ronnie Beck. The listening public were invited to vote on the performers and the actor judged the winner got a trip to Hollywood. Rod was in one of these things, playing two brothers.

'You're bound to win,' I told him. 'Because you're playing two parts.'

To speak the truth, I couldn't hear much difference in the two brothers' voices, but Rod was a great favourite at the time and he won. Off he went to Hollywood, and battled for a while but eventually established himself.

Years later, in London, I was having a drink one Sunday with Ronnie Fraser and a few other actor friends, when he told me Rod was in town and he was at the Salisbury and wanted to see me. The Salisbury is a lovely old pub with beautiful ornate Victorian glass and carved wood decor. At that time it was the actors' pub. I went there and found Rod in the bar with Lex Barker who had played Tarzan in the movies and had been married to Lana Turner.

I walked up and put a fiver on the bar.

'Rod, how lovely to see you. Welcome to London! What are you having?'

'No, baby,' he said.

I said, 'Look this is London, Rod, when you are in London I'll buy. If I come to America, you can buy.'

But he was the complete Yank by this stage with a broad accent and all the moves. He took out a wad of notes with a rubber band around it and plonked it on the bar. 'Uh, uh. I'm buyin'. Whaddya want, baby?'

He was staying at the Dorchester and invited me to join him for a drink. I arrived to find him and his lady and another couple. He poured me a beer and there was a knock at the door. It was room service. A trolley was wheeled in and the four of them proceeded to partake of their Sunday roast with all the trimmings. I was not invited to join them and felt distinctly uncomfortable. It was time to go whereupon Rod turned to me and said: 'Hey, baby, I caught that television show of yours on the BBC the other night.'

'Oh yes Rod,' I said

'Not bad, kid, not bad.'

'I must go, but could I use the loo?'

'Sure, baby, sure. On the right.'

There was the exercise bike, the massage table, all the paraphernalia of American stardom which he'd embraced so completely. But it saddened me because it seemed so cardboard cut-out and phoney, not at all like the old Rod I had known.

That's looking ahead, but in any case New York and Hollywood didn't appeal to me back in 1958. Mum was English and Dad had spent time there during the war. Above all, the lure of the West End theatre was very powerful. Kenneth Horn, Richard Murdoch, Margaret Rutherford and Spike Milligan had encouraged me to go, but I had no thoughts of them helping me to get work. I felt confident enough to risk my arm and I had saved enough money to enable Audrey, Suellen and myself to live in reasonable comfort, without income, for eighteen months. I put it no stronger. When I took the plunge and bought first-class sea passages for Audrey, Suellen and myself, I also paid for the return voyage. The booking was for a few months ahead, but I wanted to present it to Audrey as a fait accompli, heading off any excuses she might find for not making the trip. The return ticket was valid for up to eighteen months.

Spike Milligan, wearing a dinner jacket to my great surprise, had come to the opening night of *Look Back in Anger*. He was leaving the next day for England by ship (he refuses to fly), and I asked about the sailing time.

'Don't come and see me off,' he said. 'I'll be hiding in the lavatory, away from my wife's relations. I'll see you in London.'

I told him when I was leaving and mentioned that we were booked on the *Arcadia*. It happened to be the very ship he had come out on. Spike promised to write to the Captain and Purser and ask them to look after me. These sorts of promises are often easily made and more easily forgotten, but not by Spike.

We sailed in December 1958, farewelled by Mum, who had made the trip from Brisbane for the occasion, and friends from the Sydney radio scene. After the last of *The Idiot Weekly* went to air, there was a cocktail party attended by the then managing director of the ABC, Sir Charles Moses. I guess I must have been somewhat fortified, because I approached him and asked why it was that we only saw him on occasions like this when overseas artists were on hand. I can't recall his reply. I told him that I was leaving for England the following week and wondered if he would give me some letters of introduction. The next day I was mortified at what I had done but I consoled myself with the thought that I would soon be 12,000 miles away. About an hour before sailing time a woman was ushered in who introduced herself as Sir Charles' private secretary. She handed me several letters of introduction to various people at the BBC in London and apologised for not getting them to me sooner.

No sooner had we passed out of Sydney heads, than there was a knock on our cabin door and a steward appeared—bow tie, mess jacket, the complete rig. He introduced himself as Nobby Clark and said he had been Spike's steward and would be taking care of us on the voyage. We were presented with an invitation to be the Purser's guests for drinks at six o'clock. The first hours on a big passenger boat can be an intimidating time, this was a true welcome aboard.

We found ourselves launched into the VIP department. We had the run of three compartments—our main three berth cabin, another which I could use as a bar, entertaining area and dressing room, and another cabin where four-year-old Suellen could sleep should we be having a soiree, all thanks to Spike. At six o'clock every evening I would have drinks for the four stewards in my part of the first-class deck, take my bath, which Nobby had drawn for me, and change into my dinner jacket for the evening's festivities.

This sort of treatment went on for four weeks as we made our way to the 'old country', via Singapore and the Suez canal. It lulled me, I'm afraid, into a false sense of security and a feeling of being detached from reality and immune to its pangs. *Why,* I thought, *didn't I do this sooner?*

We were shuddered back into the real world with our first sight of Tilbury Docks. No Nobby to take care of us now. We faced being thrown on our own resources in a strange country and a freezing cold one at that! We were struggling to come to terms with this when a friend, Eric Sadler, emerged from the icy mist to whisk us off to his beautiful thatched cottage in the hamlet of Thorne, outside Chagford in Devon.

Eric was a friend from my Sydney sailing days. He'd led an interesting life, served in the British and Australian armies and had won a lot of prizes on a Sydney radio show in circumstances that were questionable. He was a keen sailor but not a very competent one. He once lost a boat by trying to put in at the Kiama blowhole. One time I went sailing with him along with Wally Sullivan and my brother Scott. We took his steel ketch up to Pittwater and then back to Rushcutters Bay, a nice trip. We were heading into Rushcutters Bay under full sail with a lot of boats swinging at their moorings and plenty of people about. Eric was at the wheel and all he could say was, 'Some bastard's on my mooring. Some bastard's on my mooring.'

I urged him to go about and luff up and we could sort it out but he paid no attention, just kept on about somebody being on his mooring. There was a motor boat and a yacht with a long bowsprit, both swinging, not much room and from bowsprit to boom ours was a big boat. We collided with this yacht and then it was one disaster after another. Eric's borrowed dinghy exploded when hit by the yacht's bowsprit; the outhaul hook on Eric's boom caught on the forestay of the yacht, slid up to the mast as we ploughed along still under full sail downwind, and ripped the bobstay right out of his hull. The two boats were locked together; people were jumping off the yacht and the skipper yelled at his wife to jump just before his mast snapped and crashed down exactly where she'd been. So we wrote that bloke's yacht off and nearly killed his wife. And he'd been about to set off on a world trip!

All that was forgotten now. Eric was great company and the stay at his place made for a gentle easing into our new life and by chance not far from the Barrett ancestral home, Moredon Hall in Somerset.

· 10 ·

Getting started

After a pleasant interlude in Devon reality had to be faced: the finding of a place to live in London, securing an agent and looking for work. Through Aussie actor friends, we heard that Peter Finch's ex-mother-in-law, Mumma Tchinarova, had rooms to let in her house in Lower Sloan Street. It was bitterly cold when we arrived in London and a shock to the system, after the comparative luxury we had been enjoying, to be shown a room with a single gas fire and its shilling-swallowing meter. Finding a reasonable flat became a top priority.

Madge Ryan, with whom I had worked in the Phillip Street Theatre, put me on to Dina Lom, head of the Leading Players theatrical agency and the wife of the character actor, Herbert. We found a flat above Cullen's grocery shop in the Fulham Road where a coffee grinding machine in the window was a feature. Cullen's coffee was supreme and much sought after, but with every grinding, the aroma and dust would rise through the ancient floor to our lounge room until it was impossible to smell anything else and difficult to see from one side of the room to the other. But for four pounds a week we could put up with it. The wonderful Finche's pub, an artists' hangout, was nearby and the Goat in Boots, a name that fascinated me, was immediately opposite.

My first job in England was a kind of reprise of something I'd done in Australia. I had worked with Peter Brough and his little wooden friend, Archie, in a radio series in Sydney called *Educating Archie*. Peter had developed the idea into a television series for Rediffusion and, when he heard I was in London, he invited me to join the cast. The writers were Ronnie Wolf and Marty Feldman, later to go on to bigger things. Although it was hard to take, being straight man to a wooden doll with all the funny lines, I wasn't complaining. I was feeling my way and grateful for the start and regular income. I'm sure that Dick Emery, who also worked on the show, felt the same.

In cold, foggy old London in 1959 an actor was likely to find himself put in a pigeonhole by the various forces operating in the profession. You were either a straight dramatic actor, a light comedian, a revue or musical comedy performer. I wanted to be a serious actor—Stratford and all that. I instructed Dina Lom to ensure that I was put in the first of these categories. So naturally, the world being the way it is, one of Dina's staff slotted me in for an audition for a revue at what is now the Albury Theatre. I objected but turned up for the appointment out of courtesy.

My name was duly called. I walked onto the stage and peered out into the darkness of the auditorium. The only person visible was the piano player in the pit, the 'thumper' as he was called.

A voice came from the darkness. 'Can you sing something for us?'

I thanked them for the invitation and tried to explain that I'd only just arrived in the country, that my agent had got it all wrong and I didn't have any music.

'And I don't know where Palings is,' I said.

The voice: 'Can you sing "God Save the Queen" or something?'

'Well, I'd prefer to rehearse . . .'

'No, no, just sing something.'

I thought, *Well, this is the way to get clear of being categorised as a bloody revue person.* I asked the pianist if he knew 'A Pretty Girl is like a Melody'.

We settled on a key. I asked for a few bars, ran through the verse: I have an ear for music/I have an eye for a maid/I like a pretty girlie/With each pretty tune that's played ... and on to the chorus:

A pretty girl is like a melody ...

And away I went, swanning around the stage, camping my head off.

That's fixed it I thought. I smiled politely and began to walk off.

The voice: 'Stay! Stay! Get down to Margate at once!'

I just had time to phone Audrey and tell her where I was going. Then I was on the train to Margate and there was Eleanor Fazzan who was producing the show starring Beryl Reid and Patrick Wymark. The revue was called *One to Another*; Stanley Meyers, Eleanor's husband, had written the music. I was whisked off into the pub next to the theatre (which had closed in the afternoon as was the custom), stationed by the pub piano, and I had to learn three songs there and then. Couldn't do it in the theatre because they were rehearsing the whole show. The problem was that the fellow who was doing some of the singing wasn't up to scratch and I'd been recruited to replace him.

It would be hard to imagine a more tricky theatrical predicament: there I was, expected to go on stage without proper rehearsal, only hours after auditioning, and *with* the man I was replacing. He was still appearing in the sketches but I was to sing his songs. It had all happened so quickly that I hadn't quite taken it in. I'd had no time for nerves; I felt sort of transported into the situation. But it hit me just before I was due to go on. I can remember the first scene—Beryl Reid and Patrick Wymark winding a skein of wool into a ball.

I said to Beryl, 'God, what am I doing here?'

She said, 'Fuck it, darling! Get on with it!'

I went on and did the necessary. It's a peculiar business, this one of ours. I'm sure that if I had desperately wanted that job I would never have got it. The revue played to good houses for about five months and had a run at the Kings Theatre in Hammersmith which was the nearest thing to getting on in the West End. The salary was nothing wonderful, but enough to keep us, and I was learning all the time. I met some wonderful people and enjoyed every minute of the run.

I had a brush with fame early on while working in the revue. I was sent back to London from Margate for a photo session. Management wanted poster-sized portraits for front of house dressing and, as the new boy, no photograph of me was available. I turned up in the West End at the address given me to find that the photographer was none other than Cecil Beaton.

He took one look at me and said, 'Where are your clothes?'

I was in my street clothes and explained that I didn't have time to go home and change. I'd come straight from rehearsal at Margate and had to go straight back there for more of the same.

'Good God!' he said. 'I can't possibly photograph you in that!'

He took some time to ponder the situation and appeared to arrive at a solution. 'Wait here.'

He returned in a few minutes with a garment over his arm. 'Try these on.'

Now it is a fact that Mr Beaton always wore what are known as 'pussers trousers'—sailor's bell bottoms with a flap in front fastened on each side by a row of buttons. This was the garment I was to try on.

'Wonderful,' he exclaimed at the result. 'Much better.'

I tried to tell him in the nicest possible way that I didn't think this was the effect the publicity person had in mind.

'Don't fuss, dear boy.'

He produced a bundle of safety pins and proceeded to circle me, pinning the trousers at the back, reducing the bell-bottom effect and giving them the appearance of something like normal apparel. The photograph session went ahead.

It was only to a very close circle of friends that I revealed that the trousers I wore in the poster were Cecil Beaton's.

I picked up some work in television in police shows with names like 'Murder Bag' and so on, doing anything that was going. It was a useful learning and exposure experience. I worked with different directors and understood what they were looking for and they in turn took note of me. I remember getting my first cheque from this sort of work, a paltry sum like eighty-four pounds, and I went across the road to the Midland Bank, opened an account and deposited. My savings were lodged in an Australian bank in Piccadilly and I said to myself, *Try to live on your earnings. That's the way you'll know whether you're doing all right or not.* It was a good strategy and I managed to keep those savings intact for a long time until I had need of them for something major.

I did another revue, entitled *Don't Shoot, We're English,* with Michael Bentine, Dick Emery and Clive Dunn. Again, I wasn't keen to do it but they wanted a jack of all theatrical trades—an actor who could sing and dance. I was no great shakes as a dancer but I knew I could handle the work and there was the attraction of performing with good people and touring the country.

I've mentioned being in Northumberland with the show and finding where the Storeys had lived. Although I enjoyed the work it was brought home to me what a sad race comedians are. One of the sketches was a medley of English garden songs in which Dick Emery featured, along with Judy Bruce. Dick sang these wonderful bucolic songs while everything got fouled up; Clive Dunnn was the gardener who put the watering can spout down his trousers—there were a lot of set changes in this show and they'd bring the curtain down before Dick's number and Michael Bentine would go on and do a bit of standup comedy until he got the signal that the set was ready.

'And now a pot-pourri of English garden songs performed by Mr Richard Emery,' and Miss Judy Bruce, 'accompanied by the twelve nimble fingers of Raymond Charles Barrett.'

The stage was in a sepia lighting and I was wearing an Edwardian, long-tailed coat. All I had to do was come on, walk to the piano, which was upstage left, and set up my music. To this day I don't know why, but that simple entrance brought the house down every night.

One night in Blackpool, Dick, with whom I was sharing digs, said to me, 'You bastard! You bastard! Don't you realise that's *my* sketch, *mine*! You're doing something and killing my entrance.'

He said it dead-pan and I thought he was joking and laughed it off.

'I mean it! I mean it!' His eyes were bugging out and I could tell he was serious.

I said, 'I don't want to be in the fucking thing. I've got 21 changes as it is.' In revue you peeled off after each sketch; you started looking eighteen stone and ended up looking like six, and you had to be very careful to put the clothes on in the right order. It was all very difficult and there was no energy left over for upstaging. Also, the sketch ended with me diving over a breakaway piano and I had cracked ribs from doing that. I really didn't want to be in the sketch. So I told Dick I'd walk on backwards—no chance of getting in a bit of extra business that way.

'... twelve nimble fingers of Raymond Charles Barrett.'

I walked on backwards and the house fell down. Collapsed. More than before. I don't think Dick ever forgave me, but it was all due to his insecurity and I saw the same traits in Charlie Drake, Tony Hancock and others. A straight actor is lucky in that he can hide behind his character in a way. He's an interpreter, a mummer. But a comedian, what's called a 'front of cloth man', simply *has* to be the funniest thing in the show, or he's failed. There's a lot of pressure in that.

For all the experience it gave me and all the chances to work with true professionals of the English theatre, touring in revues at twenty-five pounds a week wasn't what I'd had in mind when I came to England. Fred Zinnemann's film of the Jon Cleary novel *The Sundowners* was shot in Australia after I left, the interiors were shot in the ABPC studios in London. I played the close-up shots of a character who had been filmed in long shot in Australia.

Through the good offices of Peter Finch, who recommended me to the casting director, I secured a small part and added to my meagre experience of working to camera. I found that I felt relaxed in the atmosphere and enjoyed the work. I had, as I say, played small roles in a couple of television series and I appeared in the unmemorable telemovie, *Flagfall*. The money wasn't good. I can't recall exactly how much I was paid but I have a chit which had accompanied a cheque from the agency from a few years later recording payment for an episode of *Z Cars*. I was paid one hundred and seventy-one pounds and two shillings. After the deduction of a ten per cent commission and one pound eleven shillings and ninepence for National Health insurance, I was left with one hundred and fifty-one pounds and ten shillings exactly. A note on the bottom of the chit requested me to 'please cash this as soon as possible'. Despite the poor returns, films and the small screen seemed to offer the best opportunities.

· 11 ·

On the box

Charles 'Bud' Tingwell, a colleague from Sydney radio, had preceded me to England by several years and was in regular work as a television actor. He was an original member of the cast of the BBC series *Emergency Ward 10*, an enormously popular show in Britain in the late 1950s and early 1960s. Within a couple of weeks of its appearance it had built an audience of about eleven million viewers which it held throughout its run. Almost every young actor, male or female, making their way in the 1960s, had passed through the wards and corridors of the fictional Oxbridge hospital. The show was an institution. It was adopted and embraced by the British public in much the same way as the radio program *Blue Hills* had been taken to the hearts of Australians.

As with *Coronation Street*, viewers identified closely with the characters, worshipping some and hating others. The condition of patients was monitored daily and discussed over meals and on buses and the tube. To many people the characters were as real as their friends and relations or more so. Cakes were sent to mark the characters' birthdays.

Bud Tingwell put my name forward for the role of Dr Don Nolan, the new casualty officer. For this I am eternally grateful because the part acted as a springboard for the further advancement of my career. I stayed with the series for nine months (until the directors' strike stopped production) and gained enormously in experience. After almost twenty years in radio it might have been thought that I would find the transition to television testing. In Australia and Britain, many radio actors had found the switch painful or even impossible to make, but I was never aware of any difficulty. I don't know why this was so except possibly that I was always a visual actor. When performing on radio I would literally 'see' the action we were creating with voices and sound effects. So to have a version of that imagined reality actually happening around me presented no problem. Also, as I've mentioned, I liked working to camera.

In those days we did two half hour episodes, live, each week, shot in black and white. We would read then block the show, next day rehearse in the blocking tapes and next day do it in the studio live. Twice a week. I still remember scrambling over cables and evading the lethal menace of Taffy's number one camera as it hurtled from one end of the studio to the other. Going out live had obvious difficulties. Not only did you have to be absolutely sure of your lines, but you had to be very familiar with the props and adept in the correct use of medical equipment. We had a doctor on hand at all times to advise on the right procedure, and we actually had to practise suturing, using the materials employed in the medical schools, the needles, the grips, scissors etc.

One of my first assignments as the new Casualty officer was to suture a wound in the arm of a motor accident victim. The writer of this particular episode had not taken into account that Dr Nolan had to finish a scene at the far end of the studio in street clothes and immediately appear fifty yards away in gown, mask and surgical gloves. I was assigned two dressers—one, to stand by with the gown ready for my outstretched arms; the other with the cap and mask. The change was made on the run to the ward where my Noddy (an extra, simply nodding his head but speaking no lines which would have meant paying him at actor's rates), the patient Noddy and the nurse Noddy were waiting. Now to draw on the gloves which lay where I had carefully placed them after liberally lining them with French chalk for easy entry of my nervous fingers. I had rehearsed this procedure many times and felt confident that all could be achieved before the red light on the re-positioned camera indicated that the scene had started.

When the light came on I had three fingers in one hole, two in another and the remainder hung like empty cow's udders. Close to panic, I ad-libbed to my Noddy nurse for a swab, then for another, all the time endeavouring to fold the offending empty fingers of the glove into the palm of my hand. Real sweat was dripping from me when the scene finally came to an end and I had completed a two-finger suturing of the poor patient's arm.

I agonised for hours over how such a mishap could have occurred. I am always meticulous about preparing my props before a performance. Most of the cast used to repair to the local at Highbury after the transmission to settle their nerves, tell one another how good we were and fish for compliments. Actor stuff. I was still puzzling about the catastrophe when Bud Tingwell came up and put his arm around my shoulder.

'How were the gloves, old boy? I saw what a difficult change you had so I took the precaution of turning them inside out for you.'

A director of one of the early episodes I was in was Hugh Rennie, a sweet and kind person. After a camera rehearsal he informed me that the head makeup lady, a woman of advancing years, had queried his wisdom in coming in so close on my face. She remarked that, in black and white and with harsh overhead lighting, my acne scars were over-emphasised. Hugh said that this was his intention. She was very concerned and left the production booth muttering, 'I don't know what I can possibly do.'

Hugh asked me to be kind to her and go along with whatever she proposed. She was due for retirement soon.

Thus prepared, I arrived at the make-up room and was shown into the chair. The lady hovered over the chair with a white pencil poised, explaining the effect of the lighting on my unfortunate complexion.

'Would you mind if I make them up?'

I'd never actually counted the indentations in my physiognomy, but I calculated that if she were to apply the white pencil to each one, it would take a long time. I settled back and went along with it, feeling the white pencil being carefully applied to each of the offending craters. After completing this, she carefully plastered me with a concoction that seemed to set immediately like cement. Lastly, a dusting of powder.

'I'm afraid that's the best I can do. I'm sure it will be much better.'

She obviously came from the old school, where everybody looked like a chocolate box painting. I knew that if I uttered one word or changed my expression, the whole mask would crack and fall like powdered alabaster. I went to my dressing room and carefully washed the whole thing off.

After the performance she made a point of coming up and thanking me for subjecting myself to the ordeal with such patience. She assured me that it had been worth the effort and a great improvement.

The impact *Ward 10* had in Britain was brought home to me after I had been with the show a week. With my friend Doreen, with whom I had worked in the revue *Don't Shoot . . .*, I decided to do a 'recce' of the pubs in Holland Park where she lived. After a few pleasant stops we ventured into an ancient hostelry, whose name I have forgotten. It had a bare wooden floor and Victorian stained glass windows. The bar seemed to be a cricket pitch length from the front door and by the time we'd reached it I was beginning to think this might be a mistake.

The clientele were unsettling. Dead centre of the bar stood a man with a decidedly hard countenance. A diminutive chap with a greasy cloth cap and muffler and his lady with a black plastic hat, a Guinness and a fag, were sitting under the window on one side. Opposite, four or five young Turks in Teddy Boy suits, bovver boots and hair styles to match, whispered among themselves, eyeing Doreen's trim, attractive figure.

'Oi, Oi, 'ave a look at 'at!'

Too late to retreat. This was definitely not your run of the mill London pub. I decided to drop my voice to its lowest octave, order a drink and get clear as soon as possible. I asked the plump barmaid with the pink-dyed frizzy hair for a half of bitter and a gin and tonic.

Hard-face with the steely blue eyes said, 'Make that a pint and a double, Muriel.'

'No, you shouldn't do that,' I protested limply. 'We're only having the one.'

He bent closer to me and almost breathed the words in a husky voice, 'This is my manor, see? When you come in 'ere, you drink wiv me.'

The Teds had steered Doreen away and were slinging in a few smart remarks. Little did they know that she was a Geordie and could give as much as she got. She handled them with ease and they were soon offering to buy her the other half.

Meanwhile, back at the bar, the Guv'nor was confiding in gravelly whispers that should I ever require any 'barfroom gear' or electrical appliances, I should go no further than him. This was of interest. I had just bought a cottage in Richmond and was renovating it.

'Are you in the building trade?' I asked.

A wry smile and a quaint look. 'Leave orf, leave orf. I'm a fief, arn' I? Me son's a fief an' all.'

I wasn't sure what to say to that when Greasy Cap interjected, 'Mum's just recernised ya. You're the noo doctor, arn' ya?'

I twigged. 'Yes,' I said.

'Y' right, Ma. It's 'im.'

Ma, sucking down Guinness and inhaling smoke, responded with an affirmative cough.

'Dr Nolan, innit?' says Greasy Cap. 'Dr Nolan?'

'That's right.'

'Y' right, Ma. Dr Nolan.'

Another cough indicated satisfaction with her completely correct identification.

Greasy Cap became confiding. 'Y' know wot giv ya away, don't ya?'

'No,' I said.

'Them bleedin' 'oles in y' face!'

The power of television.

Although it did not attract anything like the audience of *Ward 10*, *The Brothers Karamazov* was a high quality TV drama serial, in six one hour episodes, that I consider myself very fortunate to have played in. Alan Bridges, the director who cast me as the oldest brother, Mitya, the most complicated character in the story, is one of many directors I would class as brilliant.

He was able to win the actors' devotion and get the best possible performances from us. We rehearsed for some weeks in London and then the whole production was moved to Glasgow. This was the BBC doing something for the provinces, but it worked very well because the cast became a unit, like a play company and we were all very keen. Judith Stott, a wonderful actress, was in the cast along with Jane Asher and my old mate from Australia, John Tate.

Judith Stott had just come back from Australia, touring in a play, and she revealed that she'd married Dave Allen, the Irish comedian. I just couldn't put the two together in my mind—the classical actress and the Irish comic—and I asked her how it had come about.

'Oh, well, I was at one of those awful Sydney parties,' she said. 'You know, the nouveau riche and the bejewelled ladies and he was the only one there with a Gauloise, so I married him.'

I got Tate the job. The actor playing the mad monk had dropped out because his wife was seriously ill. It was close to the time when we were due to go to Glasgow and we were deep into rehearsal and really needed this role filled. Alan Bridges was desperate and I told him I had just the man—a mad, eccentric guy who'd just come over from Australia. Alan said, 'I'd like to meet him'. We rehearsed all over the place in those days, in army drill halls and the like, before the BBC rehearsal rooms were built. We happened to be at just such a place in Wimbledon when Tate showed up. I was amazed by his appearance. Not normally a snappy dresser, he was resplendent in a dark mohair suit with a white shirt and dark tie. It turned out he'd borrowed it from the writer, Mike Noonan. The only trouble was that he'd split the back seam in the trousers.

Here we were walking through this immense drill hall, going to meet Alan and Tate's Y-fronts were wagging out behind him. Now on any film and television set or in any play cast there's always a woman who's a sewer or a knitter who'll have needle and thread. Tate spotted a woman who had a bit part in the series sewing away and he walked straight up to her and showed her the problem.

'Take 'em off,' she said. 'I've got some dark cotton here.'

So there's Tate—the beautiful jacket, shirt and tie, socks and polished shoes, and Y-fronts. That's how he was when Alan came over. I introduced them. Alan looked him up and down and said, 'You've got the part.'

We worked very hard in Glasgow, six days a week with only Sunday off. On Sunday we'd all get together and drive off to lunch at some restaurant or other. We'd decide on the Buchanon Arms at Lochernhead say, and there would be a genuine race between Alan and myself to get there first. The winner bought the champagne. We'd have a magnificent lunch and quite often it happened that someone would say, 'Why don't we go back and rehearse some of those scenes?' And we did—a very unusual thing to happen.

I'd read the Dostoyevsky novel but I have to admit I found it hard going. The adaptation though, by Frederick Gotfurt, was terrific and I believe I did some of my best work in television on *Karamazov*. We were working at a high emotional pitch for a lot of the time, very draining, but immensely satisfying to work with someone as sympathetic and creative as Alan Bridges. I remember that I cried genuine tears in one of the prison scenes I was so moved by the intensity that had been achieved. I hope the Beeb hasn't wiped the tapes—it would stand re-screening.

But it was very demanding, taking about three months in all, and I remember that after we finished and had returned to London I proposed to Tate that we shoot over to France for a weekend to let off steam and relax. We went to Boulogne, booked into a hotel and the next day we went to the market and loaded up on oysters, bread, cheese and wine (lots of wine) for lunch. Where would we eat? We drove up to Cap Gris Nez, where the channel swimmers set off from. There are still German gun emplacements and other fortifications in place and Tate decided that one particular gun emplacement was just the right height to open the oysters on. So we had our lunch up there, opening the oysters, drinking the wine—two long-haired, bearded characters, a bit crazed from the emotional acting we'd been doing, shouting and laughing into a howling gale blowing in from the Channel—while the quiet French farmers passed by. They must have wondered what asylum we'd escaped from.

· 12 ·

Real life

A lifetime of happiness! No man alive could bear it: it would be hell on earth.

George Bernard Shaw, *Man and Superman*

From the outside, an actor's life may seem to be made up of the roles played, the reviews good and bad, the awards won, the conflicts and harmonies with other professionals. This is because, of necessity, more of an actor's life is on public display than with most other occupations. But of course there is another life away from the stage or film and television set. In this life the actor suffers, achieves and fails and is shaped for better or worse in just the same way as other people. In my case, as I was making a career on the stage and in British films and television, important off-stage events were happening. The most significant of these were the death of my father and the breakup of my first marriage and the emotional turmoil that followed.

I had always been close to my father. I admired him and appreciated the understanding, tolerance and love he had shown me. He was not demonstrative, few Australian men were in those days, but I never had any doubt of his love. He and Mum visited me in Sydney not long after my arrival there. We were living in the awful flat in Double Bay. They stayed with us and we had the usual good family time together, but I have a vivid memory of our parting on that occasion. I had to leave on the morning they were due to drive back to Brisbane. I was due in the ABC studio for a play rehearsal. I said my goodbyes, went out the gate and walked along Cross Street towards the main road to catch a tram into the city. Dad came running out and caught up with me. He was on one side of the fence and I was on the other, on the pavement. He reached out and grabbed my hand and said, 'Goodbye, Ray,' and there were tears in his eyes. I didn't know how sick he was, but I believe he had some kind of premonition that we wouldn't meet many more times.

I saw him again on a couple of fleeting visits to Brisbane and then I was off to England. Dad had emphysema which imposes a strain on all the functions of the body and eventually leads to death from lung failure. When, in 1962, Scott phoned to tell me that Dad was dying, I was far-advanced in rehearsal for a television play, *The Frightened Sky*. I had the leading role. I told Scott I'd try to get out of the commitment and fly back but he told me not to. They knew about this job back home from earlier phone calls.

'I don't think you'd make it,' Scott said. 'He hasn't got long and he told me to tell you to do a bloody good job for him in the play.'

I didn't tell a soul in the cast, but Dad died shortly before the play, written by Jacques Gillies, went to air. It was about a bomb threat to a plane flight and was to go out live—a stressful way of doing television drama that has now disappeared. I was playing the captain of the plane. An enormous mock plane had been built on the set. I remember taking my place for the first scene in the cockpit of the plane. I was grief-stricken. In my mind's eye I can see the floor manager in his earphones as he begins the countdown—eight, seven, six . . .

For an instant I went completely blank. Then the thought flashed into my head: *This is for you, Dad*. Suddenly, everything was back and I believe I gave the best performance of my life.

Life went on but I felt very unsettled and I realised that I hadn't had the time or the appropriate circumstances in which to think through what Dad's death meant to me or how to come to terms with it. We were holidaying at Margate soon after, sharing a big house with friends, and on a Sunday evening I decided to go down to the local church and just sort of say hello to Dad and think about him. A church seemed like an appropriate setting. I went to the Anglican church and found it locked. I tried another Protestant church and it was locked too. I happened on a Roman Catholic church which was open and I went in and sat down and tried to get into the right mental state. A priest or some other church official came up and told me I couldn't stay, that he was locking the church. I tried to explain what I was doing but he wasn't receptive.

As I've said, I never had much interest in organised religion and this experience set the seal on that. Distressed, I left the church and went outside. It was a wild, windy night and I took myself down to the cliffs and sat there with the trees whipping about in the high wind, and I found I was able to do what I wanted—get a feeling that Dad was still there in some sense and communicate with him. I felt better after that, but the sense of loss stayed with me for a long time.

It was a sadness to me that I was again overseas when my mother died many years later. I've talked about various aspects of Scott's personality and behaviour that gave me trouble in my youth, but I'm glad to say that on both these occasions he handled all the difficult and distressing arrangements involved in a parent's death as well as it could be done and on his own. I felt terribly guilty that I couldn't be there to help him. It was a comfort to know that he was looking after things and he earned my undying thanks.

I had been a faithful husband in Brisbane and Sydney and remained so for a time in England. But the theatrical life plays hell with marriage, especially touring. You are thrown together with attractive, like-minded people, stimulated by performing, celebrating and commiserating and the ties get loosened. I was very attracted to a girl named Doreen who was a cast member of *Don't Shoot, We're English.* We'd been eyeing each other off for a time. I knew that she lived with a musician and she knew I was married so we held back.

Eventually we reached Edinburgh one Sunday after a horrible train journey, being shunted off to Halifax, sitting in a siding for hours. It was cold and pissing with rain and Doreen and I, who'd travelled together, were both dying for a drink. We got to the theatre and looked up the list of available digs, which are always pinned up in the stage door keeper's office with names, addresses and prices, but we were a little late and the people who'd got there before us had taken the cream.

Cold, wet, dying for a drink, I said to Doreen, 'Come on, darling, we'll get a taxi, find a hotel for tonight and look around tomorrow.'

I asked the taxi driver to take us somewhere not too pricey but comfortable. We fetched up at what I call a 'brown leather' place—enormous brown leather armchairs, jardinieres, aspidistras, wheelchairs and a musty smell. The man behind the counter had grey hair and steely blue eyes.

'We'd like a room for the night,' I said.

The steely blue eyes ran over me and the attractive young lady.

'Well . . . two rooms,' I said. 'But most of all we want a drink.'

He took an extraordinary amount of time to tell us that this was Sunday in Edinburgh and most people went to church and the drinking laws were such and such.

'Would ye be bona fide travellers?'

I said, 'Would Australia be all right?'

That intrigued him and he seemed to think we were eligible for a drink. Then it took another huge stretch of time for him to locate a set of keys, a great bunch like gaoler's keys, and then there was a trek up the stairs and along the corridors to a room and another wait while he located keys for the separate locks. At last he got the door open with much creaking and groaning from him and it, and this musty smell of non-use hit us. Doreen was having trouble stifling hysterical laughter by this stage. To my horror he approached a sort of rollerblind that shuttered the bar and there was another interminable wait for the keys to the bar and the rollerblind.

Eventually the rollerblind came up.

'Australians, ye say. What will ye have?'

'Two double whiskies—one with ginger ale and one with water.'

There was a tinkle of bottle and glasses. 'Australians. Aye. I have a whisky here ye'll no get in Australia.'

'Oh, good.'

So he produced the two whiskies and the bottle of ginger ale and a carafe of water and he put them on the bar. 'Roll it round y' tongue,' he says to me.

'I am, I am.'

He looked at Doreen. 'Ye'll put nae ginger ale in there.'

I thought, *How can I get rid of this character?* Brilliant, I'll offer him a drink, thinking he might take the hint. He paused, considered, paused some more, looked around. Sunday of course, somebody might be watching. On and on. At last he said, 'Aye, I will. I'll have a gin and orange.'

This after being such a purist about the scotch. At long last we got our door keys from him and before he took off he turned and gave us a huge, exaggerated theatrical wink.

'I've put y' in the two top rooms. Ye'll nae be disturbed up there.'

So that was the beginning of an affair with Doreen which fizzled out but led to others. I fell madly in love with Janet Watts. I met Frank, her husband, first. He was a lighting cameraman and we played golf together. We'd taken a big house at Margate for the holidays, Audrey and I and some of her friends who had kids at school with Suellen. I invited Frank down for the weekend and he brought Janet. I took one look at her and felt something like an electric shock. There were just no defences possible. I was full of guilt about hurting Frank and Audrey and Janet felt the same about me and guilty in the same way but it was as if we were helpless and there was nothing we could do about it.

It was a very passionate affair and it broke my marriage. It got to the point where Janet said that we had to be together and that she was leaving Frank and I had to break it to Audrey. She took it hard of course, but she was absolutely trumps. She could see the inevitability of what was happening and she eventually agreed to give me a divorce. She wasn't mean or grasping about it in any way. She was quite wonderful. So the time came for me to collect Janet and a few belongings and to go off together. We stayed with a friend who was a stuntman in television and is now a director. And our cohabitation lasted just one night. Janet got cold feet and went back to Frank.

I was absolutely shattered by that. All boats burned and then all hopes dashed—it was very hard to take. I was working on a series for ATV at Elstree and I felt I couldn't go on with it.

The producer was Dennis Vance and I told him I wanted to pull out, but he really took me in hand, he and his wife Clair. I stayed with them. He took me to the studio in the morning, and he was there when we broke for lunch and he took me back in the afternoon. He helped me to pull through a very black time. He got a shock when I was fiddling around with his son's .22 rifle (I was occupying the son's bedroom) and accidentally discharged it. Dennis told me later that his first thought had been, *Oh, shit. He's shot himself.* I hadn't reached that stage, but I was near to it. I learned afterwards that there was a pot plant full of .22 shells on the mantelpiece in the room. Thank Christ I didn't discover it.

After a bit, Dennis introduced me to a woman named Celia Sherman Fischer who was a production assistant at ATV. I went home with her one night after a good deal to drink. At that time I was so mortified by what had happened with Janet that another affair was the last thing on my mind. I explained to Celia that I was still desperately in love with Janet and also that I had come to the conclusion that I was bad news where women were concerned. I thought that would call a halt. But one thing led to another and an affair developed. I had a little basement flat in Hampstead by this time which I'd done some work on and made comfortable in bachelor fashion. I also had a kitten named Poo[1]. Celia began coming around, cooking for me, staying the night which eventually became two nights, then three, and she moved in.

---

[1] I acquired Poo when working on a horror film at Bray. The cat was supposed to belong to my wife in the film and when the house of horrors burnt down I had to race into the flames following its plaintive mewing and rescue it. Jennifer Daniels, playing my wife, hated cats, always brought her dachshund to work with her and consequently the cat would have nothing to do with her. It lived in the wardrobe department and slept in the pocket of my Edwardian jacket. Being the bachelor by then, I loved the thing and brought it tit-bits every day.

At the end of the shoot I asked the prop boy what was going to happen to the kitten. 'Looks like the river, doesn't it?' he said. 'My wife'd kill me if I took it home. We've already got six.' I asked him to get the cat into its basket and put it in my car. It shat all the way from Bray to Hampstead—hence the name, not as in Poo Bear as everybody thought.

Once again, I got set in my ways. I felt secure and comfortable with a companion. I'd got tired of renting so I bought a little cottage in Albert Road, Richmond. It was a two up and two down workman's cottage, and I completely renovated it, working at night after slogging away at the studio all day. It came up really beautifully. Celia moved in there and we were together for some years, getting along very well. She used to collect me at the BBC, after I'd finished working on the television series *The Troubleshooters* for the day. She was working at ATV, and one night she picked me up and I could see that she was tired and I suggested that we go and eat Chinese rather than cook at home

We went to our favourite place in Richmond. It was Friday night and packed, and we had to share a table with a group of people. There was a very handsome boy she sat next to. Within two days she left me for this fellow. I couldn't believe it. It seemed so bizarre—to be abandoned without warning for someone met in a Chinese restaurant. I was totally distraught again.

There was some unpleasantness after that. She told me she was coming around with Tony or whatever-his-name-was, to pick up her things and that got under my skin. I'd collected a lot of Victorian glass and objets d'art that I cared about and I was damned if I was going to let them traipse through together doing what they pleased. I told her that her belongings would be out on the footpath and I changed the locks. Pretty savage behaviour for me, but again I was distraught at how the bottom had fallen out of things so suddenly.

But I pulled myself together with the help of the people I had come to know and been accepted by in Albert Road, Richmond, where I had my little cottage. These little workmen's cottages, two up two down, were built around the turn of the century. I remember on the deed of my cottage the construction price was roughly 245 pounds.

Maggie, opposite, who had a sort of run-down fruit and veg shop, had long passed the days when she used to hawk her wares around in an old pony and cart.

George Baker up the road ran the off-licence, a terribly crippled old gent who held court quoting Shakespeare whilst we sat around on beer crates. It was a sort of 'before and after hours' establishment where one could help oneself and leave the money on the counter. The law turned a blind eye to George's trading hours. He was an institution.

Joe and Mary. Mary used to clean for me, a darling lady, and Joe was an assistant ranger at Richmond Park, looking after the royal deer, the ponds and general flora and fauna.

I suppose I was one of the first, shall we say, 'foreigners', to invade such a closely knit community and I felt I was intruding on their domain, of which they were justly proud. Nobody had much money but they'd give you the clothes off their backs.

When Celia left so suddenly these were the people who consoled me and rallied round. I would come home to find the house cleaned, the bed made and hot dinners in foil waiting for me in the kitchen. 'You must eat, Ducks' they'd say. I'd find the washing and ironing done. These were the people who put their arms around me, unasked, unsolicited and expecting no thanks. That was their way. True blue Londoners who'd had it hard all their lives and helped one another.

I was proud to be more or less adopted into their society and I knew I had them as a sort of family to confide in. They were my props. I have them to thank for keeping me sane and easing me through those rough times. They will always be in my heart.

Of course my old mate, Glyn Owen, was always supportive. When Audrey and I were living in a big Victorian house in Maida Vale, equipped with a vast basement that had a bathroom and toilet, Glyn was living in a nearby flatette. The rule at his place—this was the very early 60s—was that residents could not entertain guests overnight. Glyn was having a relationship with a six foot blonde woman, Margaret, impossible to overlook and the upshot was that he was kicked out of his flatette.

'I've been thrown out,' he told me. 'Can I doss down at your place for a week or so until I find another flat?'

I'd already offered him the basement when I'd heard about the restrictions on his lifestyle, so I told him that'd be fine. I supplied a nice little stove and some heaters and he moved in pro tem. The basement let out onto the garden and it was really very pleasant. Margaret moved in soon after. Glyn was still there two years later! Our local was the Star at St Johns Wood where we had many good times with people from all walks of life. We've remained close friends ever since and he is one of the first people I look up when I go back to England.

At the time of the break with Celia I was working on *The Troubleshooters* about which I'll say more later. It helped to be in steady work, to have that discipline and distraction from a pretty turbulent personal life. I shouldn't exaggerate. I was still spending a lot of time with Suellen. Audrey never put any barriers up there and in fact my relations with Audrey were good through all of this. I was fortunate in that.

The next woman in my life was Mirén Cork. She was a production assistant on *The Troubleshooters*. She was blonde, very attractive and I was drawn to her in the same way I had been to Janet. A very powerful, physical thing. Eventually, after a certain amount of coming and going—Mirén was living with a very possessive Greek who used to lock her in at night and watch her every move—Mirén moved in with me at Richmond.

We were married and my son Reggie was born in 1972. The Richmond cottage was too small for a growing boy so I bought a beautiful house in East Sheen, Surrey. It had been built originally as a stables in the 1830s and had been converted and extended over the years since. It required considerable renovation and restoration—too much for me to do myself this time. The house was near Richmond Park where the royal deer are. There are gates with wonderful names like Robin Hood gate, a very atmospheric area. We lived very happily there for the rest of my time in England.

So, after more than ten years in England, I had come full circle. I was a family man again, very settled.

There were many memorable and enjoyable family outings like the time we went out to lunch at a house on the Thames and Reggie fell in the river. No trouble, he was fished out unharmed, but a dear old friend of mine named Colonel 'Tubby' Marshall was there and he was one of the Swan Uppers. This is a select band of men who are concerned with the breeding of the royal swans on the Thames. It's an overhang from the old medieval guilds and societies, and has become a kind of social club. To be a Swan Upper you must have been totally immersed in the river at a certain point and Tubby's judgement was that Reggie had qualified. He arranged for him to be issued with a beautifully framed parchment scroll with a swan's quill incorporated testifying that he was a duly acknowledged member of the Honourable Society of Swan Uppers.

There were nice, traditional British things like that to enjoy as well as more contemporary pleasures. My career was progressing satisfactorily. I was older and, I hoped, wiser.

· 13 ·
The Troubleshooters

John Elliott was the creator of the television series that began life as *Mogul* and became *The Troubleshooters*. The series, about the fortunes and machinations of a giant oil company, ran on the BBC from 1965 to 1972 and it was my great good luck to be in it from first to last. Like *Emergency Ward 10*, *The Troubleshooters* built its audience quickly and held it. Showing on Mondays, it is estimated to have had a regular audience of about eleven million people. It also became very popular in Australia and New Zealand.

I played Peter Thornton, a hard-bitten Australian who was the company's field man. Uncomfortable in the office, Thornton was in his element in sticky, practical situations. He could negotiate a deal with a military junta, pull a colleague out of a compromising sexual situation and drive a long wheelbase Land Rover over rough ground. Intelligent and resourceful, but essentially a hands-on type. He was Australian in manner and attitude.

Some years into the series I happened to ask John Elliott how I got this role which I had found suited me so perfectly.

'I wrote it for you,' he said. 'Early on in the piece, I saw you in the bar of the BBC club. I was agonising over the Thornton character and I thought, that's the man I've been looking for.'[1]

That has to be the luckiest time I ever spent in a bar. *Troubleshooters* gave me regular work and a good income for a long stretch and raised my profile in the profession. Some years we made twenty-one episodes and some years fewer, but the job always left me free to do other work and, particularly in the early years, I made several films and telemovies. But above all, it was a good, solid part in a realistic show that tackled serious stories in an adult manner. I was working with fine actors like Geoffrey Keene and Phillip Latham and we had some input to the scripts. If we felt the story was running off the rails, getting mushy say, we would put our oar in and ask for re-writes which we usually got. I remember one occasion when a gay set designer had placed Thornton in a grimy, sleazy flat in the Portobello Road. I jibbed at that. I remember that I got somewhat annoyed and told him, 'Thornton is a chief executive of one of the world's largest oil companies. He's a man's man, but he has style. He wouldn't shack up with a bird in a slum. At the very least he'd entertain her in some style.'

After lunch I came back to find the set painted bright colours and everything changed around more in keeping with Thornton, who was a tough guy but not a low life.

Geoffrey came from an acting family and had a wicked sense of humour. I recall once sending him what I thought was an amusing postcard from Spain and getting no reaction at all when I saw him again back in England. Eventually, six months later, he said something like, 'Oh, I should have thanked you for that postcard from Spain.'

I said, 'Well, yes, I was wondering when you'd get around to it.'

'Yes, funny thing. There weren't enough stamps on it. The postie knocked on the door and he said, "Here you are, Mr Keene, here's a postcard from your mate in Spain. It needs another 20p in stamps. D'you want it?"'

---

[1] My good friend Peter Yeldham has recently reminded me that John Elliott was the producer of a television play of his named *Reunion Day* in which I appeared. Elliott subsequently revealed that it was my performance in that play that planted the seed in his mind which led to my casting as Peter Thornton.

Geoffrey said, 'No, I don't want it.'

'Orright, I'll read it to you.'

The postie read it and Geoffrey told me there was water dripping from his cap all over the card. When he finished the postie said, 'Can I take it home for me kids?'

That was Geoffrey, a whimsical individual.

Robert Hardy, a distinguished actor who joined the series late in its run, proved to be another interesting colleague. He had a farm near Bray and one day invited the cast who were shooting in the vicinity to visit. We turned up to discover him deeply involved in his great hobby—archery. He had targets set out on the lawn and a variety of bows, quivers and arrows, the works. We were invited to participate and made fools of ourselves. I hadn't realised how difficult archery was. I was surprised to learn that Robert was actually a bow-maker himself and had written several books on the subject.

Robert is a most generous host and great company. We had a fine lunch and afterwards he took me inside.

'This,' he said in a hushed tone as he ushered me into a room fitted out in green baize, 'is the Agincourt Room.'

It was filled with dozens, perhaps scores, of longbows in racks, made by the finest craftsmen in the world. I felt very honoured and had the impression that he wasn't in the habit of showing the room to everybody. He took a beautifully crafted bow from its rack and placed it gently in my hands.

'This was made by the finest bow-maker in the world, the Norwegian Olaf Ericsson. It's made from ash; the grip and tips are of elk horn, feel the quality, look at the workmanship.'

I felt as if I was handling a Stradivarius and quickly returned it to him.

It was rugged work at times on *Troubleshooters*. That physical feats I would have taken for granted as a youngster were now not so easy was brought home to me when we were filming on an oil rig being built in the River Tees. To get to the top of the rig you had to climb into a huge wooden box attached to a crane by a cable. When it took off the box swung wildly round and round until it reached the top of the structure and was manoeuvred into place. Then you had to get out of the box onto

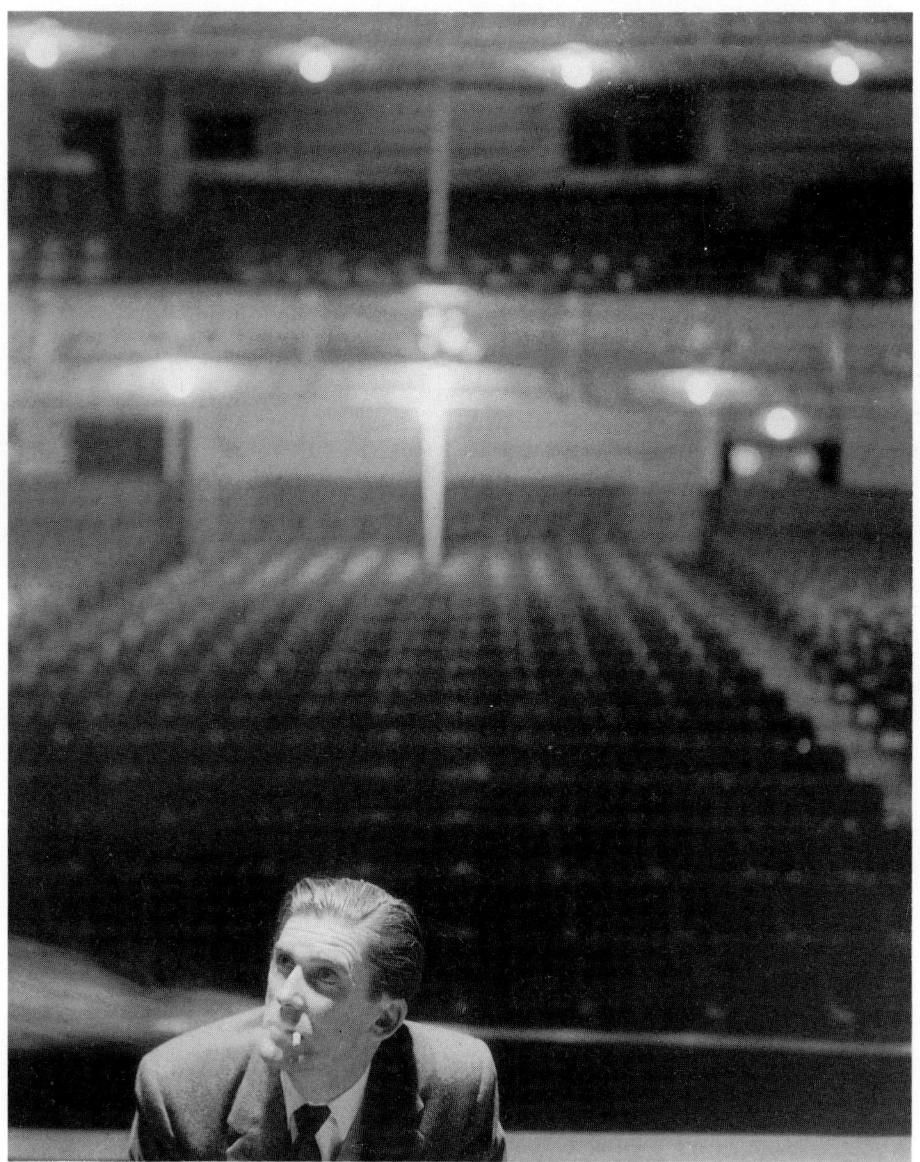

Rehearsing *Look Back in Anger* at the Elizabethan Theatre. *(Elizabethan Theatre Trust)*

LEFT: As Mitya in *The Brothers Karamazov,* BBC, 1964-5. *(H. Moyes)*

BELOW: With Judith Stott in *The Brothers Karamazov. (H. Moyes)*

TOP: Relaxing at Cap Gris Nez after *The Brothers Karamazov*!
BOTTOM: John Tate gives me a hand!

As Dr. Nolan in *Emergency Ward 10*, 1962. *(Associated Television)*

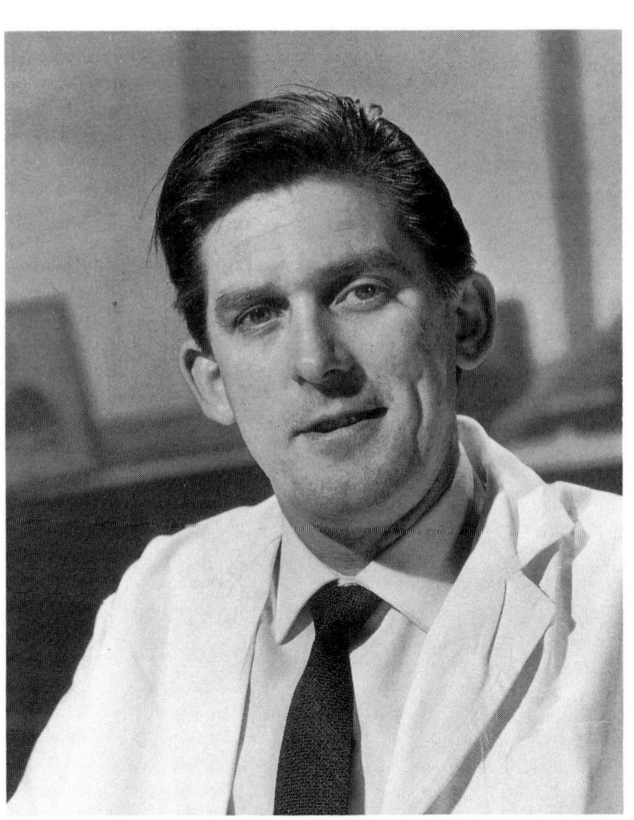

Broken arm, courtesy Bill Madders. Setting Spanish style, Formentera, 1967.

As Peter Thornton in *The Troubleshooters*, 1966. *(BBC)*

ABOVE: With Geoffrey Keen as Stead in *The Troubleshooters.* *(BBC)*

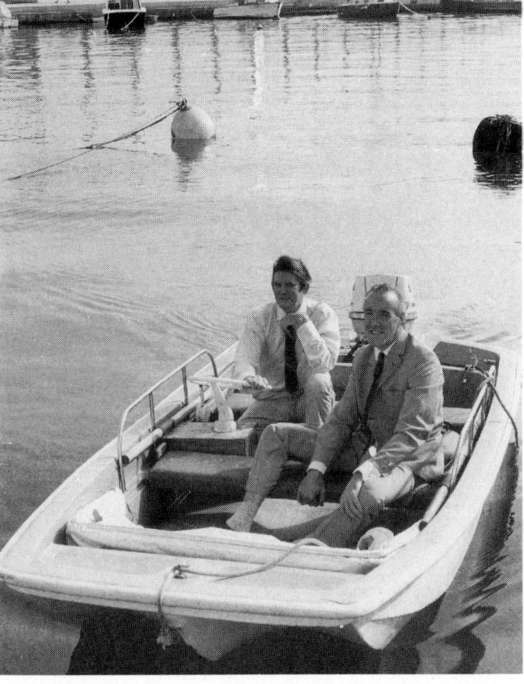

LEFT: With Philip Latham on location in Kenya for *The Troubleshooters. (BBC)*

At my cottage in Richmond, 1969. *(Rex Features Ltd)*

In the kitchen. *(Chris Ware)*

‘A Talent to Amu

An entertainment devised from the works of NOËL COW
and based on the biography by SHERIDAN MOR

Part One

Overture	
The Boy Actor *Projection from the* Mander and Mitchenson Collection	JOHN GIELGUD
This is not a Day Like Any Other Day *Projection from the* Mander and Mitchenson Collection	MAGGIE FITZGIBBON
	RICHARD ATTENBOROUGH
Early Mourning	IRENE WORTH, BETTY HARE
	ROBERT MORLEY
I've Been to a Marvellous Party *Projection designed by* Berkeley Sutcliffe	DANNY LA RUE
What's Going to Happen to the Tots? *Projection designed by* Hutchinson Scott	GRETCHEN FRANKLIN, DORIS HARE, ALISON LEGGAT DANDY NICHOLS, ELSIE RANDOLPH, DOROTHY REYN GEORGE BENSON, ROBERT COOTE, JACK KRUSCHEN, JOHN MERIVALE
Projection designed by Ronald Searle	DAPHNE ANDERSON, AMANDA BARRIE, SHEILA BERN JOYCE BLAIR, JOSEPHINE GORDON, GAY SOPER, BILLY BOYLE, NEIL FITZWILLIAM, JOHN GOWER, TERENCE KNAPP, ROD McLENNAN, TERRY MITCHELL
A Room With a View *Projection designed by* Paul Anstee	CHERYL KENNEDY, DAVID KERNAN
Ladies of the Town *Projection designed by* Anthony Mendleson	FAITH BROOK, PATRICIA BURKE, JUDY CAMPBELL, DULCIE GRAY, MARION GRIMALDI, GLYNIS JOHNS, VANESSA LEE, MOIRA LISTER, DINAH SHERIDAN, ELEANOR SUMMERFIELD assisted by KIM GRANT, LEWIS FIANDER, NORMAN WARWICK, STEPHEN WARWICK
Private Lives (scene) *Projection designed by* Hutchinson Scott	SUSANNAH YORK, RICHARD BRIERS
Green Carnation *Projection designed by* Peter Farmer	PATRICK ALLEN, RAY BARRETT, MICHAEL DENISON
If Love Were All *Projection designed by* Tim Goodchild	JOYCE GRENFELL *at the piano* WILLIAM BLEZARD
Any Little Fish *Projection designed by* Anthony Holland	CARYL LITTLE, SHEILA WHITE, JONATHAN DENNIS, GRAHAM JAMES
The Stately Homes of England *Projection designed by* Osbert Lancaster	TONY BRITTON, PETER GRAVES, JOHN MOFFATT JOHN STANDING
I've Just Come Out From England *Projection designed by* Motley	CELIA JOHNSON

The programme for *A Talent to Amuse,* a performance at the Phoenix Theatre to honour Noel Coward on his 70th birthday.

Sigh No More *ojection designed by* Tom Lingwood	ANNE ROGERS
Matelot *jection designed by* Gladys Calthrop	MARK WYNTER *accompanied by* HARVEY HOPE
Three Juvenile Delinquents *Projection designed by* Disley Jones	NICKY HENSON, JULIAN HOLLOWAY, BUNNY MAY, GARY BOND, ANTHONY ROBERTS, NORMAN WARWICK, HUBERT GREGG, GORDON JACKSON, DAVID KNIGHT, BRYAN FORBES, GUY HAMILTON, JOHN SCHLESINGER
There Are Bad Times Just Around the Corner *Projection designed by* Peter Rice	JOAN HEAL, IAN CARMICHAEL, GRAHAM PAYN assisted by TERRY MITCHELL
London Pride *Projection designed by* Carl Toms	STANLEY HOLLOWAY
London *Directed by* Douglas Squires *ojection designed by* Malcolm Pride	TESSIE O'SHEA THE YOUNG GENERATION

INTERVAL OF TWENTY MINUTES

Part Two

Where are the songs we sung?

JOHN CLEMENTS
Introduces our other guests
the programme will include:

You Were There	SUSAN HAMPSHIRE, DENIS QUILLEY
Chase Me Charlie	PAT KIRKWOOD
Twentieth Century Blues	ELISABETH WELCH
y do the wrong people travel?	MAGGIE FITZGIBBON
Mary Make Believe	JESSIE MATTHEWS
That is the End of the News	AVRIL ANGERS, HY HAZELL, STELLA MORAY, JUNE WHITFIELD
I'll Follow my Secret Heart	PATRICIA ROUTLEDGE
Nina	CYRIL RITCHARD
Poor Little Rich Girl (*piano*) **Parisian Pierrot**	RICHARD RODNEY BENNETT
Time and Again	ANNE ROGERS, JEREMY BRETT
Dance Little Lady	ANNA NEAGLE
Melanie's Aria	JUNE BRONHILL
Beatnik Love Affair	UNA STUBBS, CLIFF RICHARD
Mad About the Boy	CLEO LAINE *accompanied by* JOHN DANKWORTH
Vocal Accompaniment by	THE MIKE SAMMES SINGERS

Directed by	WENDY TOYE and NIGEL PATRICK
Produced by	MARTIN TICKNER
Lighting by	MICHAEL NORTHEN
Decor supervised by	HUTCHINSON SCOTT
Musical Director	GRANT HOSSACK
Production supervised by	ROBERT NESBITT

This Programme is subject to alteration

ABOVE AND NEXT PAGE: My new career as a singer is launched, 1969-1970. *(Fontana)*

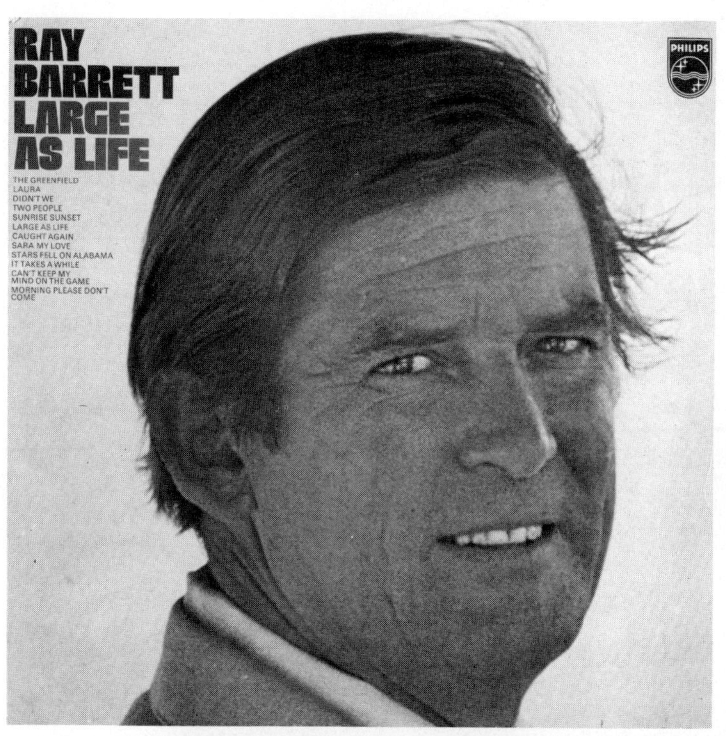
RAY
BARRETT
LARGE
AS LIFE
PHILIPS
THE GREENFIELD
LAURA
DIDN'T WE
TWO PEOPLE
SUNRISE SUNSET
LARGE AS LIFE
CAUGHT AGAIN
SARA MY LOVE
STARS FELL ON ALABAMA
IT TAKES A WHILE
CAN'T KEEP MY
MIND ON THE GAME
MORNING PLEASE DON'T
COME

No
Trouble
Now!
Ray
Barrett
fontana
I have dreamed
Without her
Lonely lonely girl
This guy's in love with you
House for sale
If you go away
The very thought of you
Can't get used to losing you
Why do they have to fall in love?
Hushabye Mountain
Don't say a word
My silent love

ABOVE: Sean Connery's Charity Golf Tournament at Gleneagles, 1970. Stanley Baker's hands are on my shoulders; Connery is kneeling at the front with Ronnie Corbett.

LEFT: When I was playing well. Richmond Golf Club, 1971. *(Rex Features Ltd)*

TOP: Charity cricket at the Oval, 1972. Note Michael Parkinson, Roy Castle, John Hurt, Mike Aspel and John Alderton in the back row. I'm sitting next to Mickey Stewart, England captain; to his left is Andy Williams. *(The Central Press Photos Ltd)*

BOTTOM: At Lord's, 1972. Back row from left: Brian Rix, Elton John, Michael Parkinson, Peter Cook, Ed Stewart, Nicholas Parsons, me. Note Wes Hall and David Frost in the front row.

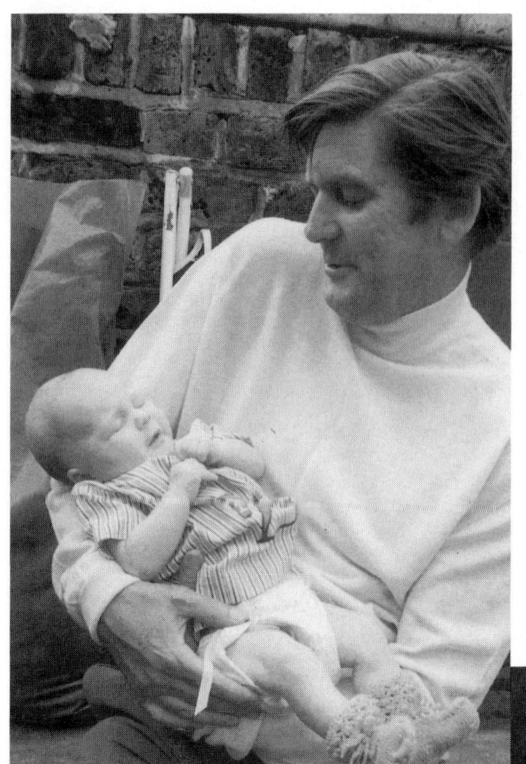

A proud Dad again. At the Richmond cottage with Reg, aged a few months. 1972.

Suellen nurses Reginald.

RIGHT: Charity cricket with Pete Murray of the BBC at Kew Green, 1972. *(Mr M. R. Singleton)*

BELOW: Freddie Carpenter introducing me to Princess Anne after the Charity Concert for Darwin Cyclone Relief, 1973. Next to me are Anona Wynne and Danny La Rue. *(J.A. Ballard)*

Suellen becomes a British Airways air hostess, 1973. *(Jon Lyons)*

With Reggie. Hillfield, 1973. *(Jon Lyons)*

a flimsy plank and then scramble up to a metal deck still being welded together.

I perched on the edge of the swaying box and made the fatal mistake of looking down. There was a gap of a few feet between the box and the plank. I felt sick and knew I was suffering from vertigo. Only the fact that the female production assistant, the wardrobe mistress and other crew members had done it motivated me to take that step. Vertigo is a terrible thing. Planes, helicopters and gliders don't trouble me, perhaps because they are moving. On the rig I had to force myself to look down through the scaffolding and maze of steel to the water below with the seagulls wheeling about and then do my scenes.

I pleaded with the director to put up some rope handrails beside the springy planks for safety's sake.

'Sorry, Ray. Wouldn't look real.'

Then the boom operator slipped as the camera pulled back. He disappeared. Everything was still and every face was ashen until we saw that he had fallen into a well that held machinery for the running of the rig. If he had been in a slightly different position, on the other side of the camera, and fallen all the way he would certainly have been killed. The rope handrails were soon in place.

I remember that I had to do some underwater scenes for one episode to do with the North Sea oil rigs. Some cables had become tangled and lives were at stake and I had to go down and cut the cables with an oxy-acetylene torch. The shot was to be done in a big tank at a Royal Naval training base. The script called for another actor to go down with me but he was ill on the day. Clever bugger. Now, while I'd been a good enough swimmer in my youth, I'd never done anything like this and I naturally thought I'd have a stunt double. I said to Peter Graham-Scott, the producer, 'Where's my double?'

He said, 'No double. You have to do it yourself. We've got the camera set up looking through one of the observation windows the instructors use to check on their students, so we'll know it's *you*!'

They had Chief Petty Officer someone-or-other on hand to run me through it. I got into the wetsuit and put on the flippers and whatnot, the lead weights. 'Hop in and swim around a bit. You've done this before 'aven't you?'

'No.'

'Oh, shit,' he said. 'Well 'ere's your tanks, slip 'em on.'

I nearly fell over with the weight of the bloody things and then he showed me the mask and the demand valve and how to breathe. 'Don't worry if your mask fills up with water. Just ease it up and blow it out with ya nose. Remember, you can swallow a lot of water before you die.' They spend weeks training people in heated swimming pools for this sort of thing and I was expected to do it right off the bat.

'Now, when you come up, come up slow and don't ex'ale or you could blow your lungs. Right?'

I swam around for a while feeling very uncomfortable because of the unfamiliarity of it and because I suffer a bit from claustrophobia anyway. Then came the crunch. I had to go down and use the oxy-acetylene torch to cut the cable.

'Now, you know how to light one of these underwater don't you?'

I said, 'No, I've never seen one before let alone used one. I don't spend much time underwater cutting cables.'

'Oh, shit.' Eventually he decided it was simpler for him to light the torch and for me to take it down lit and do the job that way. But he warned for Christ sake not to touch myself with it. I was in a state by this time, hardly likely to remember everything about the breathing and so on. But I got in, went down and did it. I trained the torch on the thick cable, two inches or so of it, and it cut straight through it like butter. I tugged on the cable, it fell away and I came up as I was supposed to.

'How was that?' I said, happy to have survived.

Graham-Scott pulled a face. 'It looked far too easy. You've got to do it again and make it look like hard work.'

I did it. I wouldn't now. I'd call for the double and sit there high and dry until he came.

Another time we were shooting in Malacca. The action called for me to be lowered into the jungle from a helicopter. We were flying over the Straits of Malacca, over the water, and I wasn't wearing any sort of harness, the only person not so protected. Ernie Christie, the cameraman, looking through his lens, kept pushing me with his foot. A helicopter doesn't bank slowly like a fixed-wing aircraft but jerks quickly and I was afraid I would just disappear straight through the wide open door down into the Straits of Malacca.

We got over the abandoned rubber plantation which was the drop zone and there were a couple of RAF guys in their helmets and gear organising the action. I was just in slacks and a light shirt. One of them, I remember his ginger moustache vividly, said, 'This is where you hop out, old chap. Have you ever done this before?'

That question again. Same answer. 'No. I don't usually do this sort of thing.'

'Just put this belt under your arm and ... whoosh ... off you go. And pull on the wire. It'll hurt a bit but you'll get used to it.'

So there I am, high above these huge trees, hundreds of feet up, twirling on the end of a bit of wire. Ernie Christie was safe and sound and I remember thinking, *I hope you get a bloody good shot, mate, and it's clear that I'm doing this bit myself.* Down I went and the undergrowth looked thick enough to swallow me up. I thought, *What am I going to land on? Some cobra or other poisonous reptile waiting to say good morning?* I knew no-one had been down to check the spot out. Eventually I lobbed into this tiny cleared spot in the middle of an overgrown rubber plantation. In white shoes, shirt and slacks, I waved them goodbye, and it crossed my mind that they might never find me again. The rub is, when you saw it on the screen, it could have been a rag doll dangling there.

The hairiest moments on *Troubleshooters* came when we filmed in Kenya in 1968. We arrived in Nairobi on New Year's Eve and, fortunately for me as it turned out, our arrival coincided with that of the Kenyan Ambassador to the Court of St James. He'd been summoned back from London by President Jomo Kenyatta to be present for the state visit by Archbishop Makarios. The main function was to be held at the President's beach complex at Mombasa.

The ambassador was a friendly man, obviously happy to be home. He gave me a brief rundown on the history and culture of Kenya and a warning.

'If you're driving at night,' he said, 'and you come across a body on the road, don't stop. Drive over it and report it to the nearest police station.' I didn't think he was serious—then.

We finished filming in Nairobi and drove south to Mombasa through some of the most beautiful country I have ever seen. We booked into the Mombasa Beach Hotel along with President Kenyatta's foreign minister, a former Mau Mau terrorist, a gentleman by the name of Mungai. My newfound friend, the ambassador to Britain, was also staying in the hotel. Mr Mungai, I was to learn, had a penchant for schnapps and a hatred for whites. The sight of his countrymen being filmed in their roles as waiters around the hotel pool greatly angered him apparently.

On the completion of our filming at the Shell refinery in Mombasa, our hosts from Shell treated us to dinner at the charming old Mombasa Club. It was the very epitome of colonial style and you almost expected to see W. Somerset Maugham descend the stairs, stick and martini in hand. After a splendid meal we drove back to our hotel, interrupted on our way by coming across a car halfway up a tree with its engine still roaring, a dead man in a ditch by the side of the road, another badly injured and broken glass everywhere. All pretty shaken when we reached the hotel we invited the Shell people in for a nightcap.

The BBC production people on the trip were determined to take as much of their travel expense allowance home intact as possible and they were notoriously tight-fisted. I treated our hosts myself. In the bar were the ambassador and Mr Mungai, in shirt sleeves, his eyes flaming red and a bottle of schnapps on the bar in front of him. He immediately started an argument with the producer and director. I carefully stationed myself at the other end of the bar with the Shell people.

Although it was getting noisier by the minute, I couldn't hear what the argument was about and didn't want to. But I was forcibly removed from where I was sitting and placed on a stool in the presence of this extraordinary red-eyed man. He screamed at me to apologise. I could see the state he was in but I had no idea of what I was supposed to apologise for. I tried, as tactfully as possible, to inquire about my misdemeanour. He hit me with a vicious right to the jaw that sent me flying off my stool and sprawling on the marble floor.

The first impulse was to come up fighting, but that was quickly dispelled by the appearance out of nowhere of two uniformed thugs with pistols on their belts. They picked me up and dumped me back on the stool whereupon Mungai swept me off it again in the other direction with a savage backhander. Red eyes aflame, he said. 'Take him out and shoot him.'

I was marched, or rather dragged, because my feet barely touched the ground, towards the glass doors by the two thugs. It seemed to take a long time and I was aware of the strangest of feelings—complete acceptance. I knew that once through those doors I'd had it. I remember thinking, '*What a place to go out in—Mombasa! This is not really what I'd planned.*'

I have no doubt that I owe my life to the ambassador who intervened and got things under control. My BBC colleagues, with the single exception of a gay dresser who stood up for me, offered no support whatever but mostly fled for their rooms when the trouble started. I recall one actor, a timid type who sweated profusely every time he boarded a plane, pleading with me, almost screaming, 'For god's sake apologise! Don't you know I've got a wife and children back in London?'

'What d'you think I've got,' I said, 'fucking monkeys?'

Piecing it together later, it seems that the trouble arose out of some light-hearted remarks the Shell people passed while some general tie-exchanging was going on. I exchanged my Richmond golf club tie for a Mombasa Beach Club tie and someone said within the hearing of the minister or one of his party something like, 'Now you black bastards are members of the Mombasa Beach Club you had better learn to wear a tie.' With three bottles of schnapps aboard, it seems that the minister took offence and attributed the remark to me.

I was rounded up very early the next morning by the nervous production team and rushed to the airport. I was anxious about what Mr Mungai might do when he sobered up, but they were terrified. The threat was real. As we waited in the furthest recess of the lounge the message came frequently over the tannoy: *Mr Barrett, come outside, please! Mr Barrett ...* We didn't hear it, did we? and after an eight hour wait caught our flight.

On my return I learned that a campaign was conducted behind my back to lay the blame for the Mombasa incident—from which some embarrassing political or diplomatic reverberations could be expected—squarely on me. This went on in the gap between finishing one series and beginning the next. When I got wind of the campaign, I insisted on a meeting being called in the holy sanctuary, the inner heart of the BBC at White City. Everyone who had been present in the bar was there including the actor who had feared for the future of his family. I questioned them one by one and the truth came out. Even our cufflink shooting Head of Drama eventually saw that I had been made a patsy by my gallant colleagues. Actors are expendable after all. End of story.

One of the problems was that some of the production people tended to treat location shoots as junkets, made sure that their favourite make-up lady was in the party, stock up on the duty-free and save as much of their per diem as they could. On a long sweep from Hong Kong through South-East Asia to India we made towards the end of the series, I got off to a bad start by picking up the tab after we all went to dinner with some wealthy people at an expensive Hong Kong restaurant. This was something the producer should have done and put it down to production expenses. That almost wiped out my expenses for the whole trip. Pretty soon I was using my own money to eat and drink.

That was bad enough, but by Bangkok it became apparent that Peter Graham-Scott, the producer (P.G. Tips as we called him), and his pals were treating the whole thing as a holiday—a chance to explore the *klongs* and pick up bargains in silk and cameras. Also, the filming was just a lot of guesswork—doing set-ups with me against identifiable backgrounds that could be slotted into stories later. This is not how an actor likes to work and it made me angry. I had a serious bowel infection by this time and was very ill. No sympathy or consideration from the producer. Moira Armstrong was directing these meaningless snatches and I asked her if she knew what she was shooting.

'I don't know what I'm shooting,' she said.

Tony Reed was the script editor. I blew my stack and insisted on him sitting down and writing scenes for the shooting that was coming up in India to get some value out of what would otherwise be a mere tourist excursion.

By the time we reached India I was in a very bad way with a severe intestinal disorder that made it perilous for me to be more than a yard from a toilet for more than five minutes. But a very famous and beautiful Indian actress had become available and nothing would do but that some filming had to done at the Taj Mahal. I was in agony, very ill, and tried to beg off but the powers-that-be insisted. We got to the Taj Mahal and the filming was to be done day-for-night, which meant at the time when the sun was immediately overhead and there were no shadows. A moonlight scene was required but there were dust storms blocking out the moonlight.

The heat was indescribable and the Indian actress promptly fainted. For religious reasons we all had to take our shoes off and I can still remember the smell of sweaty, unwashed feet.

Despite my condition, some of the production people wanted to linger to admire the edifice. 'Fuck the Taj Mahal,' I said. 'There are no toilets at the Taj Mahal!'

'How unromantic,' they muttered.

I came close to committing murder that day.

But there are bound to be frictions in the course of a long relationship, and I retain many more happy memories of *Troubleshooters* than sour ones. The scripts were outstanding and it seemed to me that I had the best part in the show. Whereas Geoffrey and Phillip, playing Brian Stead, the managing director and Willy Izard, the accountant, did much the same thing all the time—agonised and pulled the strings from the office—I was working with different actors every time and it felt like a new film each episode which was very stimulating and enabled me to maintain my interest over the long run. As far as I know, the series never lost popularity and the BBC simply decided to go out in style and finish the show while it was still rating strongly.

When I got back to Australia in the late 1970s I was surprised to find how popular *Troubleshooters* had been. People kept asking me, 'When's that show coming back?' I conceived the idea of a spin-off from it being set in Australia. I thought of calling it 'Energy' and imagined oil exploration in such places as Antarctica and New Guinea, etc. The idea was to make it of international interest and draw on foreign capital such as Japanese and American. There seemed to be many possibilities. I got John Elliott out from England and made contact with MIM, the mining company. I left the idea in the charge of a guy who had a little production company in Brisbane while I went back to England for some reason or other. When I got back the script had taken shape as virtually a giant commercial for MIM and I couldn't see any value in that. It was a pity. Properly handled, it might have worked.

· 14 ·

Finch and others

I bumped into Peter Finch in Paris one weekend. He told me a story against himself.

Finch had been 'discovered' in Australia by the Oliviers when they had toured the country in 1948. Encouraged by them to come to London, he was 'taken up' by Olivier who had introduced him to everyone of importance in the West End. A terrific start for a young man, enabling him to skip having to traipse around repertory for parts and all the dreadful business of auditions and interviews. Finch had a wonderful voice (which he had used to great effect on Australian radio), but he did have a tendency towards a falling inflection at the end of a spoken line. Olivier pointed this out to him and suggested a voice tutor to correct the fault. Very concerned, Finch dutifully went to the coach and worked so hard that he over-compensated and turned the falling delivery into an upward one.

He had a success in *Daphne Loriola* with Edith Evans and was cast as Iago to Orson Welles' Othello. Welles directed the play at the old St James Theatre. Welles, who was big to start with, wore lifts in his shoes and a padded costume and the lighting was so arranged to catch every nuance of his performance. Peter had a battle on his hands every performance to make his mark.

One memorable night Peter was informed that Noel Coward was in the audience. This inspired Peter to lift his performance to even greater than usual heights. As Finch told it, he was in a quandary after he came off. *Will I quickly take my makeup off and get ready to receive the Master, or should I stay made up and in costume in case he comes to see me straight away?* He elected to stay as he was and the inevitable happened—Noel went to see Welles first.

By the time he heard the unmistakable voice in the annexe outside his dressing room, Finch was in a state of nerves.

'Get me a large gin,' Noel said to Finch's dresser, 'I'm about to be very rude to your master.'

As Finch described it 'The tinkle in the glass came closer and closer and then I gave the worst performance of my life.'

'Ah, Noel,' he exclaimed, 'what a surprise!'

Coward held him in his gaze, sipped his gin and said, 'I've seen many Iagos in my time, dear boy, but yours fascinated me. A wonderful performance—inventive, intuitive, but one thing intrigued me. Tell me, Finchetta darling, why are you playing it in Welsh?'

The great comedy character A.E. 'Matty' Matthews was performing in the West End. He was well advanced in years and the management was concerned for his welfare. The stage manager was instructed to provide for his every need. He in turn briefed the call boy about Mr Matthews' advanced age and frailty and told him to be attentive to his requirements. The management's concern must have weighed heavily on the young man and made him acutely conscious of the great responsibility that had been placed on his shoulders.

One night, as always, he checked that Matty was in his dressing room at the 'half' (half an hour before the curtain) and that all was well. He returned at the 'quarter' and knocked. No response. He gently opened the door to see the old gentleman slumped over in front of his mirror. He patted him on the shoulder and asked if he was all right. No response. Panic!

The poor boy fled, running around the theatre shouting, 'Help! Quick! Mr Matthews is dead! Mr Matthews is dead!'

Everybody rushed in blind panic to the dressing room to find Matty sitting at his dressing table applying his makeup.

Amazed at this visitation from the majority of the theatre staff, he asked the reason and was told what had happened. After apologies the shaken staff departed, but Matty insisted that the call boy remain.

'Sit down,' Matty demanded.

The boy sat.

'I want to give you a bit of advice.' Matty paused. 'Next time you see me in a similar situation, you mustn't run around the theatre screaming, "Mr Matthews is dead! Mr Matthews is dead!" You must say, "I *think* Mr Matthews is dead."'

Whatever became of those great characters of the theatre? One such was Robert (Bobby) Newton. Bobby had just opened his Shilling Theatre at Hammersmith when a grand film industry dinner was held at the Savoy, and he had been carefully excluded from the guest list. The black tie affair was in full swing when the grand doors were flung open to reveal Robert Newton unresplendent in pyjamas, dressing gown and slippers. The excited chatter of the 'darlings' of the film industry slowly dwindled to complete silence whilst Bobby surveyed the privileged guests.

Imagine the atmosphere. The chandeliered splendour of the Savoy dining room, its glittering occupants stunned into silence. Every eye focused on the apparition framed in the grand doorway. I suspect the majority would have given anything to have made such an entrance. Slowly and with great dignity, Bobby approached the Top Table where sat the moguls of the British film industry, the Ranks, the Kordas, etc. With great resonance he deliberately announced:

'I have opened my own theatre!' and proceeding the full length of the table fixing each official guest with those piercing eyes, proclaimed 'and *you're* not invited and *you're* not invited' moving along until the entire official table had been thus addressed. Then with great aplomb made a sweeping bow and and even greater exit.

At around the same time, the great character actor, Wilfred Lawson was in a long running play in the West End where he appeared in the first act and the third act. He had invited a friend one particular evening and after the first act, went around to the stalls bar, as arranged, to have a drink with him and ask if he was enjoying the play. He sat with his friend during the second act which he was not in and bought him another drink at its end. When the bells rang for the start of the third act, Wilfred ushered his friend to his seat and stayed with him. The curtain went up and the play proceeded for a little while when he turned to his friend clutching his arm and whispered: 'Now watch this! This is the best part of the play. This is where I come in!'

I met Wilfred Lawson in the make-up room at ATV at Elstree one day. His braces were stretched and his pants were hanging down revealing his long johns and he was busily cutting himself whilst endeavouring to shave, muttering all the time 'I thought it was tomorrow, why have they got me here today? I thought it was tomorrow.' It seemed that the director of the show had pulled a fast one on him and called him a day early to shoot all his scenes and get them out of the way. The young man was scared that Wilfred might settle his nerves too enthusiastically on the day.

I didn't see him again until the end of the day when we had both completed our respective engagements. We met in the tiny bar at ATV where he seemed to be wandering around looking for someone. I approached the great actor, whose Doolittle I'll never forget, and asked if I may have the pleasure of buying him a drink. Without a pause, in that high-pitched voice, he replied 'Yes. Large. Large.' The young director then arrived on the scene apologising to Wilfred profusely for having to call him a day early and swamping him with praise for his performance.

'You were brilliant, Mr Lawson as always. You were wonderful!'

Whereupon Wilfred fixed him with a stare, saying:

'Well don't take all the credit.'

Another great character in London in the 50s and 60s was the actor Dennis Shaw, a rotund, not very pretty rogue, whose tipple was simply gin and water. Wardour Street housed the major film companies, local and international, and actors came there over the years in their hundreds to trudge from one film office to another and to kick their heels and wait for their interviews with the latest 'hot' director or producer. Agents arranged the interviews. An actor turns up thinking he is the only one for the part only to find that there are fifty other hopefuls and he has to wait his turn.

On one occasion, my friend Dennis arrived at the appointed time to be informed that interviews were running late. He was asked to come back in an hour. There is a pub on every corner in the street from Shaftesbury Avenue to Oxford Street and Dennis was in no doubt as to how to kill the hour. He went back and forth between the film office and the Wardour Street pubs for most of the afternoon and was afloat on gin and water when he finally reached the inner sanctum. He was ushered in by Ronnie Curtis, a casting director and a very kind soul.

The fourth-rate American director threw his cigar on the floor, stamped on it and shouted, 'Ronnie, Ronnie. I told you I wanted a fat man, and when I say I want a fat man I want a fuckin' fat man!'

Without hesitation, Dennis picked up the American, lifted him off the ground and slammed him against the wall, exclaiming very forcibly, *'I was fat four hours ago!'*

Another time, Dennis was thrown out of a well-known actors' watering hole, The Queen's Elm, in the Fulham Road. The late John le Mesurier happened to live in the vicinity and was on his way home when he passed by the sight of Mr Shaw being manhandled into a paddy wagon by four burly policemen. Precisely what le Mesurier did not want to happen happened—they made eye contact. Something *had* to be said, but what? Le Mesurier hesitated and then, with the rather permanently embarrassed expression known to anybody who ever saw *Dad's Army*, he said, 'Hello, Dennis . . . Er . . . working?'

I ran into Trevor Howard one day at the Red Lion, the pub that serviced ABPC studios at Elstree. ATV and MGM were in the vicinity. It was just half an hour to closing time. The practice of closing pubs in the afternoon for a couple of hours had been introduced during the war, supposedly to get more productivity out of the work force. The poor British public, subjected to these absurd licensing regulations, had accepted them without protest. One wonders how long they will survive Britain joining the EEC. It would be interesting to hear a British barman explain to a French visitor that it was illegal to serve him with a drink after 2.30 pm.

When I encountered Trevor he was feeling no pain. He was in full flight, entertaining the patrons of the Red Lion, encouraged by the publican, Alf Bartell. Trevor's driver implored me to extricate him so that he could complete his assignment and deliver his charge into the arms of Helen Cherry, his wife, a great actress and a delightful lady.

It appeared that some sort of altercation had developed at MGM where Trevor was making a film version of Ibsen's *A Doll's House* with Jane Fonda, directed by Joseph Losey and shooting had ended early for the day. (The film was not a success but Trevor's performance has been praised.) Trevor, when in a good humour which was most of the time, had the habit of slapping one's cheeks with both hands and exclaiming lovingly, 'My sporting!' After a few rounds I found myself rapidly approaching the same state as Trevor. The bar was almost empty but Trevor's driver had slipped in a few times, pleading with me to remove him.

I happened to notice the time and, with what I thought was sheer brilliance, I told Trevor that it was imperative that we should leave.

'Trevor, time to go.'

Another slap on my now already very ruddy and tender cheeks. 'Why's that, my sporting?' Another slap.

'We have to leave,' I announced solemnly, 'because it's almost opening time.'

Charlie Drake was a difficult customer, hard to work with and often not liked by cast members and crew. On one occasion he ended up in hospital with a severe concussion because the crew, angry at the way he had treated them, installed a firm window on a set instead of a breakaway for a routine Charlie was doing. I encountered him one day at Richmond golf club where I was a member. The clubhouse was a fine old Tudor hunting lodge and the course itself was glorious. I played nine holes with Charlie and a few others and then I was waiting for some people who'd come late and we were going to play the back nine.

We were sitting out in front of the club and I could see my

friends coming up the eighth fairway. I said, 'Can I get you something, Charlie? I'm off in a minute.'

'Yis,' he said in that incredible voice. 'Ay would lake, a double vodkah, a pint of bittah, a packet of Peter Stuyvesant and a large cream cake.'

I took my spikes off and went through into the bar. I knew Don, the barman, pretty well and he knew Charlie. I said, 'Give us a packet of Peter Stuyvesant and a double vodka and a pint of bitter. And you wouldn't happen to have any cream cakes, would you?'

'Yes, I've got half a cream cake here.'

'I'll take it.'

I went back to Charlie and I said, 'Here's your double vodka, pint of bitter, Peter Stuyvesant, and here's your cream cake.' And I let him have it right in the face.

His response was to be expected—one unprintable word.

I was working on a film at Pinewood called *Revenge* with Joan Collins and Jimmy Booth and Hugh Griffiths. We spent most of our off-screen moments on the set of *Fiddler on the Roof*, which was wonderful to watch. I had never seen the stage production and vowed to get there as soon as possible. I did and it was a fabulous production. I knew quite a few of the people in the cast, including Miriam Karlin, whom I adored. I decided to go backstage and say hello. When I entered her dressing room, there was Topol and a not-feeling-too-much-pain Olivier. He took one look at me, grabbed my arm and said 'Come with me.'

He raced me down the corridor to Topol's dressing room where his wife Joan Plowright was waiting, shouting

'Plowright! Plowright! Look who I've got here.' He pointed to my hair. 'It's real! It's not a wig! It's real!'

I have extraordinarily fine soft hair, like a baby. It is extremely difficult to control and always sticks up somewhere no matter what is applied to it. My unruly hair was a feature of my appearance as Peter Thornton in *The Troubleshooters.* You don't imagine that theatrical greats like Olivier and Plowright watch the box, but they do, they do.

At the time I thought that *Revenge* was one of the worst pictures I ever made. I walked out of the premiere before it finished. I notice that it is listed in *Movies on TV* under the title

Inn of the Innocent People, hardly an improvement, but I have watched it and found it passable. I assume it has been astutely cut. I remember one scene in particular that gave Joan Collins a great deal of trouble. She had just 'arrived' as a star and was rather over-conscious of her new status. This scene took place in the country pub she ran and it involved her coming down the stairs into the bar where Jimmy and I were conversing. The camera setup was behind us and the director, Sid Hayers, a very nice and reasonable fellow, wanted the shot to be done in one long take. Joan was supposed to begin speaking on the stairs and continue as she came down until she reached us. She dried and fluffed her lines several times and it was obvious to all that she hadn't learned them properly.

The more she goofed the more determined Sid became to get it in one shot and so the more she stumbled. After about a dozen failed takes she found an excuse and exclaimed, 'For God's sake, how do you expect me to act and remember the lines with all these fucking lights shining in my eyes?'

Sid said, 'They're to light your pretty face, darling.'

We broke for an early lunch after that and when we came back she got it right, straight off. I noticed that she was a little more subdued in her manner, a bit more down to size, and I asked Sid what had happened.

'Well, you know,' he said, 'I took her to lunch. That is, I had a nice lunch sent up to her dressing room and I said, "Joan, you really have to get this right, because those boys are pinching your picture. They're acting you off the screen."'

Of course we weren't doing anything of the sort. Our parts were small compared to hers, but the suggestion was enough to get her to pull her socks up. She was a different Joan entirely after that. We used to go to her dressing room and have a drink after shooting and we'd say, 'What colour knickers have you got on today, Joan?' And she was a good sport. Fragile egos are everywhere in the acting game.

I seem to attract crims and the following is only one example of the sort of thing that used to happen quite regularly. I was drinking in my local, the Star Tavern in St Johns Wood. My companions were a property developer, a solicitor, a spirits salesman from Haig and others. We were at *our* end of the bar—

strange how regulars command a particular part of the bar—and I could see at the opposite end a group engaged in animated conversation. A character with a face you could strike a match on detached himself and made a beeline for me.

'Hullo, Ray. Luvly to see you.'

My pinstriped friends gave me some old-fashioned looks as he proceeded to inform me that he had recently been released from Wormwood Scrubs prison.

'See that geezer down there in the black suit? He's a saint, Ray, a bleedin' saint. He's the padre at the Scrubs. You know how I recognised you, don't you? We're all fans of that show in the "ship of distress".'

By now my regular companions had drifted away to the fireplace, leaving me with my newfound friend.

'Now, I'll do you a favour, Ray. Give us a pound.'

Here we go, I thought. I quickly gave him a pound hoping that would dispose of him. But no, into my hand he pressed a solid object wrapped in cellophane. On inspection I found it to be a gold watch.

He slapped me on the back. 'Next time it'll be two.'

Meaning pounds of course.

It was at about the time that Sophia Loren's priceless jewels had been stolen from the mansion she was occupying while making a picture at Elstree. With my chums, convinced that I hobnobbed with the criminal classes, out of earshot, I asked him, 'Did you do that Sophia Loren job?'

The compliment brought tears to his steely blue eyes. 'Thanks, Ray. No. But I know who done it, like. Great man. I do jewels meself, like, but that's a speciality job. You gotta be a rope man. You gotta be able to come down a rope one-'anded.

'I done a place in Eaton Square. *Funny*. I was a winder cleaner, wan' I. I 'ad me bike, me ladder, me buckit and me levva.'[1]

I nodded.

'Little mop with 'er little black skirt and pinny let me in. Cor, she weren't arf a looker I can tell you. Told me to start in the basement cos Modom was still asleep. This was a blow cos I

---

[1] = leather = chamois cloth

figured to get into the bedroom pronto, where the tom[2] was most likely to be. Now you gotta be a bit careful not to show your boat[3] too much in the winder in case a legit winder cleaner lamps you from the other side of the street. I was doin' the second floor when I heard the bath bein' run. *Oi, oi,* I thinks to meself. Can't be too long now.

'Sure enough, in about half an hour, little mop comes in and says, "You can do Modom's bedroom now. She is leaving for her luncheon engagement."

'I sees her get into the limmo. *Right. 'ere we go. Don' rush it. Squeeze the levva dry and spread it on the bed. On with the gloves and empty the drawers into the levva and the buckit.* Down the apples.[4] Little mop pays me me gelt.

'"Thank you, my love. See you next time, I'm sure." Out the door.

'Now this is the caper, Ray. Don't 'urry. Ladder over the shoulder, walk slow. Get me bike and don't look across the street. Slowly round the corner. Place the bike and ladder against the wall. Jump into the *Jaguar* with me buckit and the goodies. "Shall we have it away, Charles?"'

I guess meeting characters like that in the flesh was handy when you found yourself having to play them in front of the cameras.

Barry Humphries is one the most quick-witted creators and performers in the business. I knew him slightly in the days when he was working in Australian radio, trying to establish himself in Sydney. He did much better, of course, in Britain. One day when I was working on *Troubleshooters,* I bumped into him in the BBC cafeteria in the White City complex. The building is circular with sound stages at intervals around the circumference. The different studios are adjacent to different coffee shops and cafeterias which are known as 'sectors', so that studios 2 to 3 might be serviced by the red sector, 5 to 6 by the blue sector and so on.

---

[2]= tomfoolery = jewellery

[3]= boatrace = face

[4]= apples and pears = stairs

Barry was working in the studio next to mine and we met in the red sector. He was filming one of his specials and he was all got up in an incredible silver lame astronaut's outfit for a sketch about an Australian rocket landing on the moon.

Barry took one look at me and said, 'Would you be willing to do something for me?'

He told me what he had in mind and I was willing but told him he had to clear it with the producer of the show I was working in. I agreed to give up one of my breaks and that was cleared up.

They put me under a very harsh white light that showed up, emphasised in fact, the holes in my face. Barry was in his moon landing craft and they cut between him and this intense, cruel close-up of my face, using a severe lens, magnifying the holes, to convey the impression that the landing was taking place amid cruel craters on the moon surface.

> Barry: Oh god, look at those craters! Hideous! Impossible to land. Certain death to attempt landing . . .

A slow pullback began. Back . . . beginning to reveal my face with an amiable grin and couple of blacked-out teeth; back . . . showing the hat and flies; back . . . showing me in the singlet and shorts holding up a can of Foster's. All I had to do was say, 'Gidday.'

It worked very well, all dreamed up on the spur of the moment by Barry in the red sector.

· 15 ·

Vignettes from Spain

I was working on *Troubleshooters*, getting over the breakup with Celia and in the early stages of my relationship with Mirén. We finished shooting a series of episodes and I felt I needed to get right away from things. Penny Joy, a floor manager on the show, told me that she had an old farmhouse on an island called Formentera, off the coast of Spain in the Mediterranean.

'There's no electricity,' she said, 'no phone, no made roads.'

This was sounding more attractive every minute so I got the details from her and she wrote to the man who ran the only taxi on the island. She said something like look out for the guy with the holes in his face and a lady with long blonde hair and take care of them. Mirén and I flew to Ibiza, the most westerly of the Balearic Islands, and got the ferry across to Formentera in the south. We were delivered to the house which was very, very basic. It needed fumigating and cleaning but it was charming with a huge fireplace. It had no bathtub or shower and we bought a big plastic tub and bathed in turn in front of the roaring fire. No problem to wash the rough stone floor, we just tipped the tub and used the bathwater.

The house was built right on one of the salt lakes constructed by the Romans for salt production when they occupied the island in ancient times and still in use today.

After we'd settled in I had a hankering to get down to the sea, a really passionate need. We stumbled down this rough road, stubbing our toes. I could hear the sea in the near distance on the other side of the lake and beyond the bush but we couldn't seem to get close to it. The salt lakes lay between the track and the sea. Eventually we came to a driveway into a property. I saw a sign saying 'Propidad Privado', but I thought, *Bugger it, the sea's down there and I'm going to get to it. I'll apologise when I get to the house and ask permission to go down to the beach.* I went to the *entrada* and I could hear someone speaking Spanish in an English voice, I guessed to a workman. I knocked at the door.

'Ah, come in, Max. Large gin and tonic?'

I said, 'I'm sorry. It's not Max. You don't know me. My name's Ray Barrett and this is Mirén . . .'

'Oh, super. Do come in. *Two* large gin and tonics.'

We ended up sloshed, stumbled back to the farmhouse and didn't see the beach at all.

Our host's name was Bill Madders. He was then in his sixties, stocky, grey-haired and rather pukka in manner but a man in a million. He had been a buyer for Harrods, had his finger in many business pies and wasn't short of money. He was a delightful man and the next day he came up to Penny's house and said, 'You can't stay here. It's too rough altogether.'

He insisted that we stay in his place which he'd built as a sort of complex with plenty of space for guests. The original structure he put up was right on the beach and he'd built a main house and added very pleasant and comfortable extensions. It was all right there—the beach, the fishermen's huts, an exquisite view.

So we stayed with Bill and I got to know the island and fell in love with it. After the pace of life in London the sleepy, quiet atmosphere was a tonic. I mentioned to Bill that I'd like to buy some land. He said 'Super.'

We frequented Fonda Pepe's in San Fernando, then the only *fonda*[1] thereabouts, and got to know little Pepe or Pepito as he

[1] Bar-restaurant.

was known. He spoke a little English. I told him I was looking for land to buy and he said he knew of a family with some land for sale. We got on our bicycles and cycled off to look at the land which was on a cliff overlooking Cala Enbaste at a part of the island called Ses Roques. This was the spot for me. I told Bill about it and he came up the next day. He'd been eighteen years on Formentera and had never seen this part because it had been private property only just now coming up for sale. The view was magnificent, right out across the Mediterranean and a beautiful sweep of the whole coast of the island.

'I'll buy the land next to you so you can't be built out,' Bill said.

I said, 'Super.'

That night, over dinner, we were discussing the whole idea and I said, 'It all sounds wonderful, Bill, but I've thought of a problem.'

'What's that?'

'Harold Wilson won't let us take more than thirty pounds out of the country.'

'Oh, don't worry about that,' Bill said, 'I'll buy it for you.'

'But we've only known each other a week.'

He waved that aside. 'Don't worry. You can pay me back when it suits.'

Then I hit on an idea. I asked if he came to London often and he said he did.

'Next time you come, don't bring any money.'

I used to meet him at Heathrow and give him five hundred pounds. We became good friends and he stayed with us, first in Richmond and later in East Sheen, and I'd give him the five hundred each time and reduce the debt that way. I bought the land, a modest block of about 1400 square metres, from Catalina, the wife of Juan Costa Pins. The people there are farmers and fishermen but they're also very good builders and always build their own homes. Bill introduced me to Angel Costa, a local who loved the English. He had been rescued by English seamen in the Bay of Biscay during the war. He had just begun to build houses commercially, and mine was the second he built on the island.

The building was financed in the same way, with remittances to Bill, but on one occasion much later there was an urgent need for me to get some money from Australia to Formentera. The Sydney bank was reluctant to make the transfer of about four thousand dollars to the Credito Balear on Ibiza. I don't care to speculate about what their suspicions may have been. I had to call on my acting skills, conjuring up a desperately sick relative, to convince the manager to allow the money to be transferred. Getting the money *out* of the Ibiza bank required another performance. Spanish banks tend to hang onto any funds they get their hands on for as long as possible, no doubt making a profit on them through interest juggling. I made repeated trips by boat from Formentera to Ibiza only to be told that the funds hadn't arrived. Eventually, to speak Australian, I 'bunged on a turn'—shouted, stamped, waved my arms about—and miraculously the money appeared. Spain is a passionate country and sometimes it takes a display of passion to get things done.

I designed the house myself, trying to make it as much as possible like the traditional houses on the island, although of course you have to make compromises dictated by materials and modern building methods. Work started on the *caseta*, which is a small structure put up first to house the workmen's tools and building materials. It's knocked down when the job is finished but I intended my *caseta* to be permanent. This wasn't strictly in accordance with local building regulations, but they were seldom enforced and I was sure I could get away with it. So I located it precisely and, although it was only four metres square by two and half metres high, I drew precise plans with windows a metre from the floor to give a view of the sea. The site was to be excavated so the building wouldn't obtrude more than half a metre.

Bill went up to the block one day to see how things were going. He found a workman constructing the *caseta* but appearing very puzzled because the windows were looking straight out into the dirt. He was building it upside down! Bill was a kind man and so that the workman wouldn't lose face, he explained thus:

'Senor Barrett is an Australian and he was looking at things upside down. Between *us* we'll make it right for him.'

Everything went ahead smoothly. Sometimes tact is more useful than histrionics.

The house has provided me with untold pleasure now for

almost thirty years. My sons have spent a school holiday there, numerous friends have visited and stayed and there have been memorable lunches and dinners. Like all good houses, it has needed nips and tucks over the years. The *caseta* on top of the house, which held the water tanks when we had to pump the water through by hand, became my study after we installed an electric pump.

A cool head was required when I discovered Angel Costa the builder of my house taking measurements around my block. He explained that he was fixing the boundary of the *zone maritime*, a strip of land right around the coast which is deemed to be under the control of the military—a hangover from the days of the military's dominance under Franco. According to Juan's calculations the boundary ran right through my living room. In theory, the military could order everything on the seaward side of this line knocked down. A calamity. I took a deep breath and pointed out to Angel that he was taking his measurements as if the coastline was straight, whereas in fact it had promontories and indentations and I managed to convince him that, following the actual shape of the coast, the boundary did not cross my land and so it was declared. The good news is that, as nothing is ever likely to be built on the land annexed to the military, the *zone maritime* affords me very useful protection of my view and privacy.

The great thing about living in foreign parts is exposing yourself to the different ways people have of doing things. It is always interesting, but sometimes uncomfortable and even downright alarming. Mirén and I were invited to a *matanza,* the annual ritual of the killing of the pig. The men perform the ghastly act, killing and quartering the animal while the women attend to the entrails. They take the intestines and stuff them with minced offal, blood and certain spices using recipes handed down over the generations, to make a wonderfully tasty sausage called *soperasada,* more enjoyable if you don't know what's actually in it.

The killing of the pig is a family affair and our invitation signified our acceptance into the family of Juan Costa Pins. A great honour. My childhood memory of throwing up when Dad chopped the head off the chook at Christmas time was enough to prompt me to excuse myself from the slaughtering ceremony. I pleaded important business on Ibiza and Mirén and I hid ourselves for the rest of the day. But we accepted the honour of the invitation to the fiesta dinner.

We dutifully turned up, Mirén six months pregnant, at the casa de Juan to discover that we were more or less the guests of honour. The islanders spoke a dialect that rendered my halting Spanish next to useless. Furthermore, Juan's wife, Catalina, was stone deaf. We were left to communicate by mime and gesture.

We were ushered to our seats at the head of the table. The women all wore traditional dress, the men wore hats. On these occasions I always try to spy out an escape route, but here there was none. No convenient door, not even a window. There was nothing for it but to endure it with the utmost dignity and graciousness. The first course was a watery soup made from prolonged stewing of the bones of the late pig. After forcing down what seemed like a litre of this mixture I made my first mistake by praising it.

'Wonderful,' I said to Catalina, miming my enjoyment. 'Delicious. *Muy bien. Perfecto!*'

My reward was three more ladles of the watery pig accompanied by copious quantities of the home-grown wine that troubled my insides for weeks afterwards.

With stomach already distended and bladder bursting, I contemplated the next course. Chops, tasteless as chaff the goodness having been boiled out of them to make the soup. They proved to be indescribable jaw-breakers. Desperately, I looked around for a pot plant or any receptacle where I could dispose of at least part of the heap of meat, but all eyes were upon the honoured guests. No chance to slip anything into a lap or pocket. There was nothing to do but chew and hope the teeth would take the strain.

Our next major cultural confrontation presented more serious problems. I was invited to accompany Juan fishing for calamari, another sign of acceptance. His dinghy was in one of the caves cut into the cliff under my house. The rock is soft sandstone and the ingenious islanders have cut deep caves where they can store their boats in safety, protected from even the most violent storms. These, fitted out with sliprails made of sabina saplings, become perfect boatsheds.

Juan arrived at the appointed time but, to my surprise, he was accompanied by his wife, Catalina, and her mother. It is the custom on the island, when visiting, to call a greeting and then stand back, waiting to be invited officially to enter. This is a little difficult to get used to, but it is a charming custom entirely appropriate to these formal and dignified people. It intrigued me as to why the women were there. They wore the traditional outfit of long black skirts, bodice and scarves which made it unlikely that they intended to go fishing. In any case, Juan's old dinghy could hardly accommodate so many. Very bewildering, until it was explained that they had come to take care of the heavily pregnant wife while the menfolk ventured out to sea.

Juan and I set off and were soon contentedly pulling up calamari. If he had plotted to find a private place to make his strange request he could not have chosen better than a small boat well out in the Mediterranean.

'Catalina and I cannot have children,' he confided.

I knew that for a family-oriented people like them this was an immense tragedy and I murmured something sympathetic.

'Now that we are all family,' he said seriously, 'if your wife has twins perhaps it could be one for you and one for me?'

A real bombshell, that. How do you respond. I was stunned and can't remember exactly what I said. I couldn't wait to get back to Mirén and tell her of this bizarre development. Then I got her side of the story. All the time we'd been out there catching calamari, Mirén had been positioned on the sofa between Juan's wife and mother-in-law. She'd been pampered, patted and stroked and not allowed to lift a finger. The three of them sat side by side as if on a train. Poor Mirén, it must have seemed like the longest train journey of her life. Every attempt she made to rise to offer a drink or something to eat was gently restrained and she was told to rest and relax.

The situation was clear after we'd put the two experiences together. We were concerned enough to make plans so that, if indeed we did have twins, we would leave one behind in the care of Mirén's mother, and alternate one for another every time we came to the island.

Fortunately, all was resolved when Reginald Walter, named after my father, entered the world on his own.

Whenever the old ferry *Joven Dolores* glided into the port of La Sabina on Formentera, my eyes would automatically search along the quay for my friend, Juan Forn, the fisherman. The sight of him, his bare toes in the mesh of his tuna net, the shuttle in his hand, the inevitable Ducados hanging from his lips, was confirmation that I was back home on the island I had come to love.

After a short greeting of *'Hola amigo'* and embraces, he would down tools for the day and we would cross the quay to the bar where he would enlighten me on who was alive and who was not and catch me up on the gossip of the day. His news was always interesting and he was a natural story-teller. One time he was bursting to tell me about an event that had set the whole island laughing. By now it has no doubt been much embellished and become part of the local folklore . . .

At the southern tip of the island of Ibiza is a spectacular rock formation known as La Vedera. Impressive in size, it is a feature of this part of the island and a compelling sight as it changes in colour from blue to pink and white according to the time of day, the clarity of the weather and the colour of the sea and sky. Sipping his Veterano cognac, the eyes in his weatherbeaten face crinkling with amusement, Juan Forn unfolded the story of the four German youths who had hired him and his boat to take them to La Vedera.

It appears that they had been informed, on an earlier visit to the island, that the rock had never been climbed. On their return to Germany they had conferred and made plans to return and conquer the sheer faced rock in the name of the Fatherland. Crampons, spikes, ropes, picks and all the gear necessary for mountain climbing were loaded aboard Juan's tiny vessel. Fritz, Gunter, Heinz and Gert came aboard full of enthusiasm for their intrepid expedition which was certain to bring them glory.

All day long they toiled up the sheer face of the rock, shouting encouragement one to another while Juan happily fished and calculated the pesetas. He'd been hired by the hour.

Eventually the lead climber hammered in the final spike at the top of the escarpment and proceeded to haul his exhausted companions to safety and victory over the unconquerable rock. They recovered their collective breath to find an old Spanish peasant contentedly minding his goats which were cropping at the lush vegetation at the summit. Bleeding, bruised and battered they inquired as to how he could possibly have got to such an inaccessible place.

'Oh,' he said, 'I just bring them up the path at the back every day to feed.'

It intrigued me that a peasant fisherman on one of the smallest islands of the Mediterranean should have such a command of English. I asked him about it one day and an extraordinary story unfolded.

He and some friends, lured by the promise of high wages for work on the sugar boats out of Cuba up the east coast of the USA, set out to make their fortunes and ensure the future security of their families. Even the horrific conditions of the passage in the hold of a tramp steamer could not dampen their spirits. The promise of prosperity made the discomfort of the journey bearable.

A sickening reality greeted them on their arrival. Their dreams of a brave new world were quickly shattered. Their Cuban masters treated them as inferior beings, actual slaves. Their living conditions were appalling, their rations meagre. After several years of suffering Juan could take it no longer.

'It was so bad, Raymon,' he said. 'I had to jump the ship in America. I did not have the passport. I had to ride the rattler. I was not the criminal, you understand, but we had to steal or beg our food. Anything was better than the sugar boats. I knew it was only time before the authorities would catch up with me.'

The inevitable happened and as an alien in the 'land of the free', Juan was confined on Ellis Island to await deportation. At this point he became literally poetic in his description of the famous house of detention for illegal immigrants and undesirables. His face lit up as he described the food, the beds and above all the library. He put his hand on my shoulder and in an almost confessional tone confided what he had done when his deportation was imminent, 'Raymon, I had to commit little crimes so they would put me back. It was the happiest time of my life.'

It was mid-August on Formentera and extremely hot. My holiday time was running out along with my money. In shorts and bare feet I took myself into the Banca March in San Francisco, the capital of the island, clutching the last of my traveller's cheques. There were two others in the bank—a young American, I assume dodging the draft, cashing a seemingly inexhaustible supply of cheques, provided no doubt by an adoring Mom back home—and Pepe Tur. Pepe was a self-made man who had built with his own hands the first *fonda* on the island, certainly the first in San Fernando, the smaller township on Formentera. He is a dignified and humble man of great character with lazy eyes and always the hint of a smile on his countenance.

The Banca March was one room with a straight wooden counter on which one leant awaiting one's turn. There we stood whilst the clerk clattered away on his adding machine rifling through the countless traveller's cheques of the young American. No one spoke. We just leant on the counter staring at the wall beyond. Finally, in my halting Spanish, I remarked on how much it resembled a bar and what a pity in this heat we couldn't refresh ourselves with a convivial glass. Whereupon Pepe excused himself and left the bank, presumably bored with waiting to deposit the takings from the *fonda*.

A few minutes later he returned and placed a large tumbler of scotch in front of me with one for himself and one for the clerk.

'Salud,' he nodded.

After the transaction was completed I emerged back into the sunlight and realised that I was completely smashed. It was the only time I went into a bank perfectly sober and came out drunk.

· 16 ·

Broken bones and red tape

Medical procedures were still rather primitive in Spain when I had the misfortune to break my arm on Formentera in 1967. Mirén and I were staying with Bill and Sylvia Madders in Cana Trini, their original small house right on the beach at Es Pujols while our house was being built. Bill now had a main house and several separate apartments for friends who wished to stay. Bill, a most generous man, loved having lots of people around him.

One night, for a change, Mirén and I had invited Bill and Sylvia to dine with us in Cana Trini. We had my actor friend John Tate staying with us. Pre-dinner drinks, however, were provided by Bill who was notorious for the strength of his gins and tonic. The time came to move across the inner courtyard and up three rough stone steps. There was no electricity at that time and Bill, a pace or two behind me, held the gas lamp up to light the steps.

I slipped on the second step. To save me from falling on the rough hewn steps, Bill grabbed my arm from behind and gave it an almighty yank. He was a very strong man and perhaps the g and t's made him even stronger. The snap was like a fire-cracker going off. The bone in my arm broke cleanly just below the shoulder joint. The pain was indescribable and my evening of conviviality was over. They wrapped my arm tight across my chest, found pain killers and sedatives and tied me down to a bed for two days until a doctor from the mainland would be in attendance on Ibiza.

At the best of times the trip on the old *Joven Dolores* was rough but this time it was almost unendurable. They tied me to a stanchion so I wouldn't slip off the seat and do further damage. A taxi took me to the premises—it could hardly have been styled a hospital or a surgery—of one Dr Villain Gomez. Sylvia Madders, a woman of extreme gentility and charm, still very county despite her 18 year plus residence in Spain, accompanied me and was indispensable.

We entered the forbidding building and climbed the dingy wooden steps to the waiting room. The rough seats were occupied by creatures suffering various maladies, all wearing a look of hopelessness and doom. One by one their names were called and they disappeared into the gloom never to be seen again. Pain brought on a state of semi-hallucination and I imagined that when my name was called I would be summoned before my maker to account for my past misdemeanours.

Eventually I was in the presence of the worthy doctor. He gave me a cursory examination which consisted of screwing my arm around in order to hear the bones scraping, followed by a smart smack on the unconnected area. He announced with great authority, '*Si, Si, es fractura.*' He continued to speak and through Sylvia's translation I learned that I would have to stay overnight in the 'hospital' because the swelling would have to be reduced before the arm could be properly set. I was issued with a prescription for some tablets to facilitate this process. The prescription had to be taken to the *Farmacia* by the patient and the medication paid for. Nothing was provided on the premises.

I carried out a brief inspection of the 'hospital'. With a great deal of pride I was shown the operating room. It was like a boxing ring; the table stood in the middle with a light hanging forlornly down over it. Wooden benches in raked tiers were set around the walls on all sides so that family and friends could get a good view of the surgical procedures. Antiseptic hygiene was obviously of secondary importance. There was no way I was going to remain overnight in this house of horrors and I insisted on having my arm set that day. I was told to go away and take the tablets every half hour with plenty of fluid.

I took myself off to El Corsario, a restaurant high up on a hill overlooking the port of Ibiza. I pumped the tablets, which resembled something a vet might give to a very sick horse, into myself every five minutes, feeling the tender flesh every so often to see if the swelling had gone down.

My time had come and I was ushered into a room containing a machine which took up almost all the space. This, I learned, was their newly-acquired x-ray machine. I was screwed into it, standing up of course, while switches were turned on. The operator disappeared. I was under the impression that the procedure took only a few minutes. Wrong. It seemed like an hour before the individual I later discovered was a *practicante* (a trainee doctor, not yet qualified) returned to release me. Holding up the x-ray photo and giving me yet another slap on the arm, he announced proudly that I certainly had a fracture and I was to follow him.

The next chamber I entered was square with a tiled floor, one window and desk covered with papers in all sorts of disarray but mostly holding ashtrays, some full to overflowing, some half-full with smouldering butts of Ducados. Surgical implements which belonged to my mind in sterile containers lay about in the open. The tiled walls were hung with various anatomical charts and a forlorn skeleton hung on a frame in one corner.

I stood in the middle of the room while Sylvia stood by the window, remarking from time to time on the lovely windmill on a hill nearby. She was thoughtfully attempting to distract me from what the *practicante* was up to. He was smoking and referring to a dog-eared little volume, surely a medical handbook from the Civil War. Several times he excused himself and came back with strips of sticking plaster which he stuck to the tiled wall. I was intrigued but apprehensive and asked Sylvia to make sure I didn't faint, hit the floor, and break the other arm.

Suddenly a contraption like something from the Middle Ages was introduced—a sort of corselet made of wire mesh which was pushed and bent to the shape of my chest and back. It had an arm extension at a right angle and just where the elbow would be an extension of about four inches with a lip at the end. All the while the medical man was chain-smoking, consulting the thumb-worn manual and disappearing for short periods. The last piece of equipment he produced was a long piece of rubber tubing. *What the hell does he intend to do with that?* I thought. *Has he been reading the wrong pages in the Civil War manual?* Finally, he apologised profusely and disappeared again, asking our forgiveness for neglecting to wear his white coat. When he returned I wished he hadn't bothered. The coat was completely covered with dried blood.

He removed the strips of sticking plaster and asked me to lift my arm.

'I can't,' I said. 'It's broken.'

'*Poco malo, poco malo.*[1]' He lifted the arm forcibly, stuck lengths of sticking plaster above and below my arm and tied the ends together. This was becoming more intriguing, if no more comfortable, by the minute. Then the *piece de résistance.* He removed a little square of wood with a hole bored through it from a hook on the wall and attempted to poke the rubber tube through the hole. He was unsuccessful as the hole was too small. He lit another Ducados as an aid to thought. Ah, the solution. He grabbed a pair of scissors and reamed the hole larger. In so doing he stuck the scissors into my elbow.

'Perdón.' And a laugh.

He pushed the tube through the wood, tied a knot on the outside and wound the rest around the tied pieces of sticking plaster. He then proceeded to wind the wood in a clockwise direction as if winding up a child's toy aeroplane. It was, of course, a primitive form of traction, pulling the arm and the bones into the required position before employing the plaster—every step a nightmare of pain. This routine finished, I was then cemented into my cage for the duration of the healing process.

So strapped up I could not fit into a taxi and had to walk the mile or so to the Bar Formentera, adjacent to where the ferries docked and departed. I ordered a bottle of cognac and sat at the nearest table until the ferry arrived and I was once again

---

[1] Only a little pain.

lashed to my stanchion for the journey home. My experience suggests to me that some of those seriously wounded in the Civil War may well have preferred death to being carted off to the medico.

The Spanish make it difficult to do things legitimately and legally. In the early days on Formentera, foreigners would simply buy land from the locals, put up a house and that was that. Very few registered their houses or paid municipal taxes, in most cases, including my own, because they were simply unaware of the regulations.

In 1988, when my wife Gaye and I decided to spend more time on the island, I inquired of my friend Francisco Negré, who was then President of the College or Architects, how I should go about registering my land, my house and applying for *residencia*, residential status. Although I had a survey of the land it was necessary to have it scrutinised and stamped by a *notario*. Formentera is the smallest of the inhabited islands in the Balearic group and in those days was given scant regard by Ibiza, Majorca and the mainland. It did not boast its own *notario*, but was visited by the official once a month. Consequently, long queues would form of people attempting to sort out their troubles.

We simply wanted to do things legitimately and become law-abiding citizens and were under the impression that this would be welcomed and that a signature and a rubber stamp or two would suffice. We soon learned that for official transactions in Spain you require the patience of Job, otherwise you go mad. There is a document for this and a document for that—the yellow one, the green, the blue, the white. Having jumped this hurdle and achieved the *escritura* of the land, we next made application for the registration of the house.

To my amazement Francisco Negré and his offsider turned up with tape measures and charts announcing that he had come to design my house.

'The house has been in existence for fifteen years or so,' I pointed out.

'Ray, in order to register your house you must have a Spanish architect.'

I showed him the plans which I had drawn myself and had

professionally revised by a London architect and suggested that he simply sign them, saving everyone a lot of trouble. Francisco, well aware of the absurdity of the situation, said that this would not do. He had to re-measure the whole thing and he and his assistant were there for the next few weeks measuring and re-drawing the whole house. The resultant plans would then be sent to Palma or Madrid for official acceptance and I would then receive my certificate of ownership and be properly accredited to pay my taxes. Months went by before the inscribed parchment documents arrived. Naturally they had to be scrutinised by the *notario* and officially stamped.

Now we could embark on applying for *residencia.* There was only one place to make application—the *Comisaria* on Ibiza where one woman officiated. It was necessary to catch the first ferry from Formentera in order to be as near as possible to the head of the inevitable queue. The department closed at midday. One person was dealt with at a time and there was much shouting, gesticulating and waving of arms. And Our Lady of the Documentarios would sometimes disappear for half an hour, returning with piles of manila folders which had to be gone through with much shouting as each piece of paper was scrutinised.

To be next in line with only five minutes remaining was to be in coronary territory. To make it to the window just as the blind came down was to risk instant nervous collapse. Back to the ferry, home to Formentera, back the next day, only to be told on arrival, 'Sorry, today is a fiesta. The office is closed.'

After several repetitions of this routine we finally made it to learn that we did not have the correct green form.

'Can we get it here?'

'No, it is only obtainable at . . .' Another department in a different building. Several stops and long waits in line later we returned clutching the precious green form to be informed that we needed three references—one from a *notario* and two from Spanish residents who have known us for ten years or more. Back to Formentera. Fortunately Tony Tur, a sort of acting *notario,* had dealt with the purchase of my land so I had easy access to him. Francisco Negré and the bank manager provided the other two references. Back to Ibiza once more having by now practically bought the ferry in fares.

We made it back to Our Lady with white, blue and green forms plus references, passports, bank statements, birth certificates, every document of reference we could lay our hands on. We were not going to miss out this time. I think the sight of a veritable portmanteau of paperwork was even too much for Our Lady. She shuffled through them all.

'Where are the stamps?'

'What stamps.'

It was then that we learned of the requirement for a correct stamping of each and every document. We knew nothing of this in advance. Every step has to be learned painfully along the way.

We were close to surrender, despairing of ever becoming legal when a saint appeared in the form of a woman who spoke a little English, could see the utter desperation in our faces and took pity on us. We explained our plight, the necessity for these mysterious stamps which no office we had so far encountered had any knowledge of. This woman had obviously encountered the situation before and had taken up a more or less voluntary position as protector of demented foreigners. To our utter disbelief she explained that the only person with the franchise for the stamps was a tobacconist at the end of the Vara de Rey, the *ramblas*, the shopping centre of Ibiza.

Back we went with these ludicrously decorated stamps, quarto sized, with King Juan Carlos beaming at us, his image surrounded by very official (and unintelligible to us) script. I think it was the only time I saw a smile on the countenance of Our Lady of the Documentarios. She affixed the stamps to the respective documents and beckoned us with her thumb to follow her. We were ushered into an office where she applied ink to a pad, placed our thumbs on the ink and then onto each piece of parchment. Then every document was stamped again, jack-hammer style. That seemed to be it.

We were about to celebrate at lunch over a bottle of wine when we were told that the documents would have to be sent to Madrid for approval and we could expect to hear in about three months. We were staying for a year anyway so this seemed no problem. The week before we were due to return to Australia we prevailed upon our dear friends John and Sylvia Payne, an English couple who had fallen in love with the island

and become residents and consequently knew the ropes, to ring the *Comisaria* and ascertain how much longer we would have to wait for our papers. The news was that the documents had arrived some months previously.

We rushed to the ferry once more, made the trek to the office and received, with hearty congratulations, our *residencias.* We were now proud, legitimate residents of Espana for approximately one week. We returned to Australia for a time and, as the permits have to be renewed every two years, ours have expired and we have to start the process over again. But now we know the drill and the true meaning of *manana.* We must love the place.

. . . When Gaye and I are on Formentera, we readily fall into the slow, quiet rhythms of the island. We keep a small car as a runabout and enjoy the day's shopping which proceeds in a leisurely fashion. We enjoy our trips into town, one going to the *correos,* the other to the *panaderia.* The bread is beautiful. We usually bump into mutual friends and eventually end up at the appointed bar-restaurant and catch up on things. No one is in a hurry.

I intend to have a boat one day, something solid and honest, so we can take trips to Ibiza, do our shopping, sleep on board and take our time coming home, maybe dropping off at the lovely island of Espalmador which is uninhabited with safe anchorages and secluded sculpted beaches. The climate is very like that of south Queensland—hot in summer, mild in winter. The people are kind. I am at home.

· 17 ·

Thunderbirds, *Tutankhamen and other matters*

When Gerry and Sylvia Anderson asked me if I would consider doing some voices for their new *Thunderbirds* series I was delighted. I had only the vaguest idea of what the series was about, but the experience of working in the boom years of Sydney radio made me confident I could handle the job. I had worked with marionettes before on *The Tintookies.*

I went to the studio in Slough and was introduced to the wonderful puppets the Andersons had created and was given a rundown on the show, along with Peter Dinely, Mat Zimmerman, Shane Rimmer and David Graham.

'This is John, this is Virgil, Glen, Lady Penelope, Brains, Parker.'

I liked the look of John and Gerry said, 'OK, he's yours.' I had the additional fun of playing the villain—the role of the Hood. We each had a mental picture of the character we were playing and on Sunday morning we'd arrive, collect our scripts, read through and record five episodes in the morning. The all-important sound effects and music were dubbed in later. One time, the two women in the cast were having trouble doing the voice of a dowager Duchess. They couldn't quite capture the tone required. Peter Dinely and I could see that we would have trouble making it to the pub by 2 o'clock if this went on much longer, so I suggested to Gerry that I play the duchess. He gave me a strange look but agreed to let me have a go.

My inspiration came from having met Dame Edith Evans. Her wonderful voice was perfectly described by Peter Finch as being 'like a powderpuff shot out of a cannon'. I simply gave an impression of Dame Edith and it worked perfectly. Peter and I made it to the pub.

I don't think any of us realised at the time what an institution *Thunderbirds* would become. It has a cult following all around the world, inspiring toys, games, videos, books, comics. I have been invited to conventions where adults actually dress up in the costumes of their favourite characters. It is amazing to see the fascination of grown people with these puppets—pure escapism I guess. People who have watched it since its inception and are still fans have handed on the obsession to their children. It seems likely to be around for a long time to come.

Thunderbirds has certainly been a great money-spinner for the distributors who have admitted to profits of many millions of dollars. Here I have to strike a sour note. The actors have never received their just rewards. The distributors claim to have based our residual payments on a percentage of the original contractual fee. The snag there is that no such original contracts exist! The original arrangements were all very ad hoc. It is a bad example of a too-frequent occurrence—entrepreneurs getting away with paying the artists as little as possible. So, as far as the actors are concerned, it's a case of THUNDERBIRDS ARE NOT GO and certainly NOT FAB.

My second wife, Mirén, announced to me one day that she wanted to have a baby and had not taken precautions for quite some time. But she had not become pregnant and had secretly had some tests which had confirmed her fertility. Her eminent Harley Street gynaecologist had suggested that perhaps the trouble might lie with the husband. I baulked at first, considering that I had already proved my capacity, but I eventually agreed to have a sperm count test. I was awakened early in the morning, presented with a plastic container and asked to perform. Mirén informed me that it was imperative that the sperm, once collected, be in the doctor's possession within the half hour.

Now, I don't know how others may react to this situation, but for me the sight of the small, sterile plastic container was not at all conducive to the performance of the procedure required. I stared at it for some time before venturing the suggestion that I might need a little sympathetic help. This was agreed to and, the task completed, I was despatched with all haste to Harley Street. The thought did cross my mind that had I been stopped for speeding it was going to be difficult to convince the Bobby that the sperm had to get through at all costs.

Mission completed, I returned home to await the results. The next morning my worst fears were realised—a very low sperm count. An examination was necessary. I made the appointment and dutifully fronted up at the Harley Street rooms of the eminent medico. I sat opposite the great man while he gave me a complete history of his medical career—the miraculous cures he had achieved, the countless families he had made complete. He left me in no doubt that he was the foremost practitioner in this field.

After half an hour or so of this diatribe I politely asked if he intended to examine me. He pointed to a cubicle.

'Remove your clothes.'

He held my testicles in his hand for what seemed an eternity so that I began to have mixed feelings about the whole exercise. After apparently satisfying himself as to the shape, size and weight, he asked, 'Do you always wear that type of underpants?'

'Yes, I do.'

'Ah, that could be part of the problem.'

He proceeded to lecture me on the dangers of heat in the genital area and to pronounce that the male genitals were meant to hang free. Boxer type shorts were eminently preferable to my jockey briefs. He then pulled up a chair and made close eye contact with the offending machinery.

'On the other hand, this vein might be the seat of the trouble and simple surgery would more than likely put things right.'

I vetoed that on the spot.

I was relieved to be allowed to dress while the lecture went on—danger of confinement of the testicles . . . harmful effect of heat on the ability to procreate ... The alternative to surgery was for me to immerse my testicles in ice water for half an hour each morning and evening, actually pulling them down to ensure total immersion. I was instructed to do this religiously for two weeks after which another sperm sample would be tested. Each therapeutic session was spent sitting on the bidet while Mirén ran up and down the stairs from refrigerator to bathroom with yet another ice cube tray.

I suffered this treatment for a week and a couple of days until my wife returned from a visit to our local GP, Dr Gardiner.

'You can stop the treatment, Ray,' she announced. 'I'm one month pregnant.'

When I paid the eminent gynaecologist's bill I informed him of the outcome and suggested that a reduction of his 500 guinea fee might be in order. I heard nothing further.

I went to Egypt to make a picture for the Children's Film Foundation. It was called *The Big Dig,* an original title for a film about archaeology I thought. It was directed by Freddie Good, a very amiable soul with another gentleman of similar temperament, Bill Parry Jones, as production manager.

On the flight out Freddie insisted I sit with him to discuss the script. It became a very liquid and convivial discussion. After an hour stopover in Rome I needed the help of the carabinieri to convince Freddie that taking the brass jardiniere (complete with a six foot tree) that he had taken a fancy to was not really a good idea. Our camaraderie continued all the way to Cairo where we booked into the Omar Khayam Hotel on the same side of the Nile as the pyramids. What with the drink, the heat and the jet lag I was somewhat disoriented and when I woke up in a delightful cabana in the hotel grounds I was a little unsure as to how I'd got there and what might have happened in the time elapsed. The barman with the gold tooth and the wide smile was vaguely familiar.

I accompanied Bill while he ordered lunch for the cast and crew, about forty persons.

'Sandwiches?' asked the concierge.

'No, no,' Bill replied, 'some cold meats, salad, fruit and cold drinks, that sort of thing.'

After an intrepid journey, changing taxis two or three times due to tyre blowouts or engine failure, an exasperated and flushed Parry Jones delivered me to the pyramids at Giza, still in my original London attire. He then fled back to Cairo to arrange our imminent move to Luxor and the Valley of the Kings. There I stood alone in the midday sun, apart from a few mangy camels and their equally mangy-looking drivers, observing me quizzically between spits. I learned later that we had arrived during Ramadan, the month-long period when Muslims observe a strict fast in daylight hours. It was lucky I was not of the faith because I was rapidly dehydrating. I knew I was in the last stages of dehydration, approaching delirium, when six trucks arrived and a dozen or so men alighted, dressed in full chefs' outfits complete with starched white coats and chefs' hats.

But it was no mirage. The trucks were unloaded and twenty or more gilt-edged white tables and chairs were set up on the sand with snowy linen table cloths, the best silver cutlery and floral table arrangements. A thirty foot trestle table was set up, again with an impeccable cloth. At one o'clock, the appointed lunch hour, crates of red and white wine were unloaded, a case of whisky, untold crates of beer and soft drink. The table was suddenly groaning with a cornucopia of fruit, Mediterranean prawns, delicacies in vine leaves, turkey slices fastened to a frame resembling the bird itself, cold meats of every variety, dozens of bowls filled with salads, high, three-tiered gateaux with icing melting in the sun.

The child actors, director and crew suddenly appeared from their hot stint amid the pyramids. It is beyond me to describe the expressions on the faces of the adults. What went through their minds? *I thought this was a low budget show. If this is what they give us every day I don't mind the lousy money. Let's get stuck into this lot before it goes off!*

I had only one line to deliver that day: 'Hurry up, children, or we'll miss the train to Luxor.' I admit to total embarrassment when I was invited to see the film many months later in London. I had intoned the line with the utmost, studied caution and care and it bore no resemblance to the delivery of dialogue in the rest of the picture.

Back in the Omar Khayam we were all showered, changed and well refreshed by the time the hot and flustered Bill Parry

Jones arrived. We had all been briefed carefully by Freddie to thank Bill for the nice lunch. We sat him in an armchair, settled him with a goblet and one by one we tendered our grateful appreciation. By the time half the crew had expressed their thanks, Bill's normally ruddy countenance had paled to an ashen grey. An expression of disbelief spread over his features and he fled the room. He realised that he had blown the film's entire luncheon budget in one day.

We booked into the gracious Winter Palace on the Nile at Luxor. Directly opposite lay the Valley of the Kings. We had to cross the Nile twice each day in the course of the filming which meant four loadings and unloadings of steel camera tracks and other cumbersome and sensitive equipment—very heavy labour for the Egyptian workmen who performed magnificently under trying conditions. It was incredible to see them running across the sand carrying 20 foot lengths of solid steel tracks above their heads.

We lunched each day in the house that had been occupied by Howard Carter who, with Lord Carnarvon, had discovered Tutankhamen's unviolated tomb in 1922. This was a cool, spacious building on a small hill in the middle of the desert. After the fiasco of Giza, Bill Parry Jones had tried to foist onto us at lunchtime, hand sewn brown paper bags containing a bread roll with a piece of meat that looked as if it had been stolen from a dog. We were having none of that, and each day waiters brought over from the Winter Palace silver trays of cold collations, fruit and cool drinks. Poor Bill had either decided to run at a loss or up the subsidy from the Egyptian government. I suspect the latter.

It was eerie to sit in Carter's or Carnarvon's chair, eating my lunch from the very desk on which so many plans and diagrams had been laid out in the years leading up to the discovery and to imagine what the emotions and atmosphere must have been like when success came. I felt as if I was immersed in history.

The desert was similarly charged. One day I found myself standing in the Valley of the Kings along with a *gallabia*-clad (traditional Arabian kaftan) guard with a World War I rifle slung over his shoulder. The little monsters were busy filming in the bowels of Setie's tomb, one of the deepest in the valley. The area had been cordoned off for the filming and there were no tourists about. The guard was unsmiling but I worked up the courage to attempt to chat to him in my monosyllabic Arabic. 'It's hot, isn't it? What a fine place. Your family lives in Luxor?' I think he was relieved when I asked if I could see inside Tut's tomb.

He beckoned me to follow and ceremoniously opened the tomb, gesturing for me to enter. There followed one of the most amazing experiences of my life. To be alone in that extraordinary place was privilege not given to many I'm sure. I lost track of time as I explored and gazed, totally absorbed. I experienced a weird sensation of timelessness, together with an exhilaration and sense of belonging. It was as if I had been taken by the hand and led back into the past.

I finished work on the film a few days before the children and the first thing I did when I reached Cairo was to go to the museum to see the treasures that the pharaoh's tomb had yielded up. Again I was fascinated by the amount and variety of the material. When I think of Egypt today I think not of the modern cities and all their problems, but of how the land and the river and the people must have been in the time of Tutankhamen.

I was on a train from London to Bath to start on a picture called *40,000 Suspects,* directed by Val Guest. I went into the dining car with my script, intending to use the time to get some scenes under my belt for shooting the following day. Privacy was of paramount importance to allow me to concentrate on my lines. I chose a table for two, right where the waiters emerged from the kitchen spilling the odd drop of soup. *I'll surely have this spot to myself,* I thought. The risk of a bit of this or that in the lap was worth taking. I settled down with my script on the table in front of me, in no hurry to order.

When it came time to order I thought that the roast of the day might be the safest bet and asked for a Medoc to ease it down, this being the most superior wine on the British Rail list. I had returned from France only a day or so before and considered myself quite a connoisseur of the grape. To my horror, a woman appeared and asked if the seat opposite me was vacant.

What could I say? Gone were my chances of concentration. I held the script on my knee below table level and tried to avoid conversation, I felt her eyes burning into me as I tried to read myself into a state of aloneness in which the woman did not exist.

Rattle, rattle, rattle went the train. Without looking up I groped for my glass, found it and raised it to my lips while keeping my eyes glued to the text on my knee. After a time I found I was simply staring at the words and taking nothing in. What to do? Should I give in and ask this attractive middle-aged woman to join me in a glass or would she think I was trying to pick her up?

I opted to do the companionable thing. She accepted and I closed the script, apologising for my rudeness. I felt obliged to point out that the Medoc was the best British Rail had to offer, at least in this dining car.

She waved this aside with a gracious smile. 'You obviously enjoy your wine,' she said. 'Do you have any preference in a red?'

This was my chance to show her that I was not only a member of the Wine Society, but knew a bit about French wine. She asked if I had any preference in districts.

'I prefer Brittany,' I said. 'But I found the Muscadet a little too tart at this time of the year, being winter, and moved south.'

She sipped and nodded.

'It's perfect Burgundy weather of course,' I went on, warming to the subject, 'especially with the fine cuisine of the area. I do believe what they say about the predominance of clay in the soil. One can actually *taste* it in the better vintages. Of course, it's eventually up to you and your palate. *Mood,* naturally has a lot to do with it. I mean, if one is in convivial company one doesn't really notice the subtleties, does one?'

'Mmm.'

'I find it wonderful fun to move about and taste the wine of the area. I vividly recall being delayed on my way to Paris at Nantes railway station. On the platform was an old gentleman pushing a trolley laden with quarter bottles of red with simple corks in them—from his own vines obviously. I bought a large quantity and I don't remember ever enjoying a wine so much. *Mood*, again, you see.'

'Fascinating. Do you drink spirits at all?'

'Well, yes, I like a whisky at the right time.'

'Any particular brand?'

'I suppose I'm a bit of a philistine there. I'm not really a single malt man, I prefer a blended whisky—say Bells or a Dewars, perhaps.'

'Sherry?'

'Very occasionally.'

'Forgive me, but I couldn't help noticing your script. You're an actor, obviously.'

'Yes,' said I. 'Just another strolling vagabond.'

'It must be a very interesting life.'

'Well, yes, I suppose it is ... has its ups and downs. What do you do, may I ask?'

'I'm a wine taster for Harveys.'

I was in a sort of semi-sleep one morning in my house in London when it occurred to me that I hadn't spoken to my mother for almost two years. I checked the time difference and decided on an appropriate time to call her. I was aware that the charge was one pound per minute, so I took the precaution of making careful notes on what I wanted to talk about—the doings of family and certain friends. I had my notes in front of me as I put through the call to Brisbane.

The familiar voice. 'Hello.'

'Hello, Mum.'

'Who's that?'

'It's Ray, Mum.'

Pause. 'Who?'

'It's your son, Mum. Ray, calling from London.'

'Oh, yes.' Very loud she was now, obviously thinking she had to shout over such a long distance. 'How are you?'

'I'm fine. How are you?'

'I'm fine.'

I reckoned we were up to about six pounds by the time we'd established this much.

I said. 'Forgive me for keeping this brief, Mum, but it costs a pound a minute, so I've jotted down a few things I wanted to ask you ...'

'Just a second, Ray. There's someone at the door.'

Twenty-five pounds later she was back. 'Reenie Doolan just came over to say she's wet the tea.' (This is a Queensland expression meaning waiting for the tea to draw.) 'She said to say hello to you.'

'Mum,' I said.

'Yes?'

'I'll write to you.'

Lyndall Barbour, who made a brief trip to England to work on the stage and in television, and I were cast in the leading roles in a BBC radio play the name of which I have long forgotten. Lyndall and I turned up for the read-through and, being conditioned to the pressure of work in Sydney radio, we gave more or less our complete performance in the first rehearsal.

The rest of the cast were mostly BBC repertory actors, comfortably ensconced in the bosom of the Beeb, and never in a hurry to get the job done. After our first rehearsal, Lyndall and I chatted, contemplating what the director might have to say about our performances. The English actors sat, all tweed-suited, in their corner talking amongst themselves and eyeing these strange creatures from the penal colony.

Eventually the director entered the now briar-filled room, pausing to light his pipe. He added his aromatic smoke to that of a lot of the other thespians and pondered the masterpiece on paper in his hand. He looked at Lyndall and myself in an enigmatic way for quite some time.

'You know,' he said eventually, 'that was quite good, quite good.'

We were relieved and expected that he would return to his glass booth and announce the countdown for the recording to begin. But no. There is always a sense that time is of no consequence at the BBC.

PRODUCER: (after lighting his pipe)
That was quite good. Now, all go and have a nice cup of coffee while I sort out gwams with Victor.

Lyndall and I looked at one another. What on earth could he mean? We worked out that he had an uvular 'r' and pronounced the sound as 'w'. So 'gwams' meant 'grams' or gramophones. After an hour's coffee break (the BBC runs on coffee) he returned, lit his pipe and said, 'Now, page one.'

Three more days of rehearsal and our performances were getting steadily worse. By the fourth day I didn't need a script at all, but solemnly groaned the lines, waiting for the last page so that Lyndall and I could emerge into the daylight of Piccadilly and head for the nearest pub.

I was in Spain when I got a cable from my agent—by this time Terry Owen who had represented me inside Leading Players and I went with him when he branched out on his own—asking if I would like to be a guest on *The Dave Allen Show* on the BBC. Of course I would.

The other guests were Matt Munro and Patsy Ann Noble, daughter of the Aussie comedian Buster Noble, along with dancers and musicians. The gimmick for the show was that everybody got to sing except Matt. There were hilarious send-ups of *The Troubleshooters* and other sketches with Matt all the time asking when his number was coming up. It never did. I was given a beautiful arrangement of 'What a difference a day makes' with the backing of the BBC orchestra.

It was a very happy show, very funny and I enjoyed myself immensely. To my amazement the phone rang next day, first with an offer of a recording contract with Philips Fontana, and later with an offer from another company. I went in to Philips and met Jack Baverstock.

'We want to do an LP with you. Would you like to choose twelve songs. We'll sort out an arranger.'

I was dumbfounded. We went through piles of song scores and I finally came up with twelve I liked and thought I could handle. Mike Vickers agreed to do the arranging and we worked out keys and got down to rehearsing tempos and feelings for each song in his apartment in the West End. Mike came up with some wonderful arrangements. It was all dreamtime stuff to me.

The first recording session was in Philips studios at Marble Arch. I showed up with my daughter who was attending the Sarah Siddons school just up the Edgeware Road. I felt sick with nerves at the sight of about fifty musicians tuning up. Suellen, who was about fourteen, said, 'Dad, don't be nervous. Just get on with it.'

'Which one would you like to start with?' said Mike.

I felt so daunted with all those expert session musicians' eyes on me. I could imagine them thinking, *Oh, God, not another bloody actor trying to sing*. But as we progressed I found them all charming, understanding and helpful. The sessions became a pleasure rather than a trial. I made two albums for Phillips, *No Trouble Now*, the title obviously bouncing off the TV series, and *Larger than Life*. They did very well with a single from *No Trouble Now* of 'If you go away' getting into the top 40. Thank you, Bessie Dougall.

· 18 ·

Good sports

Wanted: Iago, must be good left arm spin bowler.

Advertisement placed by old-time actor manager in charge of theatre company and actors' cricket team.

In his *The Boundary Book,* Leslie Frewins says, 'It was in 1949 that someone stirred a tankard of ale with a cricket bat and the Lords Taverners floated to the surface.'The Taverners is a society which stages cricket matches between celebrities and professional players with the purpose of raising money for charity. A great deal of money for very worthy causes has been raised in this way and I am proud to have played my small part.

If you stood at the tavern at Lords cricket ground you were bound to meet someone you knew. One sunny afternoon I stood with a pint in my hand, engrossed in an England versus Australia Test match when I felt a light clip on the ear. I turned, ready to retaliate, to find that I was facing Wally Grout, a fellow banana-bender and legendary test wicket-keeper. He had spotted me from the Aussie dressing room and invited me across to meet the boys. I recall that Alan Davidson was getting a rub down by the masseur and was also being worked on by skipper Richie Benaud.

'Just two more overs, Alan, and you'll have him.'

I forget who the victim was but I think the prediction proved to be true.[1]

There is something especially atmospheric about cricket at Lords and the tavern was a mecca for thespian cricket lovers who are many. Cricketing actors, all Walter Mittys in their way, love getting into their creams and spikes and acting out their dreams of glory in the middle. There was a close association in England between cricketers and actors, all entertainers I suppose in their different ways. Actors were always to be found willing to turn out for professionals' testimonials, to swell the crowd and perhaps make a mark at the crease.

I played in a number of these events. The pros were indulgent, not bringing us down from our dreams of excellence with too hard a bump. I remember Ben Barnett, a veteran Australian wicket-keeper, hissing at me from behind the stumps, 'Move down to the next one, Ray. Promise I won't stump you.'

Playing at the famous grounds was great, but for me nothing could beat cricket played in good weather on a village green. Hot sunny days, a blanket spread on the grass, the picnic hamper at lunch and then across to the inevitable Cricketers Arms after the match. Magic! We played with the greats, past and present. I never dreamed back in Brisbane, trying to make the school eleven, that I'd one day play with the likes of Barrington, Compton, Tyson, the Bedsers, Edrich, Sobers and Wesley Hall.

In one match I was fielding at mid on with Sobers batting. The great Garfield cracked it and the ball came at me at a height and with such a velocity that if I hadn't caught it I would have

---

[1] The great commentator John Arlott used to make much of Wally Grout's habit of moving across to first slip after each delivery and talking to Bob Simpson, his captain. 'There's the keeper, Wally Grout, moving to chat with Simpson. I wonder if he sees something the captain is missing. I wonder, with the away swinger, is he suggesting Simpson do without third slip and move the man to deep extra gully?'

I watched closely and sure enough, Arlott's observation was accurate. I tackled Wally Grout about this one day. 'What do you say to Simmo after each delivery? Surely he must get sick of you giving him advice.'

'No, Ray,' Wally said. 'It's usually something like, "*Quick, Simmo—slew left, look, red knickers!*" '

lost my head. The catch was made out of pure self-preservation. Sobers came up to me afterwards in the pub to ask me how the hand was feeling. In fact, it had turned blue and was puffed up to twice its normal size.

'It's fine,' I said, but I didn't let him see that I couldn't even pick up a glass with it.

I suspect that the professionals often got more enjoyment out of playing with us than the first-class matches. I remember walking out to the centre at Lords, the holy of holies, to bat in a charity match—the Lords Taverners versus Middlesex, past and present. I took block with David (now Sir David) Frost at the other end. Bill Edrich was the bowler. His first ball was up on my leg stump and I hooked it to the tavern fence for four. The next was on my off stump and I cut it to point. There was a run in it but Frost shouted. 'No, Ray! Tell you why later.' The next ball I read as similar to the first, attempted to play the same stroke and saw my leg stump gone.

On my way back to the pavilion with the glorious score of four, Edrich called me over and said, 'Ray, don't hit me for four off the first bloody ball.' They never forget.

Frost, I believed, carried his bat. I learned later that he had a camera team there filming the event and particularly his own performance. The film was later screened on his American TV show.

In the same match I was fielding at deep mid-on, practically underneath the Middlesex dressing room. In these games the professionals usually like to pick on a mug, hopefully someone who could take a joke, to have a bit of fun with. I was a social member of the Middlesex club and used to drink with members of the team at the Star Tavern in St Johns Wood after matches. They had obviously singled me out as the bunny. The batsmen began lobbing sky-high catches out to me. I dropped three in a row which brought roars of laughter from the crowd, whereupon a large wicker clothes basket sailed down from the Middlesex balcony, thrown by Ian Bedford, Peter Parfitt and Fred Titmuss, to land at my feet.

Again, a high ball came my way. This time I would make no mistake. I held the basket carefully, adjusted the position until I was sure the ball would hit dead centre. It seemed to hang in the air for ages. Down it came, landed squarely in the middle of the basket and bounced straight out. All dreams of looking like a cricketer vanished.

Another time, at The Oval, our showbiz side was pitted against Surrey boasting such people as the great Jim Laker, Mickey Stewart and Edrich. Among our number was a green-haired Elton John and Andy Williams who had come over from the States to make an LP. He wore whites with a red stripe down the legs of the trousers and shoes to match. When he came out to bat, the announcement of his name over the PA system was followed by a few bars of 'Moon River'.

The bowler was instructed to deliver him an up and down half-volley which he dealt with quite admirably. His shot was even more adroitly mis-fielded several times. Andy threw his bat down and raced around the boundary, leaping and waving his arms as they do in the undignified game of baseball. Meanwhile every attempt to throw down his wicket failed.

The crowds at some of these games exceeded those for many of the serious fixtures. An enjoyable time was had by the professionals and the Walter Mittys and the spectators gave freely to charity.

> 'In my opinion putting has no part in the game of golf. All greens should be of conical shape so that when the ball lands on the green it automatically runs into the hole.'
> Arnold Palmer: when he had a dose of the 'yips' and couldn't sink a putt from six inches.

I played most of my golf in England at the Richmond club, already mentioned. When I had the time to put into it, my game improved and at one point I had my handicap down to a respectable nine. (In fact it was briefly six, but that was after another member and I had beaten the club captain and the pro in a foursome and I had shot 67 off the stick on the par 72 course—a never to be forgotten but never to be repeated feat. Of course, I couldn't play to it and the mark was allotted to me by the captain in a fit of pique.) I played at other English courses and have variable memories of them the way golfers do. I have a vivid recollection of the first hole at Royal Lytham St Annes on the west coast. It's a par 3 but the wind blows straight in your face and I've played it with everything from a

3 iron to a driver and never made the green. It's one of those holes that make you consider giving the game away.

Like cricket-playing actors, golf-playing actors entertain the same fantasies about their abilities and are always pleased to play with the greats, especially in charity events. The Harry Secombe Classic, an annual event at Effingham, is hugely attended. Harry, affectionately known as Sircumference, presides. I was invited to play and made the fatal mistake of buying a new set of clubs and bag, fearing that my old equipment would attract derision alongside the grand copious bags and lustrous gear of the pros.

When I learned that I was to be partnered with fellow Australian Peter Thomson, I made a beeline for the practice fairway to get the feel of my new clubs. My daughter Suellen was there with some of her friends and the crowd around the first tee was about ten deep and lined the side of the fairway for a hundred yards.

'And now on the tee, five times winner of the British Open, the great Australian golfer, Peter Thomson.'

Thunderous applause.

Peter tips his cap, tees his ball and with that compact, minimalist swing, puts one down the middle about 280 yards.

'And now his playing partner, star of *The Troubleshooters*, fellow Australian, Ray Barrett.'

I was shaking so much it took me ten goes to get my ball on the tee. The crowd was hushed. *Better get this over with,* I thought. I took a quick snatch and there was a sickening thud. I had hit a spectator at square leg. Fortunately, he was wearing a heavy raincoat against the drizzle but I was mortified. Amid the laughter, Peter said, 'Pick it up, Ray. I'll get this one.'

This, compounded with concern that I could have killed someone, and the untried sticks, did nothing for my game. I was a shivering wreck throughout the round and didn't hit a decent shot until the last hole or so. My 67 at Richmond was a distant memory; I played as if I had never had a club in my hands before. Golfers will know the feeling. I wished the ground would open up and swallow me and one time when I glanced across at Suellen, who was obviously hoping for me to do well, I saw her turn away and I read her lips: 'Oh, Daddy.'

No actor is more generous with his time and efforts in regard to charity golf than Sean Connery. Sean took up golf after he had to play in the filming of *Goldfinger*, and became a fanatic. He also became a very good player with a 9 handicap which he can play to. I first met Sean in London when he was just breaking into the acting business. During my early days in London we struggling actors used to get cut-price drinks in a place called the Buxton Club and we'd take it in turns to be barman. Sean has never forgotten those lean times, many do. He has remained very much a product of the rougher parts of Edinburgh where he was born and he has done all he can to raise money for underprivileged children in Scotland. Charity golf events figure largely.

By the late sixties Sean was getting tired of playing James Bond in the movies, but the films were great money-spinners and the producers, Cubby Brocolli and Harry Saltzman would have been happy for him to go on making them until the day he died. He struck a deal, agreeing to make one more film for them if they would back a film he wanted to direct. This happened. Sean then decided that he'd get together a collection of show business golfers, fly them all up to Scotland at his own expense for a premiere showing of the film and then let them loose in a charity golf weekend at Gleneagles. All profits to go to the kids of the Gorbals in Glascow and the like.

He chartered a plane which we boarded at Heathrow—all sorts of actors and other notables from all over the place—Ronnie Corbett (who hits a very straight ball but not very far), Henry Cooper ('our 'Enery') the boxer and a delightful man, Mike Medwin, Jimmy Tarbuck, Kenny Lynch. Bruce Forsyth, I remember, came up from Bournemouth where he'd been doing a panto and just managed to catch the plane. Douglas 'Tin Legs' Bader, the legless fighter pilot and hero of Paul Brickhill's *Reach for the Sky*, was in the company. There must have been thirty or forty of us, all accommodated in the best Glasgow hotels with Sean footing the bill.

We all turned up to see the film which wasn't very good but that didn't matter. There was a wonderful dinner and cocktail party afterwards with the comedians like Corbett, Jimmy Tarbuck and Co. all trying to outdo each other. Some hilarious goings on. The next day we piled into luxury mini-buses and set off for Gleneagles. And of course, it being Scotland, it was freezing cold and pissing down rain. It was a two-tee start and I recall being on the tenth tee, all rugged up in the wet weather gear, and hitting a perfect shot that made the green.

'Bloody good shot,' Connery said in that voice that has become famous.

But it was a desperately awful day and after eight or so holes we had to abandon it, the water was so deep on the fairways you were wading towards your ball. We were all booked into the Gleneagles Hotel (an immense building, once owned by British Rail but now luxuriously appointed) for the night and after hot baths and a change of clothes with the drinks flowing no-one felt let down. We had a room set aside for us with a chef and they piped in the haggis and went through all the Scottish rituals. A splendid dinner and another great night. The next day was a washout too, so we all got on the plane and flew back to London. Still, some people had turned out on the first day and paid at the gate and donated more money, and the profits from the sale of food and drink had gone to the charity so it raised some money for the kids.

This kind of generosity inside and outside the acting profession comes naturally to Sean Connery and is a great credit to him. He's never big-headed, has never forgotten his humble origins, and I've never heard anyone begrudge him the success he's had. And it *was* a bloody good shot!

We had just sold our little cottage in Richmond and were preparing to move to a lovely old stables house at East Sheen just down from Sheen Gate, Richmond Park. There were tea chests all over the place—it's amazing the junk one acquires over the years. I'd nipped out to the Red Cow for a breather and on my return my wife, Mirén, informed me that I'd had a phone call from a fellow by the name of Derek Pillage who wanted me to play golf the following Wednesday. Of course I couldn't possibly go with so much to do. Miren said she would prefer it if I went so she could quietly get on with things on her own. I must have been more of a hindrance than a help. I knew Derek Pillage as I'd partnered him in a tournament at Brighton which we'd won. I phoned him up and he informed me that there would be the usual showbiz crowd and it would be a great event.

'OK where are we playing?' I asked, thinking it would be Wentworth, Mid Surrey or the like.

He said 'Rio de Janeiro' as if where else would it be.

'OK Derek, cut the bullshit, where are we playing?'

He informed me that not only was he the manager of such top golfers as Lee Travino, Brian Barnes and others, but he was also P.R. for British Caledonian Airways and it was their inaugural flight to Rio and he was taking a group of show biz personalities out there to play ten days of charity matches for the underprivileged children of Brazil of which there were many. He said 'Just be at Gatwick 10 o'clock Wednesday with your clubs, don't worry about money.' Well what do you do? I told Mirén that I was sure she would do a great job of the packing without my help and I'd send her a postcard from Rio. Things started to go downhill from the time I arrived at the airport. No one had bothered to inform me of the vaccinations required for Brazil. The plane was held and a doctor summoned, and I got the lot in one go and was bundled onto the aircraft.

We duly landed at Rio. What a breathtaking sight it was flying past the statue of Christ on top of Sugarloaf Mountain and the wonderful bay and white beaches. Then the next crunch! The stern looking Customs man took one look at my Australian passport. I was immediately placed in detention awaiting the next available aircraft to anywhere, so long as it was out of the country. I was unaware that Australia had broken off diplomatic relations with Brazil. It was a sticky moment indeed. A sales manager from Caledonian stayed with me fortunately and it took some very swift and diplomatic explanations to the Generals in Brasilia before I was grudgingly handed a piece of paper authorising my stay for the bare ten days. This took seven hours, which I spent staring at the aircraft on the tarmac which was to take me to Buenos Aries. What would I do there? Probably rot in prison and never be heard of again! All this for my services to the underprivileged children of Brazil. I had noted on the flight out from the UK that the two airhostesses were very attractive young ladies indeed, tall, and blonde. I remarked upon this to Glen Mason a musician/composer friend of mine that they had obviously been hand-picked for the occasion, in their tight plaid skirts and pretty blouses. It seemed that Derek and Stanley Baker were commanding most of their time. This was confirmed when I arrived at the beautiful house we'd been given right on Garvia Golf Course. Derek and Stanley had the two best rooms overlooking the course and it seemed to me that the two 'hosties' were more than happy with their accommodation; on the course everyone envied Derek and Stanley their blonde gamin caddies. We played a few practice rounds and after sixteen hours detention I was not in my best form. However on returning to our mansion we were greeted by our man in the white jacket with the silver tray laden with gin and tonic or whatever and our golf shoes were taken away to be cleaned. Soon any worries about form became secondary.

In the first major event, a two ball affair, I partnered a gentleman by the name of Chi Chi (I never knew his surname), a very amiable cheery soul who played off two. We had a very pleasant round and he wouldn't let me buy a drink either at the halfway house or the 19th. You're an actor?' he enquired.

'Yes' I said.

'Must be a very interesting profession.'

'Oh, yes, like everything else it has its ups and downs. What do you do?' I asked.

'Oh, I just dabble in coffee.'

Of course, I thought, coffee ... Brazil ... yes! It wasn't until the 18th I remarked to Derek what a charming partner he had been and that he 'dabbles' in coffee.

'Dabbles' exclaimed Derek, 'he owns half the coffee plantations in Brazil.'

He came to dinner with us that evening. After coffee (of course) and liqueurs nobody was feeling any pain. Derek and Stanley occupied a couch with our two English roses listening to Simon & Garfunkel's 'Bridge over Troubled Water.' Chi Chi decided to liven up the procedings and got on the phone. Within half an hour two of the most beautiful young women appeared; one of them especially had to be the most magnificent creature I'd ever seen with her light coffee coloured skin (there's that word again.) and exquisite figure. Simon & Garfunkel were soon replaced by some exciting Brazilian music. The girls danced. We all watched, spellbound by their uninhibited movements. I couldn't help noticing the expressions on the faces of Derek and Stanley. Whenever either of them made a move to get up from the settee, they were firmly pulled back against the cushions by the two blonde beauties. Chi Chi was in deep conversation with one of the Creole ladies which left my exquisite creature. I thought 'damn this, I've been in prison, I've missed out on the damsels and the best rooms'. I took her by the hand and I said 'Darling, come with me'. The eighteen holes the next morning took some getting around. I eventually made it to the 19th, 'The Clubhouse' and to the bar which was a welcome sight indeed. No sooner had I got there than I was met by an irate Stanley Baker, who approached me shouting:

'Barrett, you bastard, you bastard!'

'What's wrong Stanley?' I enquired.

'You bastard, you haven't paid her.'

I put my arm around his shoulder.

'Calm down, Stanley, calm down ... I haven't finished with her.' He could have killed me.

She wasn't one of those ladies anyway, but a relative of Chi Chi's, but I wasn't going to tell Stanley.

· 19 ·

The West End

Diane Cilento told me that her last conversation with Noel Coward went as follows:

Noel: Of course you know I'm dying, don't you?

Diane: Oh, don't be silly, Noel. You'll be better in no time.

Noel: But don't worry, darling. I shan't be gone for long.

One of my ambitions when I went to England was to play the West End of London. I'd heard about it from childhood and Australian actors who had or hadn't made it there talked about it. Working with Margaret Rutherford of course, reinforced the ambition. As I've said, my first few years in England were taken up with revues, films and television but I appeared in Russell Braddon's harrowing POW play *The Naked Island* at the Arts Theatre in 1960. The play had good reviews and one critic suggested that it should make the West End but that didn't happen. I did two plays in 1964, fitting in between *Karamazov* and *Troubleshooters.* I was in a play called *The First Fish* by the American playwright Frank Tarloff. It was a comedy and had a short run at the Richmond Theatre after which we moved into the West End. I played the scheming friend of a married couple who helps the wife in her efforts to overcome her husband's feelings of inferiority. I appeared with Moira Lister and Ronan O'Casey, as replacement for Paul Carpenter.

It is always necessary to rehearse in a new theatre. All stages are different as are the shape, size and acoustics of the theatre. On the first day of rehearsal in the Savoy, Moira and I and the rest of the cast were waiting on stage. No Paul! He had been very well-behaved on the out-of-town run, not drinking, but as there had been a break before the shift to the West End we feared the worst. As it turned out, the stupid stage manager had not told us that Paul had arrived early, said he felt tired, and asked for the use of dressing room to lie down. All the time we were waiting on stage, thinking he'd got on the piss, the poor lovely man was busy dying in the dressing room below. We buried him next to his old mate Bonner Coleno as was his wish.

I saw my name, flashing in neon, above the title as I walked along Piccadilly, and any actor who tells you that's not a thrill is a liar.

I didn't work in the theatre again until 1972, the last year of *Troubleshooters*. The play was *A Touch of Purple*, based on a novel by Elleston Trevor, a very popular writer of the time. It was a murder mystery in which I played the detective, quite a hard character. The plot involved the whittling down of clues and the elimination of suspects, all very effective dramatically.

We went on tour to the provinces at first and the play did well everywhere we went. The system was for West End managers to have scouts out all over the country looking at the touring plays and trying to tip which might make a success in the city. All very competitive and nerve-wracking. You never knew what night one of these spotters (or, indeed, a London manager, following up a spotter's report) might be in the audience—it could be a night when everything fired perfectly or one when everyone was flat and the play fizzled or there was a poor house. The actors and managers all felt that their careers were on the line because it was everyone's ambition to be on in the West End. That was where the money and reputations were made. A lifetime in the provinces didn't appeal to anybody.

Apart from the scouts' reports, it was the regular returns that determined a play's fate. Good houses in a variety of places were a good sign and there were particular towns and cities that were used as litmus tests. Some London producers believed that Birmingham, say, was the best guide, others Coventry and so on. Glasgow was the comic's nightmare. The saying was—if you go in Glasgow, you'll go anywhere. The touring managers feed the information to the London people, hoping to convince them that they have the season's next hit. So at any time there are all these plays out there—something like planes circling at Heathrow waiting to land.

We had played at Lytham St Annes and Manchester and were doing our last touring performance at Liverpool and just before the last act the stage manager let me know that we'd made it—we were going into the Globe in the West End. It was a thrilling moment but a tricky one. As far as everyone else in the cast knew this was the last night. After the last curtain call I asked everyone to remain on stage and I went out front and announced that we were going into the Globe. I can't remember getting such a feeling of excitement coming at me from both directions—audience in front, cast and crew behind me.

So my name was above the titles in lights again and it felt pretty good. It was a better money-earner for me this time because I was now able to command what was called an and/or contract. This meant that, in addition to the weekly salary, I got a percentage of the take. At the end of the first act, the business manager would come to my dressing room bringing the returns from the box office (as per the contract), for me to check.

We had a good run for a couple months; our houses were all right but we ran into a holiday period and they dropped off. To keep the numbers up the producer bought up several rows of tickets, gave them to friends and so on. This was a standard practice if the show hit a flat spot but had prospects of picking up again. Michael Codron, another entrepreneur who wanted the theatre for one of his shows, exposed this fiddle and made a fuss about it. The result was we were closed. It's a very cut-throat business in the West End.

One of the biggest thrills in my time in England was performing in the revue staged to honour Noel Coward on his seventieth birthday in 1969. Wendy Toye, a great Covent Garden stage director, put the whole thing together and directed it with Nigel Patrick. We actually rehearsed at Covent Garden. I was assigned the task of performing the song 'Green Carnations' from *Private Lives*.

Haughty boys, naughty boys,
One, two, three
We all wear a green carnation

goes the chorus.

My partners were Michael Denison and Patrick Allen who was a hot actor at the time. The joke, of course, as we sang and performed a soft-shoe routine was in these three butch blokes doing this precious song.

Wendy Toye's effort in organising the show was magnificent because she had people from America and Europe and all over Britain, working in plays and films and television, to put together for at least two or three rehearsals. Somehow she managed it and the revue, which was staged at Noel's beloved Phoenix Theatre, where he had done all those wonderful shows with Gertie Lawrence, was a triumph.

One thing that intrigued me was the nervousness and anxiety of some of the star performers, people like Stanley Holloway, as they waited in the green room. Stanley and others had their ears glued to the tannoy and you could practically hear them thinking, *My God, he's going over well. I'll have to pull something out to top that.* I would have expected such seasoned performers to be immune from that sort of thing but not so. Of course, it was a very special night with the Master in his box attended by two handsome young men, so nervousness could be excused. But this was something else—a sort of insecurity that performers are prone to no matter how successful they are.

The show was opened by Robert Morley. He came on stage with his unmistakable walk, the stomach arriving first of course, and looked up to Noel's box.

'Evening, Noel,' he said. 'Happy birthday. You're going to have a lovely evening, my dear. All your friends have come from all parts of the world to entertain you. No doubt the sketches will be familiar to you. So, ladies and gentlemen, sit back and enjoy yourselves and don't forget to buy my baby's book.'

Morley's son, Sheridan, Noel's godson, had chosen that day to release his biography of Noel, *A Talent to Amuse*, which was also the name given to the revue.

So things got underway. Joyce Grenfell did 'If Love were all',

Stanley Holloway sang 'London Pride', Danny La Rue 'I've been to a marvellous party', Tessie O'Shea 'London'. Michael, Patrick and I got through our number without any fluffs and we were sort of high on relief and adrenalin. Even Michael Denison, who isn't an exuberant sort of chap (his dog's name is Prospero after all), couldn't wait to get to the tiny bar in the Phoenix and soak up the atmosphere in the interval. It was impossibly crowded and loud and then, as I've said, Edith Evans' voice cut through in the way Finchy described, like a powderpuff shot from a cannon.

'Noel! Where is Noel? He sent me a limousine. I do hope he doesn't want me to perform. I am not prepared!'

There she was in her pink chiffon and blueish hair, quite distressed, and I thought I might be of some assistance, perhaps escort her backstage to the stage manager. I went up to her and said something like, 'Dame Edith, you don't know me. I'm Ray Barrett . . .'

And she cut right in with. 'Of course I know you. When is that program coming back on the television?'

Like Olivier, she watched the box. She followed up by saying, 'I hear you've got on to the singing lark?'

I'd just made my first LP record and I was rather proud of it. 'Yes,' I said. 'I have actually.' Feeling rather proud and waiting for the compliment.

'Mm. I'm not sure about that. I think you're much better at the other.'

Which brought me down to size. But it was such a wonderful night it was impossible not to feel good. Princess Margaret and Lord Snowdon, in happier times for the Royals, were there. It's a great pity that no-one filmed the show, but with all those stars on hand I imagine the contractual problems would have been tricky.

Very cleverly, after the conventional first half in which one act followed another, the second half was staged in a night club setting so that people could drift in from their shows and join a table. We drank French champagne throughout and people got up to sing some of those great Coward songs like 'I'll follow my secret heart'. That was Patricia Routledge, and Cleo Laine did 'Mad about the boy'. They'd make eye contact with Noel or say something up to him and there were tears flowing everywhere.

RIGHT: Reggie and me having fun at Palewell Park, East Sheen, 1974.

BELOW: Mirén and me.

ABOVE: A family photo at Hillfield, 1974. *(Jon Lyons)*

RIGHT: At Hillfield, 1974. *(Arthur Sidey)*

TOP: 'Don, you're a weak turd.' With John Hargreaves in *Don's Party*, 1976. *(Double Head Productions Ltd)*

BOTTOM: 'You can have Kath for the night.' As Mal, with John Hargreaves as Don.

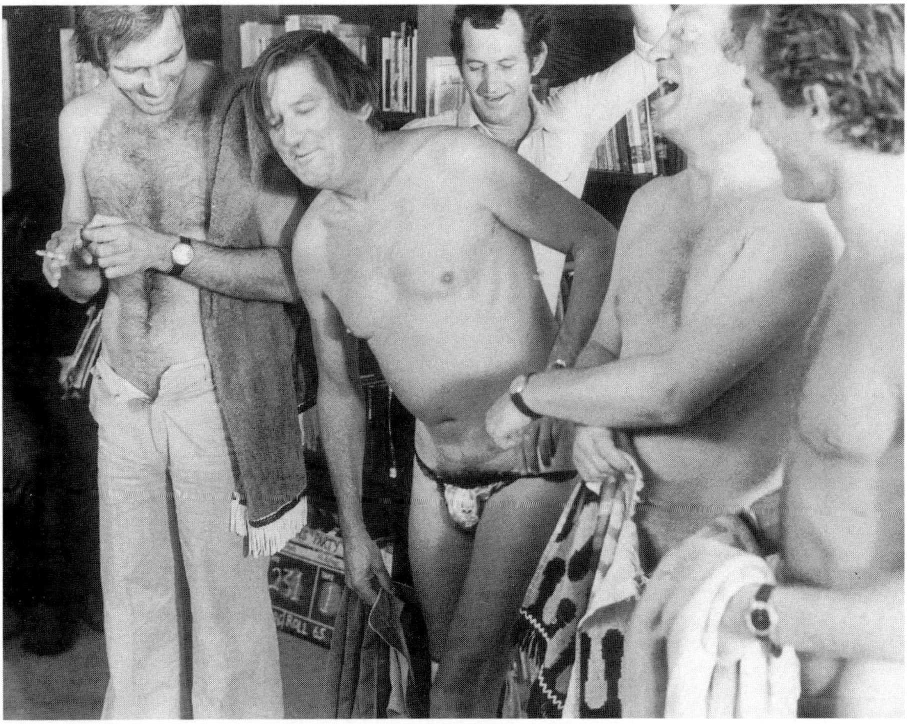

After the swimming scene, *Don's Party*. A gag for the boys!

As Sergeant Farrell in *The Chant of Jimmie Blacksmith,* 1977. With Tommy Lewis.

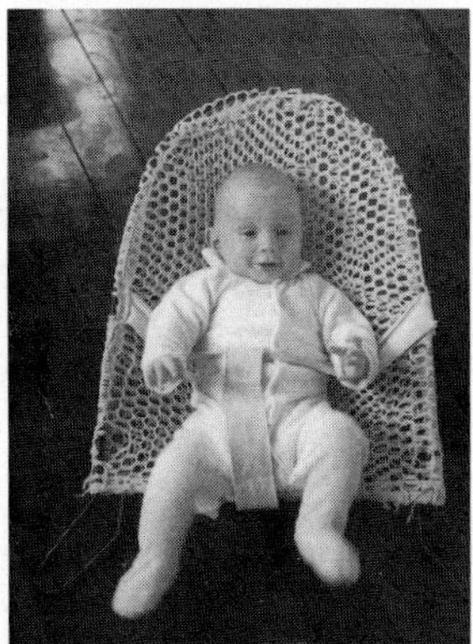

ABOVE: A comedian from the start. Jonathan at 8 months, 1978.

RIGHT: Jono about to drive off Fraser Island, aged 1, 1980.

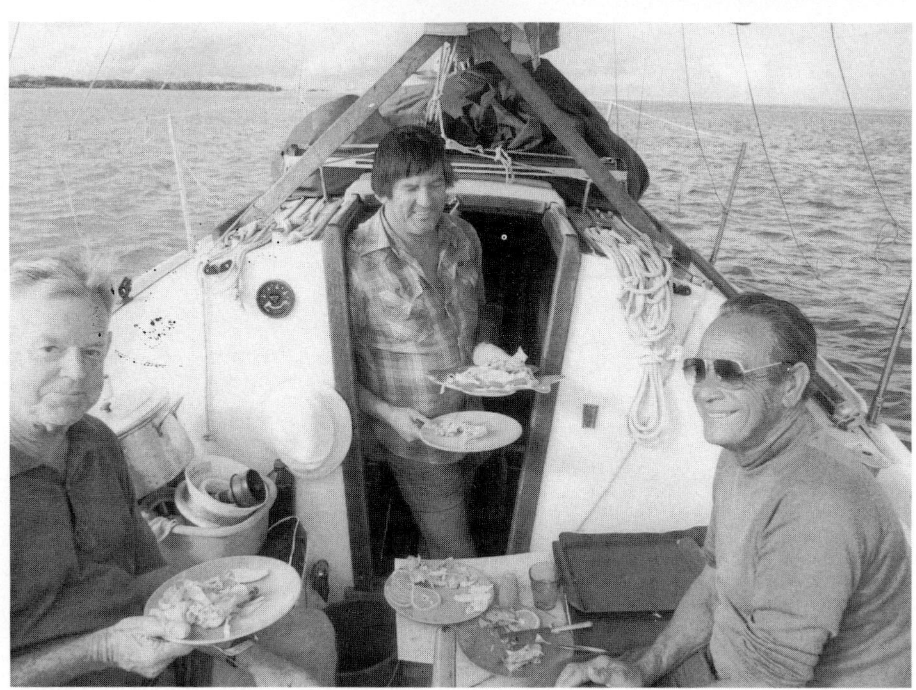

Lunch on *Odette* with Jack Collie and Jackie Borey, 1978.

Capriccio with Col Croft and Al Thomas, ABC, 1979. *(ABC)*

Governor Bligh in *The Timeless Land*, 1980. *(ABC)*

Gaye playing backgammon at her Narrabeen home, 1981.

As Robbo in *Sporting Chance,* with Liddy Clark and Richard Moir, 1981. *(ABC)*

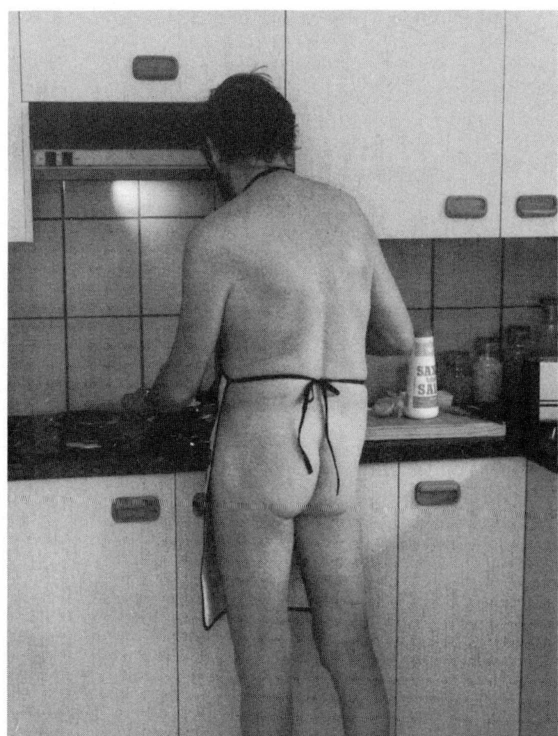

LEFT: Purely Gaye's idea! In my opinion, a good ad for Saxa salt. Ascot 1984.

BELOW: We used the image for our wedding invitation, accompanied by this text.

STATUS DOMESTICUS
CULINARIUM DORMITORIUM

A rare species found in kitchens, laundries, around clotheslines and vacuum cleaners, and occasionally bars and bingo parlours. Placid, submissive, mostly good-humoured, loving and caring.

I found this one several years ago and have decided to keep him forever!!

To celebrate this decision you are invited to a gala garden party at the Little Ship Club, Dunwich, North Stradbroke Island, Queensland, on SATURDAY, OCTOBER 4 at 12.30 p.m.

GAYE O'BRIEN R.S.V.P. 5/293 Lancaster Rd.,
ASCOT, 4007.
Phone: (07) 268 6428

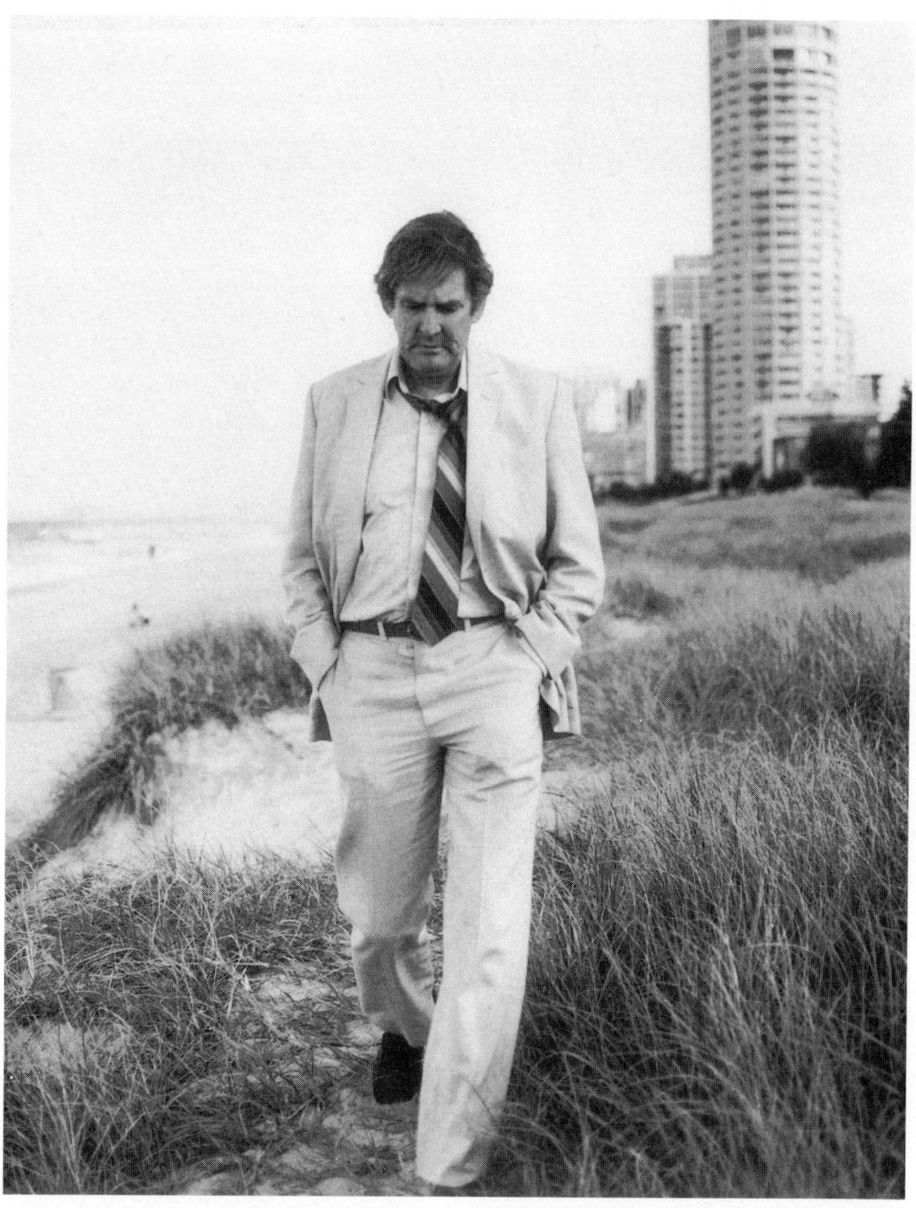

As Mike Stacey in *Goodbye Paradise*, 1982. *(Petersham Pictures)*

As Harry Moors in *Tusitalia*, 1985.

As General Blamey in *The Last Bastion*, 1984. *(ABC)*

LEFT: *Muy contento.* Gaye relaxing at Casa Barrett, 1986.

BELOW: *Tranquilidad.* Casa Barrett, 1986.

RIGHT: With Mother Morna and daughter-in-law. Formentera, 1994.

This is the life! Cruising in *Odette*, 1987.

LEFT: *Odette* under spinnaker in the Bribie Cup, 1986. RIGHT: Out for a sail, 1987.

As E.J. Banfield, 'The Beachcomber', in *A Different Drummer* by Mike Noonan at the Queensland Theatre Company. *(QTC)*

Christmas in Spain with Jono (10) and Reg (17), 1988.

ABOVE: Me and my mate, Stradbroke Island, 1990.

LEFT: With Glyn Owen at a pub in St Johns Wood, London, 1992.

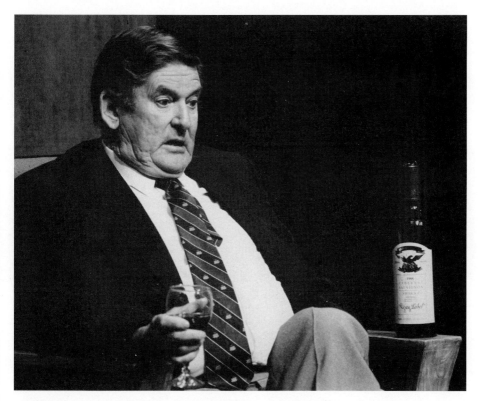

The Wolf Blass Grey Label scene from *Brilliant Lies*, 1993. *(C. William Long)*

A proud Dad with Reg and Jono at Avalon in Sydney.

With Pepe Tur (de la Fonda) at Casa Barrett, Formentera, 1995.

Getting the best advice from Pepe!

The curtain came down at 4 am, with one hundred and fifty people still captivated. No-one wanted to leave and then I think it was Gielgud who took the stage and said, 'Now ladies and gentlemen, the Master!'

Noel was suffering from some complaint that made it difficult for him to walk and he'd come in supported by his two young friends. But they'd set up a marvellous, ornate wing-backed chair on the stage and nothing was going to prevent him making an entrance. He sort of shook the boys off and stormed onto the stage and there he sat and we each went up and had a word with him. Finally, he said his thanks, declared that he had never enjoyed himself so much and was swept away in a Rolls Royce. It was a great honour to have been there and I've never forgotten it. The program is a cherished memento.

· 20 ·

Australia calling

I made a brief trip back to Australia in 1971 when filming for *The Troubleshooters* took me as close as Singapore and it seemed ridiculous not to pay a visit. My contract stipulated that Mirén should be flown out as well, and so we spent a very short time meeting friends and relations, seeing a few of the sights. Then it was back to England for more work on the series. I had no thoughts of returning permanently to Australia but circumstances seemed to conspire to draw me back.

In 1976 the Australian branch of British Leyland released a new model called the P76. It had a revolutionary alloy head and other innovative design features and the company was prepared to spend money to launch it. I had previously done a commercial in the UK for Leyland, directed by James Gatward, later the head of STV and a good friend, which had worked out very nicely for me. Part of the fee was a car which I was given with the arrangement that I could use it for two years free of charge and then buy it very cheaply if I chose to. I did. This time, I was invited to make a short film called *The Carmakers*. It was a real film, a gentle send-up of aspects of the motor industry in which the P76 would figure prominently. My old mate Wally Sullivan, Noel Ferrier and Katy Wilde were in the cast and the film was to be shown on television and in the cinema to coincide with the release of the car.

The money on offer was reasonable. It was too good an opportunity to miss and I accepted. Over the years there had been various approaches from Australian television and film producers, but the fees were miserly and the rehearsal times always too short to permit good work to be done. *The Carmakers* was the first Australian project with any appeal.

I made the trip and the film was shot to everyone's satisfaction. As I recall, it was a respectable piece of work. I had to drive the P76 a fair bit and there were no mishaps. It was good to see something of the country and catch up with people in the business and outside it. My brother Scott, to my amazement, had become a sailor of note, winning several ocean races. My mother was elderly but in fair health. However, I had no thought of staying and still saw my future in British films and television and on the stage. The P76, I should note, was not a success. Apparently there were design flaws that showed up as the car went on the road and the model never enjoyed any popularity in Australia.

In December 1974, Cyclone Tracy hit Darwin. Sixty-two people were killed and more than a thousand were injured. Forty-five thousand people were made homeless because nine out of ten houses in the city were destroyed. This was the greatest natural disaster in Australia's history and it was extensively reported in Britain with graphic television footage. Danny La Rue, who had played in Australia many times and had a great regard for the country, was approached with the idea of staging a theatrical benefit to raise money to assist the victims. He really threw himself into it and was the driving force behind the show.

I had always known that there were Australians working in London show business, but the Darwin Gala Variety Show revealed what a strong contingent it was. Dick Bentley, Leo McKern, Roy Hudd, the magician, Billy Kerr, Maggie Fitzgibbon, Frank Ifield, June Bronhill and others donated their services along with English performers like Danny and Derek Nimmo, who had fond memories of Australia, Googie Withers, Honor Blackman, Miriam Karlin, Emlyn Williams and Moira Lister. The front of house people, the band and everybody concerned worked for free.

As always, the show was difficult to put together and rehearse because the people involved were working in different places with all sorts of commitments. But ways were found. We rehearsed as best we could, sometimes with only a handful of people turning up, sometimes more. Tickets were sold through Australia House and the benefit was staged on a Sunday night on 9 February 1975 at the Prince of Wales Theatre in Piccadilly. The theatre was owned by Sir Bernard Delfont, the brother of Sir Lew Grade, and he donated its use on a night when no show was scheduled.

The theatre was packed. I went on with Dick Bentley, Bill Kerr and an Australian actor named Lewis Fiander. We did a medley of Aussie bush songs like 'Click go the shears', hamming it up of course, which seemed to go over pretty well. Everything went off as smoothly as can be expected in an impromptu event like this. Princess Anne was in the audience. She met the cast later and was obviously in no hurry to leave—a sign that she had genuinely enjoyed the evening. (When the royals have attended purely out of duty they are generally off sharpish.) When I was presented to her she asked me did we do much rehearsal for this sort of thing.

'Well, Ma'am,' I said. 'You've just seen it.'

The show had a host of sponsors like Qantas, the Commonwealth Bank, Chandris Lines and the various Australian state governments and I believe it raised over a hundred thousand pounds for Darwin.

In 1976 I played Cooley in David Williamson's brilliant play *Don's Party* at the Royal Court Theatre in Sloan Square. This was the first opportunity to appear in an Australian play in London since *The Naked Island* sixteen years before. I was surprised to see what changes must have taken place in Australia, as reflected in the play. In 1962 I had been outraged to learn that my friend Peter Yeldham's television play, *Reunion Day* in which I had appeared in the BBC production, had been banned in Australia. The play showed Diggers celebrating by getting drunk. The RSL and the 'establishment' had branded it unpatriotic, anti-semitic and obscene. I was so angry I took the, for me, very unusual step of writing a letter to the *Sydney Morning Herald* which was published on 22 May 1962.

In the letter I defended the play and attacked the 'establishment' blaming its narrow-mindedness for the outflowing of Australian talent to England and America.

> Australian artists are not encouraged to express themselves, make mistakes if necessary, and thereby create an indigenous Australian drama.

I argued that drama must show truth and expressed the belief that the Australian public was not afraid of the truth. It particularly upset me that Australians could see controversial works such as films like *A Taste of Honey* (about race, single parenthood and homosexuality), musicals like *Irma la Douce* (about prostitution) and the plays of Tennessee Williams, but not anything adventurous that dealt with Australian themes and realities.

So the vigour and frankness of *Don's Party* came as a breath of fresh air. David Williamson and his wife Kristin attended every rehearsal and I was impressed by his willingness to restructure a scene or amend a line in accordance with ideas put forward by the actors and to help us on points of interpretation. I knew nothing about the Australian Performing Group in Melbourne where David had learned and refined his craft in just this kind of collaborative way.

Michael Blakemore, an Australian who had been in England for many years, was the director. Among others in the cast were Australians Max Phipps, Veronica Lang, Barry Creyton and John Gregg. Tony Haygarth was the only Englishman in the cast. We rehearsed in St James church hall in Piccadilly and the vicar and his staff had their office just behind where we were rehearsing. There are some very coarse expressions in the play, and it was amusing to see the vicar's head popping out to catch bits of this peculiar and disreputable dialogue.

It was a bold move to put the play on in London. This was long before the TV soaps had made the Poms more familiar with Australian speech and ways. Of course they had no idea of what an election party was like, how its rhythms were dictated by the state of the polls and the level of the beer keg. The reviews were mixed and people at first stayed away. But towards the end of the seven week run word of mouth had it that this was an interesting piece of work and the houses improved dramatically so that it was standing room only for the last few performances. The producers, Eddie Kulukundis and Robert Morley, should have taken the play into the West End but I'm afraid they lost their nerve.

Unseen forces came into play again when I was offered a very lucrative contract to do a series of commercials for W D & H O Wills to promote a new brand of cigarette in Australia. Players No 6 was the brand and the commercials were to be shown in cinemas and on television and extensively in the print media. Now, the irony was, I'd never been a passionate smoker and had given it up absolutely about eight years before. I recall getting up one morning at Richmond and coughing nastily. I wasn't a heavy smoker, about ten a day and usually only when I was drinking or when I was nervous. I wasn't one of those who reach for a smoke first thing in the morning. But still, I had catarrh and a cough and the thought came to me that I didn't actually like smoking and it wasn't doing me any good. The house had sash windows. I lifted the window, picked up my packet of Craven A and Dunhill lighter, threw them out and did not smoke again. I think cold turkey is the only way to do it, and that people who say 'I'll just have two a day' are kidding themselves.

Nowadays, with what we know about the effects of smoking and passive smoking on people's health, I wouldn't consider doing tobacco advertisements if they still existed. But twenty years ago all that was less clear. And I must be honest—the money on offer was too much to turn down. Acting is a chancy profession at the best of times and you have to grab the money when you can. The other big advantage was that the deal would fly me and my family out to Australia for free. I envisaged a stay of a few months after finishing the promotion. A holiday, a chance to catch up with friends and family, do a bit of sailing, take Mirén and Reggie up to the reef. Nothing more. Little did I know.

III

· 21 ·

To stay or not to stay?

'I'll play anyone, even the women. They're all such good parts.'

RB to Bruce Beresford on the casting of *Don's Party* (1976)

The cigarette commercials were a breeze. To add to the irony of my being a non-smoker was the fact that the theme for the ads was gambling, something that has never attracted me. I made the mistake of admitting to a journalist that I didn't smoke and one of the Wills people took me to task.

'It was a misprint,' I lied.

I didn't have to actually smoke in the commercials which was a relief. I was at the races, on a yacht, playing roulette or blackjack, all togged up in the appropriate gear with attractive women hanging off me and *holding* a cigarette. There was a sort of James Bond look to some of them and everyone seemed satisfied. Whether the brand achieved its desired 'market share' or not I neither knew nor cared. I got paid.

So there we were, Mirén, Reggie and me. We traipsed around a bit, leading the gypsy life for a while that is all part of acting. We stayed with my mother in Brisbane, then with my brother. I had never felt anything other than Australian through all my time in England, but I was surprised to discover how much being back meant to me. Of course, things were far more easygoing and liberal than they had been back in the 50s and modern communications had reduced the feeling of isolation considerably. Still, my intention was to go back to the UK, taking some of the Antipodean loot with me, and pick up where I had left off.

A phone call from Bruce Beresford changed all that. I knew his name and something about his work but had never met him. He said that he was making a film of *Don's Party*. Well, you can count the number of successfully filmed plays on the fingers of one hand, so I was sceptical. Then he said that David Williamson was doing the screenplay. That made a difference. David had apparently approved of my performance in London and recommended to Bruce that I be cast. With one difference. The character I had played in London was described as 'young Cooley' in the original play and David wanted that restored. Young I wasn't. Mature actors can get away with playing young characters on stage but not in film and Bruce asked if I would consider playing Mal, the failed academic turned management consultant.

'I'll play anyone,' I said, 'even the women. They're all such good parts.'

The stay in Australia was obviously going to stretch a bit. We let the house in East Sheen and I went into rehearsal for the film.

So, nearly thirty years after my part as the fop in *Long John Silver*, I was back working in an Australian film and playing a character at the other end of the spectrum—an aggressive Aussie who propositions every woman and insults every man at the gathering. It was an extraordinary shoot in many ways and very demanding. The film was shot entirely at night as far as most of us were concerned. (Only the host and his wife and Cooley, the arch lecher, and his girlfriend had substantial outside scenes, apart from when most of the characters went skinny-dipping in the neighbour's pool.) The location was a house at Westleigh, a northerly suburb of Sydney. It seemed an odd choice but the location scouts had decided upon it because it fitted the requirements of David's screenplay. In particular, the swimming pool was in the right place. Also the house was at the end of a cul-de-sac which made it easier from a production point of view.

Don McAlpine was the cinematographer and he and

Beresford had us working within the actual confines of the house which added something indefinable but significant to the film. There is perhaps an artificiality to studio sets that was completely avoided here. There were shots through windows and using different lenses and lighting, all very imaginative stuff. We worked all night and no effort was spared to get the feeling of the piece right. Now this is no easy thing to do when the actors have to apparently get drunk and change in manner and attitude as the story progresses. I recall that John Hargreaves put it to Beresford that he should play one of his drunk scenes—a sequence that involves him offering his wife to me—drunk. We were having lunch during rehearsals when the idea came up.

Beresford was very shrewd. Some directors would squash the idea and leave the actor feeling dissatisfied. Not Bruce. 'OK,' he said, 'let's try it.'

It didn't take much to get John a bit drunk and we rehearsed the scene with him in that condition. He slurred his words, fluffed his lines and missed his cues.

'Doesn't work, does it?' Beresford said.

I doubt that it ever works. The most famous 'drunk' actor in Hollywood movies of the 30s and 40s was Jack Norton. He almost never played anything else *but* a drunk and in real life he was a complete teetotaller!

This episode reminds me of an experience I had with another fine director, Ted Kotcheff, in England some years earlier. *The Strain* was a great telemovie written by Alan Owen, in which I played a crime boss Liverpudlian, just released from gaol. His 2IC had taken over while he was away. That was the strain. My mate Glyn Owen was also in the cast, playing a priest. We rehearsed for a couple of weeks with me trying to perfect the Scouse accent. It was working well although I was perhaps concentrating more on the authenticity of the accent than the character. Eventually Ted, who was a Canadian, said, 'Ray, Ray, forget the accent. Play it Australian.'

I said, 'I can't do that, Ted. He's as Liverpool as John Lennon.'

'Trust me.'

Ted knew that I'd absorbed the Liverpool accent so thoroughly that it had become a sort of overlay to my natural accent and when I dropped it everything worked like a charm. That's the sort of thing a good director can achieve.

Beresford could sense when the actors had the chemistry right and that something spontaneous and good was happening. For example, the scene near the end, after the election result, when the characters had been skinny dipping in the pool. They are drunk, bitterly disappointed with the election result, emotionally over-extended and they tear the Graham Blundell character to shreds for his conservative political beliefs; it was entirely ad-libbed, not scripted at all. And the scene is a highlight of the film.

We worked all night and I remember that we welcomed the sound of the kookaburras at first light. It meant the end of the session. Graham Kennedy and I were staying at the Sebel Town House, way back in the centre of Sydney. We used to ride back utterly exhausted and be expected to sleep all day and be ready for the call late in the afternoon. It was shift work, nothing less, and my biological clock went haywire. I found difficulty in getting to sleep, I was what used to be called 'over-tired'. I suppose there's a medical term for it. The solution I hit on was to have an arrangement with the night porter.

'Do you want it now?' he'd say.

They'd bring a jug of hot milk and I'd pour a double scotch and add it to the milk. That helped to relax me. I'd start writing letters. The tiredness and the alcohol would catch up with me and when I saw the writing running off the page on a slope I knew it was time for bed. I suppose I should have got some sleeping pills but this was more enjoyable. I'd sleep like a log until the call and then go through it all again.

In an arduous and long—I think it was eight weeks—shoot, there are bound to be frictions. I think it was Graham Kennedy's first film and he was a bit uncertain about things. As we were staying at the same place I suggested that we could run through a few scenes together if he'd like. We did that a few times, in his room or mine, and got along very well. On the set we cracked jokes together to keep everything relaxed, when appropriate. I remember that I came up near to the camera in one of his close-up scenes to give him his eye line and I made a few remarks to keep it all light, but Graham had found his feet by then.

'Look, fuck off, Ray,' he said.

Oh, I see, you're on top of it now are you? I thought. I didn't exactly take offence but things were cooler between us after that.

David didn't come to the shoot which was probably just as well. There are enough people with their oars in on a film set, and I imagine he had confidence in Bruce. That was well placed. The film was one of the best I appeared in and I was happy with my work. It was a critical and commercial success and people still speak well of it. It's a tribute to the film's energy and life that even the Americans understood it; I see that it gets a top rating in *Movies on TV* and the critic says, 'Stunning direction, top performances by all; biting script by David Williamson'.

Hard on the heels of this came an approach from Fred Schepisi who was making (I use the word advisedly, he wrote, produced and directed) a film of Tom Keneally's prize-winning novel, *The Chant of Jimmie Blacksmith*. This was really exciting. Two top directors making films based on properties by two of the country's leading writers and wanting my involvement. It appeared that a resurgence of the Australian film industry was underway—*Picnic at Hanging Rock* had been a great success and all the signs were that *The Getting of Wisdom* would be the same. This was the era of direct government funding of films through the Australian Film Commission and the state film corporations which 'topped up' money raised from private investors. The system seemed to work well, certainly better than the notorious 10BA tax concession regime of the 1980s which brought fools and shonks into the business.

It was clearly time to think about the future for myself professionally and for my family. Mirén and Reggie liked Australia and were happy to stay. No problem there. I made some inquiries and discovered that things had gone very quiet in the business back in London. There were certainly no glittering offers to pull me back. The script of *Jimmie Blacksmith* looked like a winner and my supporting part—the brutal racist police Sergeant Farrell—was a challenge. I signed for the role and knew that I had done more than just take on another film job—signing was tantamount to a decision to stay in Australia.

· 22 ·

Settling back in, getting involved

'Ray, have you ever given any serious thought to going into politics?'

Rt Hon Joh Bjelke-Petersen to RB

I kept in touch with Spike Milligan over the years by postcard, Christmas card and the occasional meeting. One year, some time after I returned to Australia he lost my address and he sent a Christmas card addressed as follows:

Ray Barrett
Well known actor and alcoholic
Somewhere near Brisbane[1]

I found this amusing and I've kept the envelope. I acquired a reputation as a drinker. I have been what I would call an enthusiastic social drinker, sometimes *too* enthusiastic, but I have been careful not to mix drinking with working. Actors like Richard Burton and Peter O'Toole have confessed to being drunk while they were filming and to have very little recollection of entire shoots. That is incomprehensible to me. I have had too much to drink on many occasions but where work was concerned I have had a three point rule which I've stuck

[1] A Post Office employee had written in red on the envelope 'try Stradbroke Island'. It found me.

to: be on time, be sober and know your lines.

I've made the mistake, a few times, of having had too good a lunch and not being at my best afterwards. That sort of thing gets noticed and whispered about. It shouldn't happen. But I've never used the drink as a prop, to get me through a scene let alone a picture, as some people have apparently done. For one thing, it doesn't work. For another, it's dangerous. Film sets can be extremely dangerous places where having your judgement impaired by alcohol could be fatal.

I recall shooting scenes for the Hammond Innes story *Golden Soak* on the cliffs of Cornwall. I was supposed to be faking suicide by driving my car off the cliff. The set-up had to show my car rolling down the hill and over the edge, exploding as it hit a rocky ledge, turning over twice and hitting the water 500 feet below. It also had to reveal that I wasn't in the car. The camera behind had to show the car whizzing past me as it took off. They stood me on a rock just beside the wooden ramp the special effects men had constructed, looking straight over the drop.

The weather was foul with a force 12 gale blowing. I could see the unfortunate camera grips standing on ledges sticking out from the cliff at various points. They wore heavy raincoats, had their cameras covered with plastic sheets and were clinging on to their tripods for very life. There were four cameras in action and the shot obviously had to be done right in one go. I was very scared. *I'm going to be blown away here,* I thought. The boot of the car was loaded with explosives. *What if it goes up just when it reaches me?*

It was almost too much for me. I was freezing cold and had to stop myself from shivering, especially when the cameras rolled. There was only one way to look—straight ahead. To look down would have certainly brought on vertigo and who knows what might result. I just had to trust the special effects boys.

The weather abated slightly. Alert the cameras. Ready the explosives. Put Ray on the rock. ACTION!

I heard the car on the ramp behind me and wanted to run but I stood stock still as required. Whoosh, it went past me, seemingly inches from my ear, sailed off the edge, hit the ledge, exploded, turned over twice and hit the water with the cameras capturing the foam and the gurgling disappearance. I'm the first to admit that my first port of call after that experience was the pub. We were all frozen and blue, especially the grips (I could at least shelter in a car until the shot was ready) and I fronted Jimmy Gatward, the director, and prevailed upon him to shout drinks all round. But beforehand? Never![2]

As I've said, while overseas I occasionally had difficulty with weather, equipment and machinery, in Australia I seemed to have trouble with horses. I have never had an affinity with horses. Dogs I like and get along well with, but horses alarm me.[3] My role in *Jimmie Blacksmith* was the first in which I was

---

[2] The classic stunt story in the business is told of the American beefcake actor, Victor Mature. He was filming in Africa and was required to dive into a river and rescue a maiden in distress.

'All you've got to do, Vic,' the director said, 'is see the girl going under. The camera will zoom in on your eyes and catch the emotions—horror, fear, determination.'

'What do you want?' asks Vic. 'Left profile, right profile, or full face?'

The moment to shoot arrived. 'Vic, we're ready to go!'

'No,' said Vic.

'What do you mean "no"?'

'I've been talking to the locals. This river is full of crocodiles. No.'

The director, annoyed and upset over losing a day's shooting at great expense, hurried away to tackle the problem. That night he assured Vic that there were no crocodiles but just to be doubly sure he'd got a hundred people to stand side by side in the river and beat the water with sticks. 'The natives tell me that this is an age-old custom here. Crocs hate noise. There's no chance of one being around for miles upstream or downstream.

'Now, Vic. I'll put four cameras on the scene covering every angle, all with different lenses. It'll be one take. Magnificent and perfectly safe.'

'No.'

'Hell, Vic, I've explained to you. Crocs can't stand noise. Why for Christ sake won't you do it?'

'One of 'em might be deaf.'

[3] My fear of horses stemmed from an experience when I was a boy. My brother Scott and I were holidaying on a farm and took some cattle down to a dam for agistment. We were riding two farm horses which were inseparable and it so happened that the horses came to be on opposite sides of a barbed wire gate. My horse panicked, bolted, tried to knock me off on some low-growing branches, and finally came to a full stop at the fence where it could see its partner on the other side. I was thrown over the fence. Ever since I have been wary of horses and they know it. They give me a look as if to say, 'Here's one and I'll get rid of him smartish.'

called on to ride. Not only ride but 'gallop into the blacks' camp'. Reading the word 'gallop' in the script was the beginning of sleepless nights for me. As I hadn't been on a horse since I was a kid, I took a few riding lessons before the shoot began to get the hang of it. That was no problem but the horse I was assigned in the film was a gigantic stubborn brute and it was all I could do to get it to move forward, let alone perform any other manoeuvre. One scene required me to enter the blacks' camp at a gallop and to jump the horse over a campfire. The location was up near Dungog, somewhat to the east of where the real action with the Governor brothers had taken place, but very rough country. The camp was very realistically arranged with shanties, fires, snake skins hanging from branches, kids running about and dogs barking.

I hoisted myself up onto the horse and waited for Fred Schepisi's direction. I knew that I had to do it and was just determined to cling on. With any luck it would be one take and the agony would be over.

'Action, Ray!'

As per my lessons, I kicked the horse's flanks. It reared. I kicked again. Same result. I dropped the reins and clung to its neck for dear life.

'Cut!' from Fred.

'He's a stunt horse,' the wrangler said. 'And he's cued. Kick him both sides and that's his cue to rear. Kick right side and he falls over on his left side, kick him on the left and he falls to the right.'

'Why the hell couldn't they get one that's cued to go straight ahead when you kick him?' I asked.

I regret to say that the wrangler got on the beast and beat it unmercifully. But there was no chance it would perform and that was a wrap for the day. I wasn't looking forward to the next day's attempt at doing the scene but when I turned up I found Fred Schepisi sitting down on a tree stump, scribbling on his script.

'What's that you're writing?' I said.

'Hang on and I'll show you.'

He handed me the script and I saw that he'd changed 'Sergeant Farrell gallops up, leaps his horse over the fire and rides into the blacks' camp' to 'the lazy Sergeant Farrell slowly walks his horse into the blacks' camp'.

'Fred,' I said. 'You've got the character!'

Fred looked up at me with a knowing smile. I could have kissed him.

While on the subject of horses, I fell foul of them again when working on the mini-series *Tusitala* on location in Western Samoa. Peter Yeldham wrote the script and I had the wonderful part of Harry Moors, an American who becomes a mover and shaker in Samoan politics in the late nineteenth century. The story was factually based around episodes in the life of Robert Louis Stevenson. Angela Punch MacGregor was in it and John McKennery and it was a good piece of work. But, given the period, horses were the go. In one scene three of us had to ride down a shallow river up close to a sizeable and very loud waterfall. Now that's not the kind of thing a horse does every day or cares to do. My horse wanted to get away from it and I wanted to go with him. There were outcrops of rocks and tree stumps which did not fill me with confidence. I managed to hold the horse there as long as necessary but it wasn't easy.

Next thing, the director wanted us to ride across a very narrow bridge. Not much water in the stream but quite a long drop to rocks below and a rocky path on the approach and leading upwards on the other side of the bridge. I didn't know whether the horse had been trained to pick his way among rocks and across narrow bridges and no-one could tell me. I baulked at that and the wrangler backed me up. 'Don't do it,' he said.

It was going to be a long shot anyway, so I convinced the director to put the tropical suit on the wrangler and let him do it. Of course it worked out perfectly and the production budget finished in better shape than if it had had to cope with a massive compensation claim for one mangled actor.

In fact the very last shot I was in involved a horse again. I had to ride out through a gate, meet up with John and Angela and the three of us had to ride down the road. There was a barbed wire fence on the approach and I was sure the bloody horse was going to pick this moment to shy or bolt. I could feel the barbs ripping into me. But we got through it and finished up three hundred yards down the road. I waited for the magic word 'cut', waited some more until I was told it was a print and then I was straight down off that horse. I wasn't even going to ride it back. I handed the reins to the wrangler.

'Here, mate,' I said, 'your horse I believe.'

I was in the car, stripping off the incredibly hot clothes—riding coat, wing collar and all, God knows how they stood it—and was on my way to a shower and the airport before they could turn round. I hope I never have to ride a horse again but, acting being the kind of business it is, I probably will.

I'm jumping around—I did *Golden Soak* with Elizabeth Alexander, a fine actress, necessitating a week's work back in England in 1977 and *Tusitala* in 1984. I was in the swim, but it was *Jimmie Blacksmith* that cemented the decision to stay in Australia. It was a most interesting shoot with Fred Schepisi doing very innovative things with lenses and getting terrific performances from the two Aboriginals, Tommy Lewis, who had never acted before, and Freddy Reynolds, who was straight from the bush, raw and extroverted and bit of a handful off the set, turned in one of the best performances in the film. Tom Keneally had a cameo part as a shearers' cook and a whole cavalcade of Australian actors appeared—Jack Thompson, Bryan Brown, Ruth Cracknell, Liddy Clark, Arthur Dignam, Peter Carroll. I won the Australian Film Institute award for the best supporting actor in 1978 which was bound to lead to further work.

I was on the books of June Cann, one of the leading theatrical agents in Sydney, and the future looked promising. I did commercials for a clutch of retirement villages, a liquor outlet and other products. All very remunerative. Being me, as soon as I was sure I was staying, I had to buy a house and soon after a boat.

Running true to form, I bought an old 'Queenslander' in Ascot, not far from the river, and worked on it myself until it was comfortable. The boat was *Odette*, a twenty-seven foot sloop designed by Glen Schwarbrick of Western Australia. She was beautifully laid out with six feet three inches headroom and she sailed like a dream. I'd had my eye on her for a while but it took time for the money from the sale of the stables house to come through. I had to shoot over to New Zealand to do a commercial—all filmed at sea by the way, quite by coincidence—and I was worried that I'd miss out on *Odette.*

'For God's sake don't sell her out from under me,' I told the owner and I was dwelling on getting a phone call from Mirén while I was away to tell me that the money was available. When it was, I went straight down and paid cash for the boat, about $23,000 from memory.

My second son Jonathan (Jono) was born in 1978 and he, Mirén, Reggie and I did a lot of cruising in the boat, having a wonderful time. I had to sell her later when I went to Spain for a year and didn't want her to be lying idle. She later won the Brisbane to Gladstone race, that's how good a boat she was.

All in all, everything seemed very settled. At that time all the states had formed their own film corporations and what with the tax breaks and the availability of actors who had come back from overseas, there was a lot going on in the Australian film industry, a resurgence. Various people were interested in getting a film corporation going in Queensland and Joh Bjelke-Petersen, the Premier, had made this one of his election promises. Nothing seemed to be happening, but I was ignorant of this (and knew nothing of the Premier) when I was invited to a lunch meeting at the Breakfast Creek Hotel. That was a place I did know, one of the great Brisbane watering holes. It was said that if you were trying to find an old friend in Brisbane all you had to do was go to the Breakfast Creek and, if you could stand up long enough, you'd find him.

The point of the lunch soon became apparent—the film corporation was the topic. Mike Williams, a film producer, seemed to be the prime mover They put it to me that I should talk to Joh, remind him of his promise and see if he could be persuaded to get things moving. The thinking was that the Premier, who had been deaf to their entreaties, might listen to the local boy who had achieved some international recognition. At the very least he might give some hint of his true intentions.

Someone got Joh's secretary on the blower and teed up a meeting for the following day. I rolled up and Allan Callaghan, Joh's press secretary, was there and Sid Schubert, the Attorney General. After the introductions I said, 'Mr Premier, I've been informed that you promised to get behind the Queensland film industry in your last election campaign and nothing's been done. I'm here as spokesman for some concerned film people and to ask what your intentions are.'

Joh seemed to be a little taken aback by this straightforwardness and his reaction was to lay the blame on his off-siders. 'How far have we got with this? Why haven't I been informed?' Blank looks all around. He said it was a serious matter that shouldn't be neglected and that he was personally strongly in favour. To my great surprise, he then asked me if I would be willing to stay in Queensland and act in an advisory capacity to the Corporation when it was up and running. I said I would and the meeting wound up very cordially. The Premier presented me with a lovely little velvet covered box containing a set of gold cufflinks with the state's coat of arms enamelled on them and inscribed 'with the compliments of the Premier of Queensland, Joh Bjelke-Petersen'. The photographer was called in.

I said, 'Mr Premier this is a bit premature. I haven't done anything yet.'

'You will, Ray, you will,' he said.

Lo and behold, in the *Courier Mail* the next day: JOH PROMISES TO GET BEHIND QUEENSLAND FILM INDUSTRY. The article went on to say that the Premier had asked me to stay in Queensland and work in an advisory capacity.

I took the matter seriously and went around speaking at business lunches and political gatherings on both sides and having meetings with Arts bureaucrats and the like, arguing the case for south Queensland as the ideal place for major Australian film studios. I believed firmly in what I said.

The area had the right weather, abundant sunshine, the sea, the mountains and the jungle all within a fifty mile radius. I got a certain gentleman who owned a lot of land near Coomera, roughly the site of the present studios, to agree to give some land for the project in the form of a perpetual lease. The next step was to get the government to kick in some up-front money to get the thing started. Everything seemed to stall at that point. I was drawn into other things and although it remained a hobby horse of mine, the idea appeared to fizzle.

The next thing I heard, some two years down the track, was that Dino De Laurentiis had got Joh's ear and a sizeable amount of money was available to establish the studios at Coomera, very near where Russell Hinze had his property. The name 'Hollywood on the Gold Coast', which I believe I coined, was being bandied about and building got underway. De Laurentiis, notorious around the world for his financial schemes connected with films and whom I've heard called a professional bankrupt, floated a company on the Australian stock market and raised a large capital. After ten months the company announced a book loss of $22 million. Almost half of the company was owned by its American arm and when that got into trouble De Laurentiis abandoned the Australian operation and sold out to Warners and Village Roadshow.

The Queensland Film Corporation was formed with Allan Callaghan, the former press secretary, as its chairman and Mike Williams on the board along with accountants and lawyers friendly to the National Party. I heard no more of my advisory role and perhaps just as well because eventually Allan Callaghan and his wife were convicted of fiddling the books and were sent to gaol.

Joh Bjelke-Petersen had no real interest in films or understanding of what was involved in making them. It so happened that I did the narration some time later for a documentary film on the political life of Joh. Everyone concerned was invited to a showing of the film. I sat next to Joh and I saw that there were tears in his eyes.

'Isn't it wonderful?' he said. 'Isn't it wonderful?'

My only other meeting with Joh was at the premiere of *Touch and Go*, a film written by Peter Yeldham and partly financed by the QFC. At the time the Premier and Russell Hinze, who was known as the Minister for Everything, were having a behind-the-scenes struggle over the leadership of the National Party. There was a party afterwards and Joh came up to me, evidently having long forgotten his offer of an advisory role but aware that I'd addressed a lot of meetings pushing for the QFC.

'Ray,' he said, 'have you ever given any serious thought to going into politics?'

'Forgive me, Joh,' I said. 'No offence meant, but I don't think at my age . . .'

'Well, please give it some very serious thought,' he said in sincere and confidential tones, 'because I could personally guarantee you the Gold Coast seat.'

That was the seat held by Russell Hinze. Peter Yeldham was standing right next to me and has verified the story.

This seems an appropriate point to mention my relationship with two fine writers—Peter Yeldham and Mike Noonan. On a recent visit, Peter reminded me of our first contacts—back in 1956 when he directed Lyndall Barbour, John Bushelle, Walter Sullivan and me in a radio show. With due modesty he remarked that he wasn't sure whether he was directing the actors or we were directing him. He and his wife Marge left for England at the end of that year and we agreed to meet in the old country. When I was settled I hunted out his number, rang him, told him my address and asked where he was.

'If you go round the corner from where you are and walk about two hundred yards past the Paris Pulman Cinema, that's where we are.' In a city of almost ten million people, we'd ended up almost next door. One of my first jobs in television was in a crime series written by Peter and I later played in his *Reunion Day*. As I've mentioned, this had consequences for me in terms of my letter to the *Sydney Morning Herald* and my securing the role of Peter Thornton.

Peter has reminded me further that we played golf together in England and that my daughter Suellen and his son Perry considered themselves briefly engaged at the age of eight until they had a fight and called it off. We went to Paris for a mad weekend when the Algerian crisis was at its height and the word was that the paratroopers were hell bent on invading and overthrowing De Gaulle. We had coffee in a Champs Elysees cafe and deciphered a headline that read: PARIS IS SURROUNDED. CIVIL WAR IMMINENT. We set off for Calais almost immediately in Peter's old Merc and were stopped and searched about eight times between Paris and the port.

Peter and I returned to Australia at about the same time having been absent for about the same period and after achieving much the same measure of success. I worked on a number of Peter's scripts subsequently—*Run from the Morning, Golden Soak, The Timeless Land, Sporting Chance, Tusitala.*

Peter is a great writer of dialogue and I believe that it is a plus for a writer who has the talent to conceive and really *know* his character also to know the actor playing the part. The dialogue seems to fall naturally into place. I have never had any trouble learning Peter's dialogue and everything of his I've played in has been a success. As Peter has said in a recent note to me, 'It was a lot of different roles—a lot of words for you to learn and me to write, but always a lot of fun to work together.'

Like Peter Yeldham and myself, Mike Noonan, a Kiwi, was blooded in the hectic days of Sydney radio. He wrote the comedy Western *Brand of Justice* in which I appeared, and many other plays and serials. He went to England in 1957 and stayed for twenty years. Since returning to Australia he has had many successes and I have been associated with his work on the Dunk Island beachcomber E. J. Banfield. His novel about Banfield, *A Different Drummer*, he adapted for the stage and I played the role in a Royal Queensland Theatre production in 1988. Mike and I cherish the hope that we may one day do the play on the beach at Dunk Island with special lighting effects turning Banfield into a wraith appearing through the coconut palms voicing his poetic descriptions of the tropical scene. That would really be something.

· 23 ·

Goodbye Paradise *and after*

Landlady: Five more bills came for you, *and* two final notices. I put them under your door.
Stacey: Thank you. Why don't we have an affair? While I'm still a free man.
Landlady: Not while your room's in that condition.
Bob Ellis and Denny Lawrence, *Goodbye Paradise* (1982)

Just as the best part I ever had in a television series, Peter Thornton in *Troubleshooters,* was written for me, so it was with my best film role—that of ex-Deputy Commissioner in the Queensland police force turned exposé writer, Michael Stacey. Bob Ellis, one of the most talented film writers and directors in Australia, conceived the part with me in mind. He and co-writer Denny Lawrence and I went to the Gold Coast, rented a huge unit, and stayed for a couple of weeks soaking up the atmosphere, investigating the high and low life, the day and night life, talking to journos and generally getting the feel of the place. The writers were observing me I now realise, and crafting dialogue and a script that depicted me as I was at that time.

I remember being in a beer garden in Surfers some time after this recce, and Bob and his wife Ann Brooksbank approaching me and laying the final draft of the script almost reverently down on the table in front of me.

'Read that,' Bob said.

I was looking forward to reading it, but I find it impossible to read with people watching me. They say that all any writer wants is to have someone standing by the typewriter, ripping the pages out and saying, 'Brilliant! Superb!' Well, it was something like that they were asking of me and my eye just froze after a few lines and I couldn't do it. They sat there waiting for me to react, laugh in the right places and so on. Every time I looked up there were these four eyes burning into me and I wanted to tell them to go away. But when I did manage to read the script under more relaxed circumstances, I knew it was an exceptional piece of work and the basis for a very good film indeed.

So it proved. Most of the film is tight, funny and dramatic with fine performances from all the supporting cast. Robyn Nevin was wonderful to work with and I greatly enjoyed the scenes with her, especially where we sang 'Bye Bye Blackbird' and raked over the dying embers of our relationship. John Seale, the cinematographer, has made some distinguished pictures since and Peter Best, who did the music, very important for a moody film like this, is recognised as one of the top men in the business.

Not everyone is aware that films are shot out of sequence, the order being determined by availability of actors, the weather and other factors. Consequently, it's hard for an actor to tell how the whole thing is shaping. In his book *The Avocado Plantation*, David Stratton praises the film as 'a scathing satire of politics in the Sunshine state. With a very funny narration, in the best Raymond Chandler tradition . . .' He is flattering about my performance and Robyn's and rightly draws attention to 'superb cameos from John Clayton, Robert (Tex) Morton, Lex Marinos, Kris McQuade, Paul Chubb and Carole Skinner'.

The shoot was eight weeks I believe, and an arduous one for me because I was in every scene. But there were no problems. I felt comfortable on the close-to-home turf, and in many scenes—such as one where, supposedly hungover, I was transported rapidly across the water—I was conscious of just how well the filming was being done.

Happily, there were no horses, and just that last scene with Somare the brilliantly named dog. I've never had any trouble acting with dogs. Great fun.

Carl Schultz, the director, who later had such a great success with *Careful, he might hear you*, a very different kind of film, came up to the magnificent penthouse they had given me. He seemed to be a bit nervous about the rumbustiousness projected by Barrett, Ellis and Lawrence. He had obviously got wind of our few weeks of pre-writing carousing. He is a very quiet and sensitive soul and I sensed his concern. I calmed him down and assured him that there would be no drinking during the entire shoot, not from me anyway. I had too big a responsibility. The script was wonderful. It was written for me and I would have to be the biggest idiot in the world to blow this one.

'I won't have a drink for the whole of the shoot,' I said.

And I didn't. Even when we were sitting around relaxing and watching rushes.

Like all good directors, Carl Schultz was willing to listen to an actor when he had a contribution to make. There was a scene in which I had to be thoroughly beaten up and when I saw the rushes I knew that it hadn't come off. Trying to save money, the producers had hired locals who weren't real stuntmen and their punches to the jaw didn't connect, neither did their boots to the ribs. You could actually see daylight between fist and boot and body. Not good enough. I suggested to Carl that this scene would have to be shot again and that I might be able to help the 'stuntmen' do a better job. Carl agreed.

We had a rehearsal before the re-shoot and I schooled them a little in how to land a punch that connected but had no real force (pulled by them, turned away from by me), and how a boot to the body had to connect but not forcibly and, with luck, to a meaty rather than a bony part of the anatomy.

'I'll fall and I'll roll,' I said. 'Don't worry about that. I've done it a million times. Just connect with the skin but try not to bloody break my jaw or my ribs.'

I ended up with a few sore spots but no real damage. On film, it looked brutal.

I won the AFI best actor award for *Goodbye Paradise,* and on the professional front things had never looked better.

On a personal level, things were coming apart. When I got back from the *Goodbye Paradise* shoot it was clear all was not well. Anyone who has ever been through it knows the signs—the silences, awkwardnesses, subterfuges. It was not difficult to see that something was radically wrong. There were threats, confrontations, recriminations and eventually Mirén left me. On reflection, trying to put things into context, one of my worst memories is of a young Reggie lying on his top bunk saying, 'You don't really want us to go do you Dad?'

At the time I was stunned by this question, but more or less fobbed it off with a half laugh saying, 'Of course I don't want you to leave. Whatever gave you that idea?' I was still unaware of what was happening.

The next day I was shocked to discover that her departure had apparently been planned for some time. I awoke one morning to find Reggie had gone to school and there was no sign of Mirén or Jonathan. I went downstairs (our house was an old Queenslander up on stumps) to see if the car had gone only to find Mirén and Jono plus packed bags waiting under the house for a car to collect them. I cannot describe the sick empty feeling in my stomach. That moment is etched in my memory forever. Was this really finality? Could this really be happening? On reflection I am grateful that Mirén waited until I finished making the film before dropping the bombshell. I certainly did not want my family to break up, but events moved very quickly and were largely out of my hands.

This was a decidedly low period in my life. About the only positive thing that could be said about it was that I continued to have full access to Reggie and Jonathan, never pressed for any formalisation of the arrangement, and the very good relationship we enjoy today suggests that this was the right approach. Still, the breakup shook me and I found my major comfort in whisky. I did comparatively little work around that time.

Part of the stress was financial. It took three years for the property arrangements to be finally agreed, during which time I paid temporary support for Mirén and for the boys which was fixed by the Family Law Court at a level that I could ill afford. It was crippling. Whilst I was willing to give Mirén the Ascot house unencumbered (I had cashed in some insurance to pay out the mortgage to put it in that condition), I wanted to keep my boat 'Odette', my house in Spain and some land we owned in Avalon, Sydney. Naturally I was happy to contribute child support at whatever level the court decided.

At the end of the day we settled before any serious argument. I gave Mirén the Ascot house and the maintenance I had been paying for her discontinued. I was allowed to keep my boat, the Spanish house and the land in Sydney. I continued to pay maintenance only for the children. This greatly reduced my financial burden although my savings had been almost totally depleted.

I know I am not easy to live with immediately after a film shoot, but there were rights and wrongs on both sides. The separation came totally unexpected and for more than two years I hoped in vain for a reconciliation. As I've said, my main concern was that the children weren't affected. I continued throughout to pick Reggie up and take him to football training and Mirén and I attended matches together, more or less cordially. But underneath the surface, when I didn't have to keep up appearances, I was in bad shape and it was Gaye O'Brien, now my wife, who helped me to pull myself together.

I'd met Gaye in Sydney where she was working as a sales representative for Roussell, the pharmaceutical company. Gaye was a keen sailor, a very good forward hand, very athletic and positive in everything she did. She was a great cook and threw wonderful parties. We'd got along very well and June Cann, my agent, sort of recruited Gaye to help me straighten myself out. I was hitting the scotch pretty hard, spending too much time on my own, brooding and letting my friends and interests slip. Gaye took me down to Sydney and I stayed with her in her house at North Narrabeen. I took up sailing again, met up with some old friends and made some new ones. I got off the scotch—I haven't drunk spirits for ten years—and sorted myself out.

After a time it became clear that Gaye and I could make a go of it. In 1984 she sold her house in Sydney and got a transfer to Brisbane with Roussell. In October 1986, when all the dust had settled, we were married. A great day. The wedding party and about 50 guests went to Horseshoe Bay at Peel Island, in Moreton Bay, aboard Tommy Tickle's motor cruiser, the *Mascarin III*. We had a tremendous party with a couple of hundred people present at the reception at the Little Ship Club, Dunwich on North Stradbroke Island, the scene of my youthful adventures with Bonty Dixon and Jackie Borey and aboard the old *Countess*.

Of course we spent a good bit of time aboard *Odette*, cruising the Bay islands and down to the Gold Coast and up to Bribie. In the same year Gaye became my agent and manager and acted in that capacity for four years, during which she proved to be a formidable negotiator and a protective ally. In short an extremely competent business woman.

I took Gaye to Spain and she loved the island. One of the difficulties in a new relationship is whether old friends can adjust to the change. Gaye got on extremely well with people on the island, especially Sylvia Madders from my earliest days there and new friends like John and Sylvia Payne. One day Sylvia Madders took me aside and said to me, with a knowing look, 'I'm very happy for you, Ray.'

Third time lucky, you might say.

· 24 ·

The ups

'Wolf Blass, grey label. It gets better and better. The man's a genius, a bloody genius . . .'

David Williamson *Brilliant Lies*

Not long after I got back to Australia I was invited, quite out of the blue, to take over the breakfast program on radio 4KQ for three weeks while the regular man took his holidays. This was the very job I'd held so many years before. I didn't exactly fancy getting up at 5 am day after day, but I was intrigued by the prospect. For a good many years in Britain I'd taken over Pete Murray's program on the BBC while he went on his annual holidays. This was a plum job and I always enjoyed it. Coincidentally Pete's program and the show on 4KQ had the same name—'Family Favourites'.

It struck me that it would be a good idea to have Pete Murray as my first guest so I arranged for 4KQ to ring him at the BBC and I went in on a Wednesday evening to record the interview. Of course it was a two-way process and the BBC put little Brisbane radio 4KQ straight on the air—quite a coup.

Pete Murray said, 'Ray, you'll never guess who I've got in here with me as my first guest. An old mate of yours, Danny La Rue.'

So we had a three-way conversation and I played the tape on 4KQ the next day—a big scoop for the station. The advertising people were bemoaning the fact that it wasn't in the ratings period because their listening audience had shot up. I invited people to phone in and talk on the air and old friends came out of the woodwork.

'Remember me, Ray? George Whitty. Remember when we used go camping and cook snags in the bush?'

And we'd yarn away.

'Remember me, Ray? I used to play on your Dad's tennis court.'

Sometimes it was hard to squeeze a record in between all the people who wanted to have a chat and recall the good old days. Harry Secombe happened to be in Australia doing a show and so I got him on the blower and he was vastly entertaining as ever. Of course the technology had changed absolutely since my time in Australian radio. The turntables had gone, replaced by huge tape decks and racks of tapes and monitors that completely bewildered me. They gave me an operator to run all that while I broadcast from the other side of the console and he handed me the copy. I enjoyed it all. It was great nostalgic fun and an interesting way of fitting back into life in Brisbane. The early starts were a trial though.

At around the same time an old friend from the radio days named Andy Stevens got in touch and inveigled me into performing at the annual show he did at Tattersalls Club in Brisbane. I'd worked with him in radio doing talent quests in the country towns which were partly designed to recruit advertisers for the station. Andy was by way of being a 'colourful racing identity', very keen on the turf and all its atmospherics. I got up to sing a few songs and tell a few jokes and I spotted Mr Charles Carson in the audience.

I was quite taken aback. Here was Mr Carson, who must have been in his eighties by now, my former mentor and a gentleman to the core, and here am I, thirty years later, putting across some slightly blue material. I was rather embarrassed. I could imagine him thinking, *There's young Ray Barrett and hasn't he gone down the drain.* But I recovered and took the opportunity to pay him a tribute. I said something like, 'There's a certain person in the audience who gave me encouragement when I was fifteen or sixteen. He was the person who had faith in me, nurtured me in the early years and I doubt I'd have done as well as I have without him. I'm delighted to have this opportunity to thank him in front of you all. Thank you, Mr Carson.'

He was gracious as you'd expect. We often look back and see where someone has been kind and helpful and don't get the chance to tell them so. I was glad I'd been given the opportunity.

I did some worthwhile work on television in the eighties, in particular the mini-series *Waterfront, The Timeless Land, The Last Bastion, Tusitala* and *The Challenge.* In the series *Sporting Chance,* I played Robbo, a disenchanted journalist who hires Liddy Clark as his assistant. There was good chemistry between us and we shared a common sense of humour which I believe translated well to the screen. The stories tackled tricky subjects such as the gay football coach, the failed male tennis player latching on to the rising female star and the lady golfer with problems. The guest actors were good and the show was lapped up by sports lovers who could handle some intelligent presentation of the material. I thought it had the potential to run for years and said so, but the ABC only made six episodes for reasons I've never understood. I suggested we do one on the America's Cup. There were at least three 12 metre yachts in Sydney we could call on, but the producer was not interested. Look what happened.

During the 80s I made nine films. I enjoyed my part in *The Empty Beach* although it wasn't a huge success. *Rebel,* due to disastrous editing, was made to look like a promotional video for one of Debbie Byrne's albums. For some reason I was cast in a batch of films dealing with the supernatural or the extraterrestrial—*Frenchman's Farm, Contagion, As Time Goes By.*

Working on *Blood Oath* (incidentally at the Coomera studios) was very valuable in a number of ways. I played the president of the court sitting in judgement in 1945 on Vice-Admiral Baron Takahashi and others, accused of war crimes on Ambon Island. I think it was the first time I became aware of how interesting and involving it could be to play older, more mature characters. The part was very well written by Denis Whitburn and Brian Williams and I had quite long passages to deliver in the summing up and the sentencing. We rehearsed it pretty thoroughly and had useful discussions between the actors and writers and Stephen Wallace, the director. In the middle of this process someone located a man who had actually officiated at the Ambon trial. He was well into his eighties and had gone through law school with the man I was playing. He was nearby, retired to the Gold Coast, and I was able to sit with him and talk quietly about the experience.

After a run-through of the sentencing speech, Stephen Wallace commented that he had seen things in my delivery he hadn't thought of before. I believe that I had injected little things—mannerisms, reactions, emotions—that I had picked up from this charming old gentleman. Stephen made sure he caught them in the filming. Over the years Australian film crews in all departments have proved to be the equal of, if not better than, any in the world. Whilst I was making *On our Selection* in Australia in 1994, Leo McKern (who played the leading role) remarked on this. While filming Randy Kleiser's remake of *Blue Lagoon* in Fiji (an American production) the makers chose a wholly Australian crew. While clearly showing the Americans how good they were Leo found the same excellence in all Australian productions on which he worked, such as *Travelling North*. McKern has worked with top directors like Fred Zinnemann and David Lean but found no teams better than those in his home country. The image of the easy-going Aussie drops from the mind when watching the expertise, enthusiasm and speed of an Australian unit crew.

Working with David Williamson has been one of the great pleasures of my acting career. My part in *Sons of Cain*, of course, was a doddle. All I had to do was perform once for the cameras and my stuff was shown on television sets around the theatre as the play developed. I would describe David as a chronicler of the Australian way of life and the Australian way of thinking. I admire the way he has the guts to tackle any topic, expose things, hit the raw nerves. He shocks people into seeing themselves and into admitting that yes, I've done that, I'm like that. That's one of the major functions of a playwright.

The part of the father in *Brilliant Lies* is perhaps the best drawn I've ever had on the stage. It came about in an odd way, as good things often do. At a time when I was not busy I was sent a David Williamson script by the Queensland Theatre Company. The character they wanted me to play only appeared right at the end, just two scenes where he was dying of cancer. He sat in his beloved garden and pointed out the lovely birds, saying things like, 'If you plant the right trees the birds will come back.' It was beautifully written, very easy to play, quite funny and sympathetic. *Well, why not?* I thought. *I can just pop in on the last act, get all the tears and thank you very much.* I wouldn't have to expend myself too much and, as the play was scheduled to tour, I thought I could just drift around Australia and catch up some old friends. So I said yes.

The next script I saw was entirely different and involved a great deal more work. David told me that, after he heard I'd accepted the part, he got to thinking and re-writing my role and ended up with a completely different play. My character was now the father in a dysfunctional family, a boozer and womaniser and a child molester as it turns out. In discussion with David and the director Aubrey Mellor we evolved the idea of playing the character as a complete innocent. Avoiding the flasher in the park by the swings stereotype altogether and having him utterly unaware of what he's done, indeed incredulous that *anyone* could do such things until the very end of the play when he finally realises the harm he's done and breaks down. This interpretation gave the character great depth and made it a very satisfying and subtle role to play.

As always with Williamson, there was a good deal of humour and I had the tremendous boost of getting a great laugh from the audience on my very first speech. The situation was that the reluctant children are cajoled into attending the birthday party of their monster of a father. One of the daughters tells the other to buy a cask of red wine. She's got a couple of Wolf Blass bottles to decant it into and the old man won't know the difference because his palate's long been shot. The audience takes this on board.

I make my first appearance sitting at a table with a Wolf Blass bottle in front of me, tipping down a glass and saying, 'Ah, Wolf Blass. Grey label. It gets better and better. The man's a genius, a bloody genius. He's done more for the Australian wine industry than any other man. Bloody genius . . .'

Of course the audience goes up because they know it's chateau cardboard. We toured the play all over Australia—Brisbane, Melbourne, Adelaide, Hobart, Sydney, Canberra—for nine months which I found rather taxing. But it was a great success and I asked David when next I saw him, 'When are we going to London?'

My real success in the eighties though, was my relationship with Gaye and with my children. Gaye had no hesitation in selling her lovely house in Sydney and making the move to Brisbane. After the divorce and settlement I was literally flat broke, holding on to my boat, the house in Spain and some land in Sydney, but with no cash reserves and little coming in. Gaye provided not only an emotional foundation for me but a financial one as well, and it was her money that bought the house on Stradbroke Island and provided the base from which we put things back together.

We took a cruise to Stradbroke, decided that it was where we wanted to live and found a house for sale going at a reasonable price. It was the only one we looked at, a very pleasant brick house, only two hundred yards from the water with a spot to moor *Odette*. Gaye could work in Brisbane and commute and it was a blissful existence. We also got involved in an environmental struggle. Vast amounts of fresh water are held in reservoirs under the sand islands and the Redland Shire Council wanted to pipe the water from Stradbroke to the mainland. Along with some of the other residents we formed the Water Watch Committee to oppose this plan. No one quite knows the source of the water and the mechanisms that keep it trapped, but many experts believed that to tap it could put the existence of the islands in jeopardy by altering the balance of the natural forces involved.

Hundreds of people attended the first meeting we held in the little hall on the island, but things had gone too far to be stopped. The engineers had put the spears in and the pipelines were already being laid. The politicians took no notice of us beyond promising to monitor the water flow and keep it to within safe levels. Whether they have or not, I don't know.

Reggie and Jonathan were often on the boat, as I've said, and on the island. We remained close. I treasure a memory of watching Reggie play Australian football. Mirén and I were barracking and cheering him on in typical parental fashion and the moment arrived when the ball was close, no opponents in sight and he had a clear line to the goal.

'Go, Reggie, go!'

But he was too busy enjoying the nice day and waving to his excited parents to do anything about it. Some other kid came up and booted the goal. Didn't bother Reggie. I asked him another time about how the match had gone the previous day.

'Pretty good, Dad,' he said. 'We came second.' He has the competitive spirit in perspective, has Reggie.

· 25 ·

The downs

'It's only a few scenes, but it's a wonderful character and it'll be a . . . good shop window for you.'

Common producer's 'softener' justifying
a poor rate of pay to an actor

It pains me to say it, but management attitudes to actors in Australia haven't changed nearly as much as they should have since the time they took the front of house dressing down at the Elizabethan Theatre. Ask any actor at any level, and he or she will have stories of humiliation and disregard that are seldom heard by the public. This is not to say that actors are easy people to deal and work with. By nature, training and experience, actors are volatile and moody, often suspicious, sometimes erratic in behaviour. But without us the show cannot go on; it's a pity that often, those putting on the show consider the actors' needs last.

As a small example, I made myself unpopular early on in the five week rehearsal period in Brisbane for *Brilliant Lies*.

'When,' I asked, 'are the understudies going to rehearse?'

'What understudies?' was the response. 'There are no understudies.'

The management was perfectly happy to take a play on tour for nine months without a single understudy for any part. I suggested that they were taking a risk. I was thinking about the sorts of experiences I'd actually had—people falling ill with screaming dysentery or being hurt in an accident. If this happened a performance or a string of performances might have to be cancelled. The response was a slap on the shoulder and a 'She'll be right, Ray.' This penny-pinching showed no regard for the actors; in the course of that tour several people had to go on stage when they really weren't well enough to do so and one performance was cancelled on this account.

Another problem, in both the theatre and the film industry, is the presence of people who, quite frankly, are incompetent, dishonest or both. The results can be disastrous as they were with *The Sunshine Boys*. By the end of the eighties I realised how long it had been since I'd done anything on the stage in Australia (*Sons of Cain* not really counting as I've said), and I began to look around for something that would take me back to the theatre. *The Sunshine Boys* is a very funny Neil Simon play about two old Jewish vaudevilleans who argue all the time, and insist on communicating through another party. They are persuaded to get together to do a television special and there are lots of good one-liners and nostalgic business. George Burns and Walter Matthau had appeared in a very successful 1975 film version. It appealed to me and I took the part when it was offered, even though I had been offered work in two films due to go into production at about that time. One was David Parker and Nadia Tass' *Ricky and Pete*, and the other I forget. So I made a considerable professional investment in the play.

Spike Milligan had originally been intended for the other part but he withdrew for reasons I'm not sure of. Perhaps he or his agent got wind that all was not right with the production. The producer was Patrick O'Neill. He asked me if I could wait until Eddie Bracken, who was then appearing in *Sugar Babies* on the Gold Coast, became available. Now I'd seen and admired Eddie Bracken in Hollywood movies of the forties, things like *Life with Henry*, *Happy Go Lucky*, *The Fleet's In* and many others. He was a first-rate light comedian and dancer and he'd played in *The Sunshine Boys* on Broadway. I was keen to work with him and I agreed to wait.

We rehearsed during the day while he worked in the show at night and then went into a full rehearsal period of five weeks before taking the show to Perth. We did five or six weeks there, admittedly to not very good houses. I wasn't too concerned because my main intention was to appear in Melbourne and Sydney and gauge the reaction there. I had a contract for five months at good rates. We got to Adelaide, performed several times and one night were asked to remain on stage by a man who was a business associate of O'Neill's. He announced that we were closing on account of the poor houses. We discovered that our cheques for the whole of the season had bounced. Furthermore, O'Neill could not be found.

In a properly regulated environment this would not be a complete financial disaster for the players because producers would have lodged a bond with Actors Equity guaranteeing them some remuneration, something like severance pay, if the producer defaulted. No such bond had been lodged. Shocking negligence on the part of the union. The financial loss was considerable for me, given that I'd turned down the two films, and the professional damage was difficult to swallow. The financial mismanagement and dishonesty is never properly revealed and the word goes around that the show was a failure, nothing more. In any such failure the performers are at the sharp end and their reputations slip a notch or several notches. Equity's only response was to say that they would greylist the producer. From experience this should properly be called a blacklist, such crooks have a way of bobbing up again.

I have no objection to actors from overseas working in Australian films. Indeed I think it should be encouraged as anything else leads to insularity and provincialism. I have been happy to play support roles in Australian productions to actors like James Mason and William Holden and expect to do so in the future. *But* I bitterly resent being treated as a second-class citizen in this context and it happens all too often. I vividly recall reporting for work at the Gold Coast studios in a film which is better forgotten. I had worked in *Blood Oath* at the same place so I knew the lie of the land. I arrived with two other Australian actors and we were received by a very young second assistant, quite possibly on his first ever job.

'Mr Barrett, would you please go straight to wardrobe and makeup.'

I said, 'Yes, I will, but could you show me my dressing room please. I'd like to leave my bag and things there. I'll collect the costume and change in the dressing room and then go to makeup. Right?'

'You don't have a dressing room.'

'Where do you expect me to leave my things? Where do you expect me to change?'

It turned out that the makeup room and wardrobe were set up in buses and that was where the extras did their changing. I was expected to do the same.

When I heard this I asked for the driver of the car that had brought us to stay. 'I'm sorry,' I said to the assistant, 'what's your name?'

He told me his name. He was very nervous by this time and I felt for him but I wasn't going to wear this.

'I must have come to the wrong place. I didn't realise I was expected to sit in the gutter between scenes.' I pulled him to one side and pointed in the direction of a large building separate from the sound stages. 'Do you see that building there?'

'Yes.'

'Well, that building consists entirely of dressing rooms and wardrobe. We are not on location. We are making this film in a film studio with sound stages and full facilities. I'll tell you what I'll do. I'll just go back to the hotel and you go to the production office and see what you can do about a dressing room. Then you can ring me up at the hotel and send a car and we can take it from there.'

He begged me to stay, hurried off and came back with the news that there were dressing rooms for me and the two other locals. By this time I could have been changed, made up, on the set and ready to go and we were still standing about. The Americans working on the picture had what they called their Winebagos, vast caravans fitted out with everything that opened and shut, and we had nothing.

On location you expect to change in a bus and makeup is usually in a converted bus. Nor am I above changing with extras; I've done it often, but this was different. The reason was to save money; the hire of the dressing rooms would go on the production budget. The *thinking* was that locals didn't matter and wouldn't complain. If the studio was full and all sound stages were being used and all dressing rooms were occupied it would be a different matter. But this film was the only one in production at the time. Where was one supposed to sit between scenes and study one's lines? It infuriated me and I'm afraid I was quite severe with the two other Australians (who had spent the whole time skulking behind the buses) when they thanked me for standing up for our rights. I told them what I thought of their attitude and that they *deserved* to change in the gutter.

I think what could be one of the more dangerous additions to the film industry is the advent of the 'casting agency'. I suppose they are necessary to overseas producers and directors not familiar with the local scene, but I have doubts about their impartiality and the influence they are coming to wield. One casting agent in particular seems to me to have acquired a degree of power that is unhealthy. I have it on good authority that this person has a list of actors 'to be used' and 'not to be used' and the choices of producers and directors who come to the agency are governed by this arbitrary arrangement.

Sources and experience tell me that I am in the 'not to be used' category with the agent in question. On at least three films in recent times I have been cast, only to be told at the eleventh hour that plans have changed. The bad news usually comes from the director him or herself and the excuse is invariably lame and unconvincing: 'You are too strong for the part' or 'the chemistry between you and X would be wrong'.

The casting agent I have in mind has, to my knowledge, met me only once and briefly. I can think of no sound basis for the adverse opinion. One director, unsolicited, has told me of the agonies he went through in trying to get the actor he wanted. The casting agent said flatly that he could not have that particular actor because, in the agent's opinion, he was unreliable. I think it is dangerous and unhealthy when a handful of people have manouvred themselves into such a position of power that they have a virtual stranglehold on the industry. They have engineered a situation whereby they are practically indispensable and it is criminal that one person can hold the future of some talented artist in the palm of her/his hand and possibly destroy a potentially promising career, because they don't like the cut of his/her jib. Unestablished producers and directors, anxious to get their productions up and their names in the credits, are particularly vulnerable to this kind of pressure.

Inevitably, people in the business being inveterate gossips, these tales of ruthless manipulation get back to the victims. Perhaps one day the tide will turn. In the meantime, my advice to producers and directors is to have the guts to insist on having the actors they want and be prepared to carry the can.

I wish to complete this list of gripes with a shaft in the direction of those producers who are attempting to pay actors by the line rather than for what they bring to the project in the way of experience and talent. Whereas in overseas productions cameo performances are valued and highly (sometimes ludicrously) paid, there is a tendency in Australia to try to get the talent on the cheap. Various softeners are employed, one of the most common being, 'It's only a few scenes, but it's a wonderful character and it'll be a good shop window for you.'

To which my reply is, 'I've been in that shop window for fifty years and I don't like the dress.'

· 26 ·

Wire coathangers

I am not in the least superstitious. I will walk under a ladder and people can mention Macbeth in my presence as much as they like and whistle in my dressing room. But nobody is completely rational, and I do have a number of pet hates, things that annoy me beyond endurance. To balance them, there are simple things I love to do and emotions and sensations I take delight in.

I know that wire coathangers procreate the minute you close the wardrobe door. They seem to be perfectly in order and well behaved when you leave them, but in the morning you catch them intertwined and refusing to be separated. Tug at them as you might, they will not untangle. I have been known to tear them apart in rage, twist them into grotesque bundles and hurl them against the wall.

As someone who has made his living through the use of language, I hate seeing it abused. This list mostly comes directly from radio which I listen to constantly. Newsreaders, professors, politicians, teachers: various experts in their fields are the culprits:

haitch
somethink
irrevalent
libry
nucular
artheritis
bronichal
pleece
amblance
Austraya
jewry
cutelry
simily
Antartica
envionmental
reelistic
anythink
gunna
jist
Antibees (Antibes)
exetera
pree (pretty)
regalar
compnees
goverment
knowen
histry
Sinny (Sydney)
aideen muntz (18 months)
off or to instead of from
vunrable
excape

The dangerous thing is that the more they are used the more likely they are to become acceptable. Our new generation will grow up with these mispronunciations along with adding machines and computers. Will they ever be able to read a book?

Some time ago I was in the studio of radio 4BH in Brisbane to give an interview about a play I was appearing in. 'You are listening to four bee haitch,' the interviewer said. 'Today we have in the studio Ray B . . .'

'Excuse me,' I interrupted. 'What did you just say?'

'Oh, I identified the station and I was about to introduce you.'

'The name of the station is four bee aitch, not haitch. Do you know how to spell it?'

He didn't know what I was getting at.

'Aitch is spelt a-i-t-c-h.'

I must admit he carried it off quite well. 'Oh, listeners,' he said, 'I think I've been taken to task, here. You are listening to 4B aitch!'

Air travel is taxing enough at the best of times, but the stresses stewardesses put on words in their announcements irritate me beyond measure. I fear that, if enough people travel by air, the whole society will adopt these abominations:

'The captain HAS turned off the seat belt sign, but it IS suggested that you DO keep them fastened because there IS some turbulence. This aircraft WILL be carrying on to Melbourne. Passengers ARE required to stow hand luggage ... The bus WILL depart ... Hire cars ARE available ...'

Unlike some unfortunate members of my profession, I've never had my sanity threatened or had to resort to therapists. Some of the things that give me immense pleasure and I believe help to keep me sane are:

Sitting in the magnificent square at Sienna for a few hours, soaking up the atmosphere, thinking about the history of the place and observing the people.

Having a four hour Sunday lunch with Gaye and friends at Les Chiens just inside the walls of St Malo.

Sitting naked in the rock pool at the bottom of my property on the island and letting the Mediterranean sea break over me.

Enjoying my house and the things I have collected over the years—fine glassware for which I have a passion and certain paintings.

The pleasure of watching my sons grow into fine men and being thankful that they are intelligent, healthy and caring and looking forward to seeing my grandchildren develop similarly.

Sitting in front of the fire on Formentera in winter when a storm rages outside and thinking how lucky I have been and how fortunate I am.

Epilogue

I'm now sixty-seven years of age. I don't feel it. I sometimes think that the birth certificates have been tampered with in some mouldy Queensland government office. My life has been eventful and has taken some surprising turns. With very little planning involved I seem to have done a lot.

'Regrets, I've had a few', as the song says, but not many on the professional front. I would have liked to have worked with Peter Finch but the chance never came. I would like to direct a film. I wish I had played a Shakespeare season in Britain. The opportunity to play a whole season never arose. I was offered one play as part of a season and refused. Perhaps I should have taken it. I've well and truly missed the bus for Romeo and Hamlet now; I might still get a shot at King Lear. Who knows. I would have liked to play Professor Higgins in *My Fair Lady*.

My childhood was great. I built boats and sailed them. I've modified houses, designed one, seen it built and enjoyed it for twenty-seven years. Three marriages, two divorces, love affairs and broken hearts—a rocky passage through life perhaps, but no suicides, no tragedies. My profession is one of the chanciest of all, from the time of the vagabond strolling players down to the present. I've been in almost constant work in Britain and

Australia for close to forty years and have enjoyed moderate success in a number of the branches of show business—theatre, films and television, comedy and drama, singing.

My daughter Suellen and her husband, Tony Meehan, the original drummer with the legendary British rock group The Shadows have made me a grandfather twice over, with Ruari, a sensitive, handsome boy and the beautiful tearaway, Lorcan.

I have two wonderful sons by my second wife, Mirén—Reginald Walter, a twenty-two year old as I write, a good-looking and caring young gentleman who is about to get his degree in hotel management, and Jonathan Raymond, also handsome and an interesting fellow with a natural artistic talent which I hope to encourage.

My wife, Gaye, pulled me up by the bootstraps from what could have been a long slide to the bottom, helped to end my romance with the bottle and has shown faith in me through thick and thin. She is a positive and joyful person, a great cook who gives me the best diet in the world and loves the things I love—wandering around France and Spain, keeping things shipshape at Formentera. In professional matters, she compensates for a great lack in me by confronting when confrontation is needed. She nags me into doing what's best for me.

So what more can a man ask for? My health is good. The parts I'm given these days are more interesting and enjoyable. With the current vogue for nineteenth century subjects, there is talk of dramatising a series of Charles Dickens' novels—the books that sat in leatherbound splendour on my father's shelves. How I would love to play some of those rich characters. Again, who knows. The world has shrunk. From Spain I can be on a film set in England in one day and in Australia in two or three.

I look forward to many more years working around my house in Spain. My idea of boating these days is a modest ketch with an auxiliary engine and cruising quietly across to Ibiza. No more of the force 12 gales I used to weather off Queensland and in the Solent for me. I will re-read some of my favourite writers, Oscar Wilde, John Steinbeck, James Thurber, Damon Runyon. And Gaye and I will drift through the vineyards of Spain and France, meeting old friends, and in good company we will eat our way judiciously around the sea ports of Brittany.

Facts & figures

Date of Birth	2 May 1927
Place of Birth	Wooloowin, Brisbane, Queensland, Australia
First Professional Performance	Brisbane Radio 1939
Brisbane	1927–1953
Sydney	1954–1958
London	1959–1975
Brisbane	1976–

Feature Films

1959–60	*The Sundowners*
1962	*Touch of Death*
	Mix me a Person—With Anne Baxter
	Jigsaw
1963	*To Have and to Hold*
	Moment of Decision (Sleep Long My Love)
	80,000 Suspects

1964	*The Big Dig*
1965	*The Amorous Milkman*
	Just Like a Woman—With Wendy Craig
	Time to Remember
1966	*Reptiles*
1971	*Revenge*—With Joan Collins
1973	*Hostages*
1975	*Touch of Death*
1976	*Don's Party*
1977	*The Chant of Jimmie Blacksmith*
1979	*The Earthling*—With William Holden
1981	*A Dangerous Summer*—James Mason and Tom Skerritt
1982	*Goodbye Paradise*
1984	*The Empty Beach*
	Rebel
1985	*Relatives*
1986	*Frenchman's Farm*
1987	*Contagion*
	As Time Goes By
1989	*Blood Oath*
1990	*Waiting*
1992	*No Worries*
1994	*Hotel Sorrento*
	On Our Selection

Telemovies

1960	*Flag Fall*
1962	*Time to Die*—With Harry H. Corbett
	Reunion Day
	Man of the World
	Dumb Martian
	The Frightened Sky
	Recruiting Officer
1963	*The Strain*
	The Buried Man
	Peer Gynt—As The Button Moulder
	31 Backyards—Susan Hampshire

1965	*Naked Island*
	Luther—As The Knight
	Come into my Parlour
	Call me Friend—Blackmail Series
1973	*The Carmakers*
1974	*Colditz*
	Dock Green
1976	*No Room to Run*—Co-Lead
1979	*Burn the Butterflies*—Lead
1980	*Departmental*—Lead
1982	*Conferenceville*—Lead

TV Series

1959	*Educating Archie*
1961–62	*Emergency Ward 10*
1962	*Harpers West One*—Guest
	Stingray
1963	*Z Cars*—Guest
1963–64	*Ghost Squad/GS5*—Guest
1964–65	*The Brothers Karamazov*—As Mitya
1965	*The Thunderbirds*
	Dr Who—Guest
1965–66	*Mogul*
1966–72	*The Troubleshooters*
1974	*The Double Dealers*
1975	*Barlow*—Guest
1976	*Arena*—Pilot
1978	*Golden Soak*
	Run From the Morning
1980	*The Timeless Land*
	Home Sweet Home—Guest
1981	*Sporting Chance*
1983	*Waterfront*
1984	*Five Mile Creek*—Guest
	The Last Bastion
1985	*Tusitala*
1986	*The Challenge*
	The Flying Doctors—Guest

1989 *GP*—Guest
1989 *Paperman*

TV Documentaries

Prelude to Greatness:
Joh Bjelke-Petersen
A Shifting Dreaming—Dramatised
Wings over Australia
The Australian War Museum
Beyond Cape York

Awards

1978 AFI AWARDS
Best Supporting Actor
THE CHANT OF JIMMIE BLACKSMITH
1982 AFI AWARDS
Best Actor
GOODBYE PARADISE
SYDNEY FILM CRITICS' CIRCLE
Best Actor/Actress
GOODBYE PARADISE
1985 TELEVISION SOCIETY OF AUSTRALIA
Commendation for Performance by an Actor in a Supporting Role
THE LAST BASTION

Theatre

1951 *The Sacred Flame*
1952 *Young Wives' Tales*
Cockpit
1953 *The Vigil*

1954	*Hit and Run*—Phillip Street Revue
	Happy Returns—Phillip Street Revue
	Ring Around the Moon
1955	*Happy Birthday*—Phillip Street Revue
	Tintookies—Marionette Voices
1957	*Peter and the Wolf*—With the SSO
	The Happiest Days of Your Life
1958	*Time Remembered*—Margaret Rutherford
	Look Back in Anger—As Jimmy Porter
1959	*One to Another*—Revue
1960	*Don't Shoot, We're English*—Revue
	Naked Island
1962	*Jack and the Beanstalk*—Pantomime
1964	*The Uncertain Heroine*
	The First Fish
1965	*Hey You, Light Man*
1972	*Touch of Purple*
1973	*The Dragon Variation*
1975	*Don's Party*
1986	*Sons of Cain*
1987	*The Sunshine Boys*
1988	*A Different Drummer*
1991	*Love Letters*
1993	*Brilliant Lies*

Variety

Crunch
Dave Allen Show
Don Lane Show
Danny La Rue Show
This is Your Life
Capriccio
John Singleton Show
Mike Walsh Show
Tonight Live—Steve Vizard
Good Morning Australia—Bert Newton
Midday with Derryn Hinch

Radio

1939	*The Browning Version*
1941	*ABC School Broadcasts*—Various
	The Housemaster—Play
1943–50	*Breakfast Programme 4BH and 4KQ*
1945	*Smokes for Sick Soldiers*—Variety
1947	*Saturday Morning Sing Song*—Variety
1949	*The Painted Veil*—Play
1950	*The Last of Summer*—Play
	Morning Departure—Play
	George: Conversation Piece—Play
	The Piper—Play
	Theseus & the Minotaur—Play
	Dr Faustus—Play
1951	*The Women Have Their Way*
	Plot and Counterplot—Play
	The Flowers are Not For You to Pick—Play
	They Knew What They Wanted—Play
1952	*Unborn Tomorrow*—Serial
	The Ridge & the River—Book Reading
	Background to Tomorrow—Dramatised Documentary
	Skipper Next to God—Play
	Jam Today—Play
	Spaceways—Play
	Smoked Mackerel—Serial
	Release—Play
1953	*Stop the Roundabout*—Play
	The Amazing Dr Clitterhouse—Play
	Cry, the Beloved Country—Play
	Road Going North—Book Reading
	Dr Knock—Play
	The Warden—Play
	Once a Crook—Play
	Three's Company—Musical Variety
	Melody Menu—Musical Variety
1953–4	*Big Red*—Book Reading
1954	*Voyage on a Dinner Table*—Play
	Julius Caesar—Play

	Much Binding—Comedy Series
	The Overcoat—Play
	Work of Art—Play
	A Place Where You Whisper—Play
1955	*The Mirage*—Play
	Bushman's Holiday—Play
	Smilin' Through—Play
	You Belong to Me—Play
	Tea With The Thomases—Comedy Series
	Bedtime Story—Play
	A Flame in the Air—Play
	The Caine Mutiny—Play
	Pygmalion—Play
	The Mariner's Story—Play
1955–6	*Brand of Justice*
1956	*The Misanthrope*—Play
	Justin Bayard—Book Reading
	The Laughing Woman—Play
	Henry IV—Play
	Kind Hearts & Coronets—Play
	The Third Man—Play
	Colin Robin's Catalogue—Variety
	My Six Convicts—Play
	The Great Temptation—Play
	The Enormous Shadow—Play
	The Steeper Cliff—Play
1956–7	*We're Asking You*—Quiz Show
1957	*Once in a Blue Moon*—Play
	Mary Southern—Serial
	Famous Trials—Series
	Address Unknown—Series
	No Love for Linda—Serial
	Around the World in 80 Days—Serial
	A Many Splendoured Thing—Serial
	Child's Play—Variety Series
	Holiday Task—Play
	The Ghost Peak—Play
	Bandwagon—Comedy Series
	The Shadow of the Vine—Play
	Danger with Grainger—Series

	The White Rabbit—Serial
	The Rescue of a Lady—Play
	Return Engagement—Play
	Educating Archie—Comedy Series
	Tarzan—Serial
	The Adventures of Robin Hood—Serial
	Strike a New Note—Comedy Series
	Jukebox Jackpots—Musical Series
	The King & Mrs Candle—Play
	The Idiot Weekly—Comedy Series With Spike Milligan
1974	*Ricochet*—Serial

Discography

1969	*No Trouble Now*	Fontana
1970	*Large as Life*	Philips
1985	*Henry Lawson Short Stories*	RBC

Index

Index